W9-ASU-800

THE
MAISEL REPORT

College Football's Most Overrated
and Underrated Players, Coaches,
Teams, and Traditions

Ivan Maisel

TRIUMPH
B O O K S

Triumph Books and colophon are registered trademarks of Random House, Inc.

Library of Congress Cataloging-in-Publication Data

Maisel, Ivan, 1960–
    The Maisel report : college football's most overrated and underrated players, coaches, teams, and traditions / Ivan Maisel.
        p. cm.
    Includes bibliographical references.
    ISBN-13: 978-1-60078-092-9
    ISBN-10: 1-60078-092-X
    1. Football—United States. 2. College sports—United States. I. Title.
    GV950.6.M32 2008
    796.332'63—dc22
                                                                2008012319

This book is available in quantity at special discounts for your group or organization. For further information, contact:

Triumph Books
542 South Dearborn Street, Suite 750
Chicago, Illinois 60605
(312) 939-3330 I Fax (312) 663-3557

Printed in U.S.A.
ISBN: 978-1-60078-092-9
Design by Patricia Frey
Page production by Amy Carter
Photos courtesy of Getty Images unless otherwise indicated.

To Herman Maisel (1925–2007);
I remain lucky to have him.

Contents

Foreword

Visit the corner drugstore in Auburn, Alabama, or the campus creamery at Penn State. Tune in talk radio, surf to any of a thousand Internet fan forums, or eavesdrop in Atlanta's airport terminal each fall Friday, when mobs dressed head to toe in various team colors take their support on the road.

You cannot escape it or deny it: college football is a sport driven by opinions. In fact, more than any other sport, it is *shaped* by opinions. Weekly polls have been a part of college football forever, and thanks to the nutty, frustrating Bowl Championship Series, it is opinions that determine which teams are showcased in the biggest bowl games. Opinions shape which two teams play for the national championship and which teams are excluded.

Which player is immortalized as winner of the most famous individual trophy in any sport? The opinions of more than 900 Heisman voters settle that issue, but hardly end the discussion.

Now, opinions are products of particular points of view, usually filtered through a fan's distorted lens and loaded with built-in biases. They are easily attacked and debated. Do we really expect fans from, say, Ohio State and Florida to agree on most topics?

But to each of us, our opinions are precious. The strong allegiances and deep passions inspired by college football mean that the debates will never die. Maybe that's why college football is so tightly woven into our culture. What's more American than strong ideas, hotly debated?

Ivan Maisel has as much passion for the sport as any journalist I know. After 25 years traversing the landscape, he is armed with plenty of opinions. That's what makes *The Maisel Report* so compelling.

Ivan attacks conventional wisdom and provokes fresh thought on time-honored topics. His opinions are well founded and well expressed. But that doesn't make them right.

USC-UCLA the most overrated rivalry? Nebraska's 1997 team an over-rated champion? You might beg to differ. Strongly. That's your right as a fan.

You're certainly not going to agree with everything that follows. But you will learn something.

Ivan is convincing, but I surely take issue with a few of his opinions, too. Reasonable people can completely disagree. That's what makes college football (and this book) such enduring fun.

—Chris Fowler

Acknowledgments

Acknowledgments, like Oscar speeches, should be brief. So before Bill Conti strikes up the orchestra:

Thank you to Michael Emmerich of Triumph Books for cold-emailing me last year to gauge my interest in writing this book, and for remaining in good cheer as I plowed through deadlines. Surely I am not the first author to have a parent die and a spouse undergo surgery as I tried to turn around a book, but Mike never blinked as I pushed the goalposts back.

Developmental editor Adam Motin done cleaned up my grammar—just kidding, Adam—and made sure I spelled Cappelletti correctly. Thanks to Mitch Rogatz and Tom Bast of Triumph, as well.

My editors at ESPN.com—Rob King, Patrick Stiegman, David Albright, and David Duffey—cleared my schedule to give me the time I needed to write. Working with them has made ESPN.com the best employer I've had, and I've had a few.

Gene Wojciechowski—the ESPN.com national columnist and best-selling author—and Mark Blaudschun of *The Boston Globe*—the best reporter I know—served as equal parts sounding boards and cheerleaders.

My colleagues Pat Forde, Mark Schlabach, and Joe Wojciechowski of ESPN.com, my podcast partner Beano Cook of so many ESPN platforms, as well as my traveling partners Chris Dufresne of the *Los Angeles Times*, Tony Barnhart of *The Atlanta Journal-Constitution*, and Dennis Dodd of

CBSSports.com didn't hesitate to suggest ideas when asked. The genius of a book like this is that everyone who follows college football has an opinion. Some of mine, thanks to the wise counsel of these writers, never made it to the keyboard.

Thanks to my friend and colleague Chris Fowler of ESPN for making time to write the foreword, and to Brian Barlaam, the one and only, for moral support and red wine.

My wife and best friend, Meg Murray, and our children, Sarah, Max, and Elizabeth, always understood when I headed up to the attic to work on this book. If they didn't understand, they kept it to themselves, and I'm grateful for that, too.

Introduction

With no offense to Jayson Stark and Sal Paolantonio, my ESPN colleagues who wrote the first two books in this series, I don't know why Triumph Books didn't start with me. Not me, specifically, but the sport I cover. Opinion is the mother's milk of college football. The polls—opinion polls, lest we forget—owned exclusivity over the national championship until recent years, when the conference commissioners created the BCS formula.

Me, I believe that mother's milk holds more nutrients than formula.

You have your opinion. Trust me, I know. It lands in my inbox at ESPN.com with a thud every day. I think I have been accused of having either a love affair with, or a grudge against, nearly every region or major conference in the country, not to mention a few minor ones. I grew up in an SEC state, went to school in the Pac-10, worked in Big 12 country for seven years, and have lived the last 14 in the Big East (slogan: "Sometimes Relevant Since 1991"), and every one of those facts has been used to justify my readers' spewfest when they disagree with me.

So we all have our opinions. But here's why you should listen to mine:

I have covered about 300 games since 1987. My work has taken me to 85 Division I-A campuses. I have covered 26 national championship games in 21 seasons, math that adds up only in college football. I have interviewed seven Alabama head coaches in the same building, including, yes, Mike Price. I have covered every major rivalry except, to my embarrassment,

Army-Navy. That includes Alabama-Auburn, Ohio State–Michigan, USC–Notre Dame, Miami–Florida State, Texas-Oklahoma, Georgia-Florida, and Stanford-California, not to mention Texas–Texas A&M, Michigan–Notre Dame, Michigan–Michigan State, Tennessee-Florida, USC-UCLA, and Washington-Oregon.

You get the point.

I have covered six Rose Bowls, 10 Orange Bowls, five Fiestas, five Sugars, and some assorted GMACs and Gators along the way.

No one has covered college football on a national basis without interruption longer than I have. That makes me the dean of the college football press box, at least at the big games where the Verne Lundquists and Brent Musburgers are lurking about. As B.B. King sang in "Better Not Look Down": "I've been around, and I've seen some things."

(That same song contains one of the great lyrics of all time: "If the arrows from Cupid's bow that had passed through her heart were sticking out of her body, she would look like a porcupine." But I digress.)

I haven't covered only the big games. I sat in the stands at a Baylor-SMU game with the Tulane football team, five days after Hurricane Katrina. Speaking of which, I stood on the sideline at Virginia Tech, reporting for ESPN.com when Hurricane Isabel blew through a Thursday night game at Lane Stadium. I have covered Bennie Blades, and his son, H.B. Blades, and watched them both go on to the NFL. I have seen Oklahoma die and be resurrected. I have seen USC die and be resurrected. I have seen Nebraska and Notre Dame die and…well, we're still waiting on those two.

I voted in the Associated Press poll for 16 years, from 1987 to 2002. The AP doesn't allow any media outlet to have more than one vote; some guy named Fowler votes for ESPN, so my ballot got taken from me. It turns out this Fowler guy has a Saturday morning show that's all about college football. Who knew? There's a former quarterback on the set, and the two of them flank a guy holding a pencil and wearing a mascot head. Maybe you should check it out.

In his foreword to the book you hold in your wonderful book-buying hands, Chris Fowler talked about the power of opinion in college football. I like it. I am a poll guy. I enjoyed voting, although I don't miss the frantic calls from the AP office in New York wanting to know where my ballot was. I recall one year at the Fiesta Bowl when I wandered into a postgame buffet at the media hotel about 3:00 AM only to discover that the AP had all but filed a missing persons report on me. It's nice to be wanted.

I have always liked the polls, perhaps because I grew up when the polls made the champions. And you know what? When we had split national championships—and we had 11 of them from 1954 through 2003—the world kept spinning. Nothing bad happened. Balfour made twice as many national championship rings, and the T-shirt makers sold twice as many T-shirts. The value of the split national championship, once fans get past the hurt feelings of being voted down, is just as rich. My point is that living on opinion alone is possible, and perhaps even preferable, to the dog's breakfast of a formula we have now. As math wizards go, conference commissioners make great former athletic directors. The BCS commissioners do a great job of changing the formula to solve the previous year's problem. However, they will never have a formula that accounts for every squirrelly permutation in the sport.

I like the idea that No.1 and No. 2 play. The BCS Championship Game is a showcase for the sport.

But let's not be in too big a hurry to shun the power that opinion plays in college football. Which brings us back to *The Maisel Report: College Football's Most Overrated and Underrated Players, Coaches, Teams, and Traditions.*

What you are about to read is my opinion, and I figure that I owe you an explanation of how I went about my overrating and underrating. First of all, you can't really confuse them with rating. It's one thing to rate the best rivalries in college football; what I'm doing here is *judging* the ratings. For the next couple hundred pages, I invite you to meet me at the intersection of Reputation Road and Performance Parkway. I'll be wearing the media badge and carrying a bag of roasted peanuts. You can't watch a college football game, in person or at home, without a bag of peanuts. Those stadiums that don't sell peanuts in the shell—that would be you, Big House—are about to hear about it.

Any disparity between reputation and performance big enough to catch my eye made the book. Take the role that tradition and reputation play in developing the public's opinion of players who win awards and teams that win national championships. It hasn't always been fair. It hasn't always been right. Those are the entries in this book.

It's worth pointing out that the judging of players, coaches, teams, and conferences has some basis in fact. Statistics can be used to bolster an argument, although I tried not to compare statistics across generations. For instance, in 1939, Iowa back Nile Kinnick rushed for 374 yards and five touchdowns. His passing statistics (31-of-93, 638 yards, 11 touchdowns, 13 interceptions) that season wouldn't get him a look from a Division II coach today. But that's the year he won the Heisman Trophy, and the state of Iowa will suspend the First Amendment if you suggest he shouldn't have. The eight interceptions on defense, the 39.9-yard punting average, and the 604 return yards point out why Kinnick did win. The standards have changed, so there is a little cross-generational dissing here, but not much.

With players and teams, stats matter. When judging traditions and stadiums, not so much. You may agree. You may disagree. That's the point. One man's Golden Egg is another's Script Ohio. My take on fight songs, for instance, has as much to do with clef notes as cleft chins. So I will stipulate—a word I learned watching *Law & Order*—that those ratings have more to do with personal taste. However, I hope you came here for the same reason that Lonely Planet sells a lot of travel guides: I've been around, and I've seen some things.

The office in my home has a wall of books that I have collected during my career. If there's a used bookstore near campus, I like to go in there the day before a game and scour for college football books. I've saved a few credentials and the media guides from a few national champions, but other than that, my office is no shrine to college football. In fact, there is only one item hanging on my office walls that pertains to our—your and my—favorite sport.

It is a letter dated October 18, 1966, on Alabama football stationery. The text of the letter reads:

Dear Ivan:

I certainly appreciated your note of October 17. Thanks so much for your interest and support of our team.

Best of luck in your school work.

Sincerely,

Paul Bryant

It is signed with a thick black marker, the crossing of the "t" slanted from left to right. He responded three days after No. 3 Alabama defeated Tennessee 11–10, coming back from a 10–0 deficit in a driving rainstorm to take the lead late in the game. The Vols' Gary Wright missed a 20-yard field goal as time ran out. The 1966 team, which finished 11–0, won every other game by at least 10 points. The Tennessee victory helped turn Bryant into a legend. That could be why I wrote Bryant. But I doubt it.

After all, I was only six years old.

To tell you truth, I'd really love to see the letter I wrote him.

When you disagree with *The Maisel Report*—and there's something in here to torque off just about every fan—just keep in mind that I didn't just arrive on campus on a truckload of watermelons. I've got a letter from the Bear to prove it.

CHAPTER 1

Programs

What's the difference between a college football "program" and a college football "team"? Oh, about three assistant athletic directors, a video department, a marketing department, a development ("development" is non-profitese for fundraising) department, 95 skyboxes, and about $80 million. *Annually.*

"Program" is a buzzword, coachspeak that sunk its roots into the sports pages decades ago and will never leave as long as there's a college football arms race. A program represents the bureaucratic, financial behemoth that college athletics has become. For all the excess, however, the success of a program still comes down to whether a bunch of 19- and 20-year-old kids can focus longer than the bunch of 19- and 20-year-old kids they're playing. Programs, like teams, must win to survive.

Otherwise, a coach gets a seven-figure severance check and a new guy arrives, promising to bring the program up to speed. Rather than rate the best programs by how well they're doing in the arms race, we'll stick to measuring them the old-fashioned way: how many wins and losses they're getting compared to what they should get, given their tradition and the resources available.

1

How the mighty have fallen—the University of Miami is the most overrated program in college football today.

The Most Overrated Program in College Football

MIAMI

Miami has been the most successful college football team over the last 25 years, and its fans will be the first to tell you.

The Hurricanes won five national championships in the span of two decades, beginning with the upset of Nebraska by Howard Schnellenberger's underdogs in the Orange Bowl to end the 1983 season, going through Jimmy Johnson's 1987 team, and then to Dennis Erickson's 1989 and 1991 teams, on through to Larry Coker's 2001 Canes, which embarrassed—full circle, please—Nebraska in the Rose Bowl.

The coach didn't seem to matter. The stadium didn't seem to matter. Orange Bowl, Sugar Bowl, Rose Bowl—the Canes dominated.

And those were just the successes. Just one loss—really, when you get down to those games, one *play*—prevented the Hurricanes from winning in 1986, 1988, 2000, and 2002 as well. That would have been nine titles in 20 years, including four straight. Instead, Miami finished second in the final poll in each of those seasons.

(In the case of 2002, only one late whistle in the first overtime of the Fiesta Bowl kept Ohio State alive and prevented the Hurricanes from celebrating. I can still see the fireworks exploding over the rim of Sun Devil Stadium. Enough time passed between the pass interference call on Miami and the flag that someone got the go-ahead to light the fuses. In fact, enough time passed between the pass interference call and the flag that someone sitting in the stadium could have left, gone and bought fireworks, returned to the stadium, and set them off.)

The foundation for that success is in the gold mine of football talent that exists in south Florida. In the month of January, you can't swing a stuffed mascot in the lobby of the Harbor Beach Marriott in Ft. Lauderdale without hitting a football coach from some major out-of-state university. Miami retains a cachet with those players. They want to represent The U, especially now that Randy Shannon, one of their own, is the Canes' head coach. In February 2008, the homegrown Shannon signed seven ESPN 150 players who played high school football within a half-hour of the Miami campus. That might be why ESPN ranked Miami's signees the nation's top class.

All of which may explain the high regard in which Hurricane fans hold themselves and their team.

If you like Yankee fans and their arrogance, you'll love Miami fans. Judging by email I've received, you're either for the Canes or you're some Anglo-Saxon adjectives and body parts that are better left unsaid. Faith in The U is absolute. If Miami gets bogged down, it's only one spring practice/game/season from returning to the top five. If enthusiasm untainted by reality accounts for anything, there is no better fan than the Miami fan.

I would be a lot more impressed with Miami fans if they supported the Canes through thick and thin. The fans have got the thick part down; it's the thin that they have trouble with. When Miami stops winning, its fans scatter as if someone threw a stink bomb into the high school lunchroom. In 2007, Miami averaged 43,589 fans per game, or 60 percent of capacity. In 2003, coming off their two most successful seasons in a decade, and, as in 2007, without archrival Florida State on the home schedule, Miami averaged more than 58,000 per game.

Maybe that's life in a city with beaches, nightlife, and four pro franchises. But that doesn't mean it's kosher. The Miami fans may profess greatness, but my view of Miami football is based on fact, not fiction.

Since 1991, Miami has won *one* national championship. That's one fewer than Florida State and Florida—that's right, the Canes are third in the state—and two fewer than Nebraska, the team that served as the Hurricanes' final step in three of their five national championship seasons.

Since 2001, when Miami won its most recent national championship, the Canes have either had the same record or lost more games in each successive season. Watch the numbers on the left go down, and the numbers on the right go up:

    2001: 12–0
    2002: 12–1
    2003: 11–2
    2004: 9–3
    2005: 9–3
    2006: 7–6
    2007: 5–7

When I had the temerity to suggest before the 2007 season that Miami might struggle—let's see, a 7–6 team with a first-time head coach and the same nucleus of players; hmmm, what will it do?—I got a screenful. The biggest surprise is that the AP poll voters agreed with me, which gets to the crux of why Miami is the most overrated team in college football.

In the last 15 years, Miami has been ranked in the preseason poll 13 times. In 10 of those seasons, the Canes finished the season ranked lower than they began. In four seasons, Miami finished at the same ranking or higher. Do the math: the Canes have been overrated—literally.

Granted, polling is about as exact a science as phrenology—the 19th-century practice of studying character and personality by the shape of the skull. So let's loosen the definition. In six of those seasons, Miami finished the season ranked more than three places lower than it began. Here's another chart for you:

Year	Preseason Rank	Final Rank
1993	No. 5	No. 15
1994	No. 6	No. 6
1995	No. 9	No.20
1996	No. 12	No.14
1997	No. 13	unranked
1998	unranked	No.20
1999	No. 12	No.15
2000	No. 5	No.2
2001	No. 2	No.1
2002	No. 1	No.2
2003	No. 3	No.5
2004	No. 6	No.11
2005	No. 9	No.17
2006	No. 12	unranked
2007	unranked	unranked

That makes it four straight seasons without a top-10 finish, closing in on five straight from 1995 through 1999. More important, that's two consecutive seasons finishing out of the rankings, which hasn't happened since the early 1980s; since Miami became, well, Miami.

When times are difficult, the most successful programs have the cushion of their past on which to land. That clearly has been the case with the Canes. But it may be time to conclude that the Emperors of Coral Gables have no uniforms and won't have them before 2009 at least.

For one thing, no matter how well a program recruits, it's rarer than rare that freshmen can step onto campus and into the starting lineup. Central Florida coach George O'Leary first told me the freshman rule of thumb—the farther away a freshman lines up from the ball, the quicker he can contribute. That explains how Texas Tech freshman Michael Crabtree won the 2007 Biletnikoff Award as the best receiver in the nation. Meanwhile, of ESPN's three top-rated offensive linemen in 2007, Tray Allen played in nine games at Texas, while Josh Oglesby redshirted at Wisconsin and Kevin Bryant did the same at North Carolina.

Also, no matter how much Shannon means to Miami and vice-versa, he has to learn how to be a head coach. If he negotiates the learning curve well, then Miami will rebound quickly. The first year didn't go well. Most teams improve as the season continues; Miami went into reverse. After a 4–1 start, Miami lost six of its last seven. The first three defeats came by a total of 12 points; the last three, by 92 points, including a 48–0 loss to Virginia in the last game played at the Orange Bowl.

And here's another thought: could it be that the ACC is tougher to negotiate than the Big East? I don't think so, if only because Virginia Tech made the same move as Miami and continues to succeed. But it's something to consider.

Miami will begin the 2008 season without a quarterback who has ever thrown a college pass and with little experience on the defensive line. Given the performance at both positions in 2007, that's not necessarily a bad thing. But it's indicative of how far the Hurricanes have to go before they return to national relevance. When they do, the poll voters and the Miami fans alike will be awaiting, hosannahs at the ready.

The Rest of the Most Overrated

2. TEXAS A&M

The Aggies have always talked a big game. When Bear Bryant arrived in College Station in the mid-1950s to take over a program left for dead, he found that out. Speaking of Aggie Exes in his autobiography, Bryant said, "You could never sneak up on anybody because they bragged too much."

Aggies have always spared no expense, whether approved by the NCAA or not. On the plus side of the NCAA Manual stands the $27 million Bright Football Complex. On the outside, it resembles a modern office building. On the inside, there's a locker room with 130 oak lockers and a 10,000-square-foot equipment room.

The noise and the money make Texas A&M seem like a program that should be ranked among the elite. No longer is the campus a military, male-only institution that gives new meaning to the word *desolation.* The university is an academic showplace. The campus sprawls halfway to Houston, and a bigger, fancier Kyle Field continues to showcase the passion of its fans as well as any stadium in college football.

Now, if only the Aggies could win more games than they lose.

The trick for Texas A&M throughout its history has been to convert that devotion, financial and otherwise, into success on the field. It has been 10 years since the school's last Big 12 championship. It has been 69 years since the school's last national championship. With rare exceptions, most recently for a decade under coach R.C. Slocum beginning in the late 1980s, Texas A&M football has been all helmet, no cattle.

No group of fans or alumni take greater pride in their university than do the Aggies. They figured they had made the big time in 2002, when they pushed the devoted Slocum to the curb and lured Dennis Franchione away from Alabama. The move had a historical symmetry about it, gaining revenge for how Bryant departed College Station for Tuscaloosa 45 years earlier.

But paying Franchione in the neighborhood of $2 million per year produced a five-year record of 32–28, 19–21 in the conference, and 2–8 against Oklahoma and Texas. The latter record would explain why Fran's Aggies never finished higher than third in the Big 12 South. It also explained why he resigned at the end of the 2007 season.

I have a theory about college football in the state of Texas. There may be an enormous number of players in the state, but I am convinced that there are only enough blue-chip players to support two great teams. Where the fun comes in is predicting which teams get the blue-chippers. It used to be Texas A&M and Florida State, Texas A&M and Colorado. For this decade, a long one in College Station, it's been Texas and Oklahoma. New coach Mike Sherman, the former Green Bay Packers head coach, worked on Slocum's staff. He knows the Aggies. He knows how much they'll brag. If he can make the Aggies half as good as their fans believe they are, Texas A&M will be overrated no longer.

Clemson enters the 2008 season searching for its first ACC championship in 17 years. (Photo courtesy of AP Images)

3. CLEMSON

The Tigers have a lot in common with the Aggies: an agricultural school, looked down upon by The State University, pours its heart into football as a way of declaring itself an equal. That profile extends to the Atlantic Coast Conference itself, where Clemson has always been a pair of brown shoes in a room of tuxedos. The ACC may have expanded to 12 teams, and it may have a football championship game, but basketball remains the First Sport of Tobacco Road. Among the conference's original members, only Clemson poured its heart and soul into football. That's how the school made its mark.

As North Carolina, Duke, and company made basketball a religion, Clemson played hoops because it had to. Before defeating Duke and playing for the championship in 2008, Clemson had played in one ACC Basketball Tournament final in the previous 54 years, a 77–66 loss to Wake Forest in 1962, so long ago that Billy Packer started for the Demon Deacons.

Football has always been what makes Clemson fans get up in the morning, and the results on the field have shown why. When Florida State joined the ACC in 1992, Clemson led all schools with 13 league championships.

But here's the problem: going into 2008, Clemson still leads all schools with 13 league championships. Florida State is in second place with 12. Clemson's performance is not matching its fervor.

Which, by the way, shows no sign of abating. The Tigers lead the ACC in average attendance, with upwards of 81,000 filing into Memorial Stadium every Saturday. Other than the Seminoles, no other ACC program is within 15,000 per game. The problem for Clemson has been twofold. One, the state of South Carolina doesn't produce enough football players to support two state universities at the level they would like. Two, a good chunk of the state's best players always find the road out of town. Among the All-Americans who have crossed the state line: Georgia Tech quarterback Joe Hamilton, Penn State defensive lineman Courtney Brown, Florida State linebacker Peter Boulware, defensive lineman Jamal Reynolds, and offensive lineman Alex Barron.

Clemson has a good coach in Tommy Bowden. When Arkansas tried to woo him away after the 2007 season, Clemson gave Bowden a long-term extension. He has beaten his father Bobby's Seminoles three straight seasons and four out of the last five. Last season, the Tigers fell a game short of the ACC Atlantic title, losing at home to Boston College 20–17 in the final conference game of the season. Clemson junior Aaron Kelly, an All-ACC wideout who led the league in receiving yards (1,081, on 88 catches) and touchdown receptions (11), dropped a pass at the Eagles' 1-yard line in the waning seconds of the game.

Sigh.

Clemson lost only a handful of seniors off the 9–4 team that fell in overtime to Auburn 23–20 in the Peach Bowl. In 2008, Bowden will have a new contract and a veteran team, which is certainly preferable to the alternative. If the 17-year championship drought doesn't end with these Tigers, Clemson may never live up to its expectations.

4. PENN STATE

As long as Joe Paterno is coaching, Penn State football will get more attention than its performance on the field deserves. Journalistically speaking, there's not even a debate. The 81-year-old coach is a living, breathing piece of history in thick glasses and white socks. He will make news until he retires. At age 48, I just hope I'll live long enough to cover the retirement.

Since Penn State arrived in the Big Ten Conference in 1994, the Nittany Lions have done little to change the power structure. Before Penn State arrived, Ohio State and Michigan dominated the league. After Penn State arrived... I think you know where this is going. In 15 seasons, Penn State has won two Big Ten championships, the same number as Northwestern and Iowa. Good news: that's two more than Michigan State or Minnesota.

The 21st century started out rough on Paterno. His teams had four losing records in five years, and you could hear the grumbling from Pittsburgh to Philly. The shadow of Eddie Robinson fading away at Grambling fell over the Happy Valley. To Paterno's credit, the Nittany Lions rebounded. He brought new blood to his coaching staff. Galen Hall, who played quarterback for Penn State in the Pleistocene Era (1960–61), returned to open up the offense. Tom Bradley took over the defense and plugged its holes. Voilà—the 2005 Big Ten championship. In the last three seasons, Penn State has gone 29–9.

While that's a good record—two games better than Michigan, in fact— no one confuses the Nittany Lions with the national powers. The Big Ten has become Ohio State's sandbox, and the rest of the kids are invited for playdates.

The power base from which Paterno has operated for more than four decades is shrinking. Pennsylvania high schools are consolidating and producing fewer players. The fence that Paterno once built around the state has a few missing planks. In the last three years, 21 Pennsylvania recruits made the ESPN 150; Penn State signed just three of them. Among the schools who raided the state for its top players in 2008: Florida, North Carolina, and—this makes Nittany Lion fans wince—Ohio State.

To the east, Rutgers is flexing its muscles. To the west, Pittsburgh is signing the top players in the state. Paterno soldiers on. The Penn State administration tried to get him to resign after the 2004 season. He refused and went out and won the Big Ten. There is one thing regarding his resignation of which you can be certain. When Paterno does take his leave, the profile of Penn State will shrink. So great is the program's identification with one man that when he goes, the Nittany Lions won't be overrated any longer. They'll be lucky to be rated at all.

5. ALABAMA

We interrupt this chapter to bring Alabama fans this news bulletin: Bear Bryant has been dead for 25 years.

Since Bryant's death—an officially recognized measurement of time in the state of Alabama—the Crimson Tide has won exactly as many national titles as Brigham Young and Georgia Tech, and only one more than Florida International.

Crimson Tide fans want to hear that about as much as they do the scores of the last six Iron Bowls, all won by Auburn. But not just because they believe that their rightful place is among the powers that be. Oh, Alabama fans believe that. They believe their place in the top 25 is guaranteed by the U.S. Constitution.

But 25 years in the wilderness, with one national championship (1992), two severe NCAA probations, and, in the last 11 years, four losing records and five coaches, have forced Crimson Tiders to adjust to life among the middle class. Bringing up the silver anniversary of Bryant's death would bring a sigh of sadness and of boredom. They've heard it all before.

The same can't be said for the rest of us. There's still a goodly section of the national media that comes running the minute that Alabama starts winning. They still believe.

Exhibit A: in 2005, when Alabama reached 5–0 by routing No. 5 Florida 31–3, up went quarterback Brodie Croyle on the cover of *Sports Illustrated*. "Bama is Back!" crowed *SI*. A probation-wracked team that hadn't had a winning season in three years was back? Sort of. After reaching 9–0, Alabama lost its last two regular-season games, to LSU and Auburn, and limped into the Cotton Bowl.

Exhibit B: the arrival of Nick Saban in Tuscaloosa in 2007 generated another *SI* cover. It was Saban whom the networks clamored to have on national television and Saban whom recruiting services hailed for signing the top class of recruits in the nation in 2008. Oh, by the way, Alabama went 7–6 in Saban's first season. A 6–2 start dissolved with four consecutive losses.

It is a tribute to Alabama and its legacy that it has remained a marquee name in the sport when Gene Stallings, who retired in 1996, is the last Tide coach to have three consecutive winning seasons. But facts are facts. This program has maintained its national profile because of its history and its problems, not because of what it has achieved on the field. Crimson Tide fans maintain their optimism by looking forward. They believe that Saban will bring them back to the Promised Land. The rest of us wait around for the glory days to return. I think that's why the national media flocks to Tuscaloosa at the first hint of the good times, the same way it flocked to USC when Pete Carroll revived the Trojans. Legends are legends. When legends don't play like legends, they're overrated.

The Most Underrated Program in College Football

BOSTON COLLEGE

When Boston College ditched the Big East for the Atlantic Coast Conference in 2003, your genius of a correspondent wrote the following:

> Nearly a decade ago, after a lot of political infighting, a small religious school became the 12th invitee into a conference, even though it had little in common with the other schools.
> On Sunday, Boston College became the Baylor of the northeast.

Not only was I wrong, I was loud wrong.

Baylor remains a competitive drag on the Big 12, the kid brother tagging along at the insistence of the parents—in this case, the Texas political power brokers at the time of the breakup of the Southwest Conference. After the 2007 season, Baylor fired another coach, Guy Morriss, a Texas native who didn't win much more than the three coaches who preceded him.

Boston College could have played that role in the ACC: a private religious (Jesuit) institution that had been competing against private universities in the East decided to join a league with eight public institutions. That doesn't stack up as a fair fight.

Besides the financial mismatch, you don't have to be Rand McNally to figure out that Boston College doesn't fit in the ACC. Massachusetts, the state that raised cigarette excise taxes in 1992 to fund an anti-smoking campaign, is a long way from Tobacco Road. To put it another way: Teddy Kennedy, meet Jesse Helms.

Boston College remains a cultural mismatch for the ACC, and no matter how much hype the league manufactures, the heat generated by the Eagles' new rivalries couldn't warm up a beach house in Miami. The best rivalries share geography, history, or both. Boston College shares none of the former, and very little of the latter, with the 11 other teams in the ACC.

Boston College can't control geography or history. It did have control over how it left the Big East for the ACC. After pledging fealty to the Big East, Boston College leapt at the opportunity to leave. Judging by the lawsuits filed and settled, and the hard feelings that remained after the settlement—for instance, don't hold your breath awaiting a Rutgers–Boston College nonconference game—the Eagles couldn't have handled it worse.

Competitively speaking, however, Boston College has been no Baylor. The Eagles have finished first in the ACC Atlantic Division in two of their three seasons in the league. Boston College's cumulative record in league play is 16–8, tied for second with Georgia Tech and trailing only Virginia Tech.

In 2007, the Eagles, led by first-year head coach Jeff Jagodzinski and a group of seniors that included quarterback Matt Ryan, climbed as high as No. 2 in the polls before finishing 11–3 and No. 10. That's the school's highest ranking at the end of the season since they finished No. 5 in 1984, when another underestimated Eagle, the undersized quarterback Doug Flutie, won the Heisman Trophy.

Three seasons do not a definitive statement make. But it's safe to conclude that Boston College is faring better in its new league than Baylor is doing in the Big 12. The Eagles have 16 league wins in three years. The Bears have 11 wins in 12 years of their league games. I didn't major in math, but I'm pretty sure that averages out to fewer than one victory per season.

Give credit to Tom O'Brien, who took over in 1997 after the Dan Henning era. In three years, Henning presided over one winning season and one betting scandal, proving that he was a helluva offensive coordinator as a head coach in college as well as in the NFL.

O'Brien, a former Marine who instilled discipline and preached physicality, transformed the Eagles into a winning team. He took them to eight consecutive bowls and he churned out offensive linemen good enough for the pros. O'Brien sent 21 Eagles into the NFL Draft. Ten of them—nearly half—played the offensive line.

O'Brien bolted for North Carolina State after the 2006 regular season with a record of 75–45 (.625). Why? He thought leaving the Big East for the ACC put Boston College at a disadvantage. He argued against it both privately and publicly, which didn't do much for his relationship with athletic director Gene DeFilippo. By going to Raleigh, O'Brien stayed in the ACC (re: football) and moved to the ACC (re: geography) at the same time, always a neat parlor trick.

So even the guy who coached there for 10 years is skeptical about the future of the Eagles. Join the crowd. Enrollment (9,081 undergraduates) is small. Expense (tuition, fees, room and board: $47,374) is large. It's located in the northeast, which is to college football what SEC country is to cricket. Academics are tough. Jesuits are not known for their kinesiology classes. It's enough to make the most logical, seasoned sportswriter believe that Boston College isn't going to succeed.

Which is where this gets interesting.

In three of the last four seasons, Boston College began the season unranked and finished it ranked. In the fourth season, 2005, the Eagles began the season ranked (No. 22) and finished it ranked higher (No. 18).

That's pretty much the definition of underrated, and it extends to 11 seasons in the past 25 years. Either the Eagles do a great job of keeping expectations low, or, more likely, they haven't taken up enough space in the college football firmament to register on anyone's radar.

There are a few reasons for that. O'Brien finished with a winning record in his last eight seasons, but he finished first only once—and no one wanted to celebrate. In the Eagles' lame-duck 2004 Big East season, when they generated the love and respect usually reserved for divorce mediation, the Eagles needed to defeat Syracuse in the last game of the regular season to win the league championship and BCS berth. Syracuse, playing for the pride of cuckolded spouses everywhere, walloped Boston College 43–17. The Eagles fell into a four-way tie for first, Pittsburgh went to the Fiesta Bowl, and the Big East lived happily ever after.

Another reason goes back to geography. Not only does Boston College play in the Northeast, they play in the same market as the Patriots and Red Sox, who between them consume most of the passion of New England. In October 2007, No. 2 Boston College prepared to play No. 8 Virginia Tech.

Head coach Jeff Jagodzinski and the Boston College Eagles have quietly built one of the most underrated programs in college football. (Photo courtesy of AP Images)

Pretty big game, right? Four days before the game—Boston College's first top-10 matchup in 15 seasons—also happened to be the day that the Patriots raised their record to 7–0 and three days before the start of the World Series. That's why exactly three reporters covered the Eagles' practice: two Boston newspaper guys and yours truly.

The problems of college football in NFL markets are not new. In fact, Boston College has thrived compared to schools such as SMU, Houston, Tulane, Vanderbilt, and Northwestern. But the Eagles haven't made the footprint that a team winning seven of every 10 games over the last nine seasons should make, either at home or nationally.

That began to change in 2007 with the dramatic 14–10 victory over the Hokies, when Ryan led the Eagles to score both of their touchdowns in the final 2:11. Boston College, 8–0, faded down the stretch, splitting its last six games. But the ability to come back under Jagodzinski made an impression. If the Eagles can rebuild in 2008 without falling too far back, maybe someone outside of the 02467 zip code will notice.

The Rest of the Most Underrated

2. AUBURN

You may point out that Auburn has defeated Alabama six consecutive years, a source of delight for the victors and an "enhanced interrogation technique," as the CIA might call it, for the Crimson Tide.

You may point out that the Tigers have won five of their last six bowl games, that they have finished first in the SEC West five times this decade, or that in 2005 Auburn became the first SEC school ever to have four players selected in the first round of the NFL Draft.

All true, and all irrelevant alongside the one fact that explains why the Tigers are the second-most underrated team in college football.

Let me put it this way: can you imagine a 12–0 Alabama team being shut out of a BCS Championship Game the way that 12–0 Auburn got shunted to the 2005 Sugar Bowl?

I didn't think so.

That loss in the polls turned Auburn coach Tommy Tuberville into a crusader against Big, Bad ESPN and forced the conference commissioners who run the BCS to rebuild the formula that produces a No. 1 vs. No. 2 yet another time. The current system has operated three seasons without a significant problem, which presumably means we're one year closer to the next disaster. Stay tuned.

But the point is, in a league in which five coaches have won national championships, no coach has been as consistent a winner as Tuberville. He is 80–33 in his nine seasons at Auburn. That's the best record in the SEC over that length of time. Tennessee's Phil Fulmer, one of those guys with a national championship ring, is 80–34 in that same period. It says something that Tuberville has lasted at Auburn for nine seasons. Alabama has been through five coaches in that period of time.

Tuberville's ability to read people and operate politically is second to none, and it was a big reason that he survived the university's clumsy attempt to fire him in 2003. You remember the plane that carried the Auburn University president and athletic director to Louisville to negotiate a deal with then-Cardinals coach Bobby Petrino? Tuberville not only parried that thrust, he turned it to his advantage at the negotiating table. The embarrassed Auburn administration signed him to a seven-year, $18.2 million contract extension.

Though Petrino participated in the attempted coup—hard to believe, I know—he's an example of another reason for Tuberville's success. A head coach's ability to assemble a good staff is one of those talents that goes underappreciated until it's absent. Tuberville has an eye for coordinators. Two of his former coordinators—Petrino, now at Arkansas, and Gene Chizik of Iowa State—have become head coaches, and a third, Will Muschamp, now the defensive coordinator at Texas, will be a head coach soon.

Tuberville has established Auburn as the dominant team in the state. That's not an easy task at Auburn. Pat Dye did so for most of the 1980s, and Shug Jordan did it in the 1950s before Bear Bryant arrived in Tuscaloosa. Yet the national media still considers Auburn an afterthought, when it thinks of Auburn at all. In Tuberville's nine seasons at Auburn, by the way, Alabama's record is 63–49, 17 games in arrears to the Tigers.

Over the last nine years, no team in the SEC has a better record than the Auburn Tigers.

Somehow, I don't think Auburn will cede its position atop the state without a fight.

3. OHIO STATE

Do not adjust your book binding. Do not check the battery in your Kindle. That's right: Ohio State, 2002 national champion and winner of four of the last six Big Ten titles, is underrated. The Buckeyes have made the gross misjudgment and humiliating misstep of losing consecutive BCS Championship Games. They lost in 2007 to Florida 41–14, and in 2008 to

LSU 38–24. That's a cumulative deficit of 41 points, and in our snap-judgment, win-it-all-or-hit-the-road world, it's a wonder that the Buckeyes will even bother to field a team again.

True story: in an ESPN.com story that I wrote leading up to the 2008 BCS Championship Game, I pointed out that if the Buckeyes lost, they would be halfway to the Buffalo Bills and their four consecutive Super Bowl losses. It didn't matter that I had praised Ohio State's ability to overcome the disdain of fans and media a year after such an embarrassing loss to the Gators. Judging by my inbox, you would have thought that I suggested that the university had endorsed drowning puppies. Buckeyes didn't like it. More than a decade later, the Bills' four consecutive Super Bowl losses continue to be a symbol of failure.

That's dumber than an episode of *America's Next Top Model*.

It says here that Ohio State is in the midst of its greatest run in a history of winning. Jim Tressel is achieving more than Woody Hayes ever did, and all without attacking a single sideline marker. Buckeye fans shouldn't wallow in nostalgia for the program's glory years. They're standing in them. In seven seasons in Columbus, Tressel has gone 73–16 (.820). In 28 seasons in Columbus, Hayes went 205–61–10 (.761), and against lesser competition. My friend and ESPN podcast partner Beano Cook lays into the current edition of Ohio State for the lack of muscle in its nonconference scheduling. But the Buckeyes play more difficult teams now than they ever did in the days of the Big Two and the Little Eight.

Tressel is 6–1 against archrival Michigan, which means his players have so many pairs of golden pants that they could open a jewelry store. Buckeye players receive a gold charm of a pair of football pants for beating the Wolverines, a tradition begun by Ohio State coach Francis Schmidt in 1934. Even then an Ohio State coach could get fired for losing to Michigan, a rule that still applies today. John Cooper, Tressel's predecessor, went 2–10–1 against Michigan, and it didn't matter that Cooper went 109–33–3 (.762) against everyone else. Cooper got canned.

Tressel is a good teacher. His teams represent the university well. His players stay off the arrest blotter more than Cooper's did. More important, and it can't be said enough: losing two consecutive national championship games by double-digit margins is a lot more impressive than not making the game. I believe the first sportswriter to say that was Alfred Lord Tennyson, perhaps when he covered the 1850 Rose Bowl: "Tis better to have loved and lost…"

4. TEXAS

Without speaking for everyone with a lifetime membership in The Cynics Guild, this member pleads guilty of once believing that Texas under-achieved under Mack Brown. The annual failures against Oklahoma in the pre-Vince Young years echoed the failures of Peyton Manning and Tennessee to overcome Florida in the mid-1990s. The inability to win the Big 12 championship, piggybacked on North Carolina's doomed challenges to Florida State in the late 1990s, hung the "Best Coach Never To…" weight around the neck of Brown.

When Young left after leading the Longhorns to that dramatic BCS championship victory over USC in the 2006 Rose Bowl, Texas resumed finishing behind Oklahoma in the Big 12 South. Those cynical thoughts took up residence in my head again.

Mack Brown didn't win that national championship. V.Y. did.

Mack Brown: great guy, good coach. Most fans want those adjectives switched.

Forget what I said about Ohio State. *This* analysis is dumber than an episode of *America's Next Top Model.* When you take a step back and look at what Texas has achieved under Brown, it will convert you, too:

- Texas has won at least 10 games for seven consecutive seasons, the longest current streak in the nation.
- Yes, Brown lost five straight games to Bob Stoops, from 2000 to 2004. But Brown has won three of his other four against Stoops. Speaking of big games, the Longhorns are 7–3 in bowls under Brown.
- Two Longhorns have been selected in the first round of the NFL Draft in six of the last eight years.
- Including his days at North Carolina, Brown has won at least nine games in 12 consecutive seasons. He has produced 18

winning seasons in a row, which means the last time Brown coached a team to a losing record, Barry Bonds's hat size was in the single digits.

- Texas has sold out Darrell K. Royal-Texas Memorial Stadium for 45 consecutive games.
- Texas is 103–25 (.805) under Brown.

Brown has wiped the dust off one of the most legendary programs in college football and made it a national power again. If that were so easy to do, Alabama and Notre Dame wouldn't have been wandering in the desert for most of the last decade. For that matter, Texas wouldn't have been wandering in the desert from the late 1980s to the late 1990s. In the 12 years before Texas hired Brown, the Longhorns had only six winning seasons. It's human nature to take for granted what you have while searching for what you don't. It's journalistic nature to criticize the program that is the perennial contender but not the perennial champion. Texas has achieved a level of success under Brown that is reminiscent of the glory years of Royal during the 1960s.

In other words, the rise of Texas is upon you.

5. BYU

No program has suffered from the rise of the BCS more than Brigham Young. The gulf created between the six conferences that get automatic BCS bids and the rest of college football has made rickety the bridge that the Cougars built to national respectability under the legendary LaVell Edwards. In 29 seasons, Edwards transformed BYU from a regional mediocrity into a national champion known for innovative offense in general and passers in particular: Virgil Carter, Gifford Nielsen, Marc Wilson, Jim McMahon, Steve Young, Robbie Bosco, and Ty Detmer made the Cougars synonymous with high-powered offense.

Regardless of whether BYU should have finished No. 1 in 1984, the Cougars had sideline cred. But in the 1990s, when the big conferences made the postseason a private party, even BYU suffered. In 1996, the 13–1 Cougars climbed no higher in the polls than No. 5, while Florida and Florida State played a rematch for the national championship. In 2001,

A high-octane offense has helped turn head coach Bronco Mendenhall and his BYU Cougars into a powerhouse in the Mountain West Conference.

when first-year head coach Gary Crowton won the first 12 games of the season, BYU climbed no higher than No. 8.

Crowton followed that 12–2 season with three consecutive losing records and headed out the door. His successor, Bronco Mendenhall, has restored BYU's luster but from the other side of the line of scrimmage. In 2007, when the Cougars went 11–2 and repeated as champion of the Mountain West Conference, they ranked from ninth to 18th in the four major statistical categories (rush, pass, total, scoring) for defense. They ranked anywhere from 14th to 67th in those four categories on offense.

What's more interesting, however, is that after a 1–2 start, BYU ran off 10 consecutive victories and gained next to no attention for doing so. The

Cougars didn't even enter the AP poll until they reached 8–2. The final three victories, including avenging a 27–17 regular-season loss to UCLA by beating the Bruins 17–16 in the Las Vegas Bowl, moved BYU only to No. 14.

An optimist would point out that in the previous season, when the Cougars also went 11–2, they rose no higher than No. 15. But that just proves the point. Having established their return to winning football in 2006, the Cougars established no foothold whatsoever among the opinion makers. The BCS bowl victories of Boise State and Utah notwithstanding, every Mountain West/WAC/Conference USA team still comes to the plate with an 0-and-2 count. BYU committed the error of losing two of its first three games. As every LSU fan can tell you, no two-loss team even played for a national championship before 2007, much less won one. As the Cougars continued to improve and mature, they did so in the relative anonymity of Mountain Standard Time. In a season as rudderless as 2007, when teams moved in and out of the top five as if it were a Motel 6, no one bothered to look at BYU, no matter how many wins it continued to accumulate. Hey, everyone, BYU is back. Time to take a look.

CHAPTER 2

Conferences

The Most Overrated Conference in College Football

THE BIG TEN CONFERENCE

Welcome to Big Ten football, or as it should be known, *That '70s Show*. One look and you see that these people are hopelessly outdated. Is it Red's polyester wardrobe? Jackie's feathered hairdo? The Formans' orange-brown refrigerator?

Big Ten football is the same way. Who's getting its butt kicked with regularity in the Rose Bowl? Whose talent base is drying up like a Georgia lakebed? Who has started its own cable network to exploit a football product that has passed its sell-by date?

That last question cements why the Big Ten is the most overrated conference in the sport. The league has managed to combine arrogance with irrelevance, a trick usually reserved for reality show stars and former Bush White House officials. But let's take the questions one at a time.

In this decade, the Big Ten is 0–4 in the Rose Bowl and 4–9 in the BCS overall, with seven of the losses by at least 13 points. Only one of the four victories, Ohio State's 34–20 defeat of Notre Dame in the 2006 Fiesta Bowl, has been by more than a touchdown. Two of the victories (Ohio State

The Big Ten Conference likes to think it's still the premier league in college football; its teams' performances in recent bowl games say otherwise.

over Miami in the 2003 Fiesta Bowl and Penn State over Florida State in the 2006 Orange Bowl) came in overtime.

In the Capital One and Outback, the bowls that get the Big Ten's next best teams, the league is 8–8 this decade. If the league's fans want to use that as a defense, have at it—The Big Ten: Where Our Fourth Place Team Is As Good As Yours.

There are losing records for nonconference games in the regular season, too, both overall and for the Big Ten's ranked teams alone. But rather than continue to drown you in statistics, let's try to figure this out.

Let's say, for the sake of argument, that the Big Ten's strength is in parity, that it's difficult for a champion to emerge unscathed from a league so difficult. That's not a bad argument. However, in the 16 seasons since the

Southeastern Conference expanded to 12 teams, adding a conference championship game that creates another hurdle for its best regular-season team to straddle, the SEC has had six teams win a national championship. Six out of 16 is .375, an average that usually wins you a batting title in baseball.

Think about how the power in college football has shifted south over the last decade.

From 1998 to 2007, 11 schools won or shared national championships. Number outside the Sun Belt: one.

From 1968 to 1997, 37 schools won or shared national championships. Number outside the Sun Belt: 16.

"Anyone can have a bad decade" is not an explanation.

I don't buy the argument that the Big Ten gets outcoached, or outgameplanned. That decade has included coaches such as Lloyd Carr of Michigan, who won a national championship (1997), and Barry Alvarez, who won three Rose Bowls with Wisconsin (the 1993, '98, and '99 seasons). Both men will be in the College Football Hall of Fame. The late Randy Walker won a Big Ten championship at Northwestern, which may be harder than splitting the atom.

Not to mention JoePa and TresselBall. Joe Paterno of Penn State and Jim Tressel of Ohio State—I hope I'm not insulting your intelligence by identifying them, but editors are sticklers for that sort of stuff—have the conference's aforementioned four victories in BCS games. I don't think Tressel had his 2006 Buckeyes ready to play against Florida in that BCS Championship Game. I'll go along with pinning that one on him. But the team that lost to LSU in the Louisiana Superdome in January 2008 played well.

LSU played better. Why? I don't mean this to sound simplistic or condescending, but LSU had better players. That's the biggest problem facing the Big Ten. What's worse, it's nothing that the Big Ten has done, but rather what has been done to it. As the manufacturing base of this country dries up, the populations of the upper Midwest are drying up, too.

According to the US Census Bureau, between 2000 and 2006, the population of the nation rose 6.4 percent. In five of the eight states that are homes to Big Ten universities, the population rose less than 2 percent. This just in—people are moving to the Sun Belt.

Meanwhile, jobs are hemorrhaging in Ohio and Michigan. The Pennsylvania General Assembly commissioned Standard & Poor's in 2007 to study school-district consolidation. Fewer schools means fewer football players.

If there are fewer football players, there are fewer *good* football players. Take the ESPN 150, the list of the best recruits signed in February 2008. Pennsylvania had eight players. Ohio had five. Michigan had four, and Minnesota and Wisconsin, one apiece.

By comparison, Florida had 13, Georgia seven, Alabama and Texas six apiece—*among the top 50.* We all know the accuracy of recruiting rankings sits somewhere between 50 percent and a dartboard. But when I say that the talent in college football has gone South, and that the quality of Big Ten football has gone south, they don't exactly mean the same thing.

Commissioner Jim Delany is an extremely smart guy. That's what made his comments after the 2006 season so stunning.

"I love speed and the SEC has great speed, especially on the defensive line, but there are appropriate balances when mixing academics and athletics," Delany wrote in a letter "To Fans of the Big Ten and College Football" on February 9, 2007. "Each school, as well as each conference, simply must do what fits their mission regardless of what a recruiting service recommends. I wish we had six teams among the top 10 recruiting classes every year, but winning our way requires some discipline and restraint with the recruitment process. Not every athlete fits athletically, academically, or socially at every university. Fortunately, we have been able to balance our athletic and academic mission so that we can compete successfully and keep faith with our academic standards."

Delany did everything but break into song, covering Randy Newman's "Rednecks": "College men, from LSU, went in dumb, come out dumb, too."

But people in glass stadiums shouldn't throw stones. As Dan Wetzel of Yahoo! Sports pointed out, the Big Ten schools' Academic Progress Rate, an arcane NCAA formula used to make sure that that universities graduate their student-athletes, trailed that of the SEC schools, and by a noticeable margin.

Delany preached patience, the message being that success in football has been cyclical in the past and that the Big Ten will rise again. You can believe

Delany or you can believe Arizona Senator John McCain, who told the Michigan voters during his campaign for the Republican presidential nomination in 2008 that those jobs aren't coming back. If that's the case, the Big Ten's players may be gone, too.

The Rest of the Most Overrated

2. THE ATLANTIC COAST CONFERENCE

It is one of my go-to movie quotes, and it applies to football as waged by the Atlantic Coast Conference. The quote comes from *Working Girl*, the 1988 comedy starring Melanie Griffith as the New York secretary who wills her way into a corporate finance job. Griffith's best friend Cyn, played by Joan Cusack, thinks Griffith is overreaching.

"Sometimes I sing and dance around the house in my underwear," Cyn said. "Doesn't make me Madonna. Never will."

The ACC decided to sing and dance around in its Under Armour in 2003, when it raided the Big East for Miami and Virginia Tech. Boston College, after admonishing those schools for leaving and pledging solidarity with the rest of the Big East, swooned when the ACC came calling a few months later. With friends like that....

Commissioner John Swofford and officials at schools around the league believed that the ACC's survival depended upon extending the league's television footprint to the Northeast and to south Florida. By expanding to 12 teams, the league could play a conference championship game, which would bring more money.

It worked, in theory, at the time. All I want to know is, which mortgage broker did the ACC use? The league looks like every other American who overexpanded this decade, buying an unaffordable house with an adjustable-rate mortgage. I don't mean that the ACC is in financial trouble. There are too many guys in suits on too many campuses to make a financial mistake. I mean that three years into the expansion, the ACC is in over its football head.

The ACC Championship Game has been a flop in Jacksonville, with attendance spiraling from 72,749 in the inaugural game between Florida

State and Virginia Tech in 2005, to 62,850 in 2006 (Wake Forest–Georgia Tech), to 53,212 in 2007 (Boston College–Virginia Tech). At this rate, in five more years, the league could stage the game at a Greensboro middle school. Think of the savings in overhead.

That's one reason the league is moving the championship game to Tampa and Charlotte for the next four years. The other is that the Gator Bowl didn't like bringing a team back to Jacksonville four weeks after it played there. That's a tough way to fill hotels.

The ACC hitched a ride to football relevance on the back of Florida State, which joined the league in 1992 in the midst of the Seminoles' streak of 14 consecutive top-five seasons. But when the league expanded again in 2004, the Seminoles' national power had waned. Miami decided to join the league fewer than six months after playing for a second consecutive national championship and its sixth in 20 seasons. Those aren't the Hurricanes that have been playing in the ACC. Miami's record in four years of ACC play is 16–16.

When Florida State and Miami vacated the top of the league, they created a power vacuum. The rest of the league has been a bunch of poseurs. Clemson has been a model of consistency and, in terms of winning even a division title, a model of disappointment. Maryland, Wake Forest, Georgia Tech—each has had its moments on the national stage but hasn't been able to sustain that success.

Only newcomer Virginia Tech has maintained a consistent presence atop the league—two championships and a division title in four seasons—but the Hokies have struggled among the national powers. They lost all three games they played against top-10 teams in 2007.

Virginia Tech's upset loss to Kansas in the 2008 Orange Bowl made the ACC 1–9 in BCS games, with four of the losses by double-digit margins. But let's not pick on the Hokies. The league lost six of eight bowl games, including its last five, after the 2007 season.

The ACC may be a victim of its own selling ability. The rhetoric that flowed after the league expanded raised expectations on a grand scale. Tobacco Road now had hash marks.

But the ACC hasn't come close to meeting those expectations. That's why six schools have introduced new coaches in the last two years. Miami went 6–6 and fired Larry Coker. Georgia Tech went 7–5 and fired Chan Gailey. Hey, no one in college football has patience anymore. But the reasons that there is no more patience are the increased expectations and financial demands on football. In the case of the ACC, the league brought those expectations and demands on itself.

When ACC commissioner John Swofford said in 2003 that the league had to expand in order to survive, I didn't believe it (neither did the University of North Carolina, which voted against expansion). I still don't. The ACC had a solid financial model with nine teams. When you have "only" nine teams, each piece of the financial pie is bigger. I'm going to stay out of financial analysis, because you didn't pick this book up in the business section of the bookstore. I just want to point out that four years in, the ACC has done nothing to change my original belief that it expanded to grab power and money, and that it raided the Big East Conference for no good reason.

We can trot out here the cyclical nature of college football, how conferences rise and fall with regularity. If that's the case, the ACC managed to time its expansion just as it plummeted. Sell high, boys, sell high.

There's some evidence that the ACC's time will come again. In February 2008, the ACC schools signed 32 players in the ESPN 150, 13 of them in the top 50. Miami finished first in the website's recruiting rankings, signing 12 of the 150. Clemson had 10. A year earlier, the ACC schools recruited 23 players in the ESPN 150, six of them in the top 50. Perhaps the incoming players, sensing an opportunity to play quickly, are buying low.

If the cause of the ACC's downfall is not cyclical, then it means the league has made a promise of big-time football that it can't keep. It may be that the ACC dancing around in its underwear doesn't make it Madonna. Or it may just be the league got caught with its pants down.

3. THE PAC-10 CONFERENCE

To be perfectly honest, I don't know whether the Pac-10 is overrated or if the 2007 season opened my eyes fully to its faults. But as someone who championed Pac-10 football when others dismissed it, the 2007 season turned out to be a disappointment…or maybe just a reality check.

The failures of Washington, Arizona State, and UCLA to break through the ceiling that USC has installed above them says more about the deficiencies of the league than any of its detractors ever have. Since King Pete ascended his Trojan throne, all three schools have threatened to topple USC and failed.

I left Oregon out of that triumvirate for a few reasons:

1. The Ducks beat the Trojans in 2007.

2. The Ducks may continue to challenge the Trojans for the Pac-10 championship in the next couple of years. Coach Mike Bellotti must find a way to keep offensive coordinator Chip Kelly, who parachuted in from I-AA New Hampshire in 2007 and transformed the Duck offense into the most dangerous in the nation. Before Kelly, quarterback Dennis Dixon played like a wildly talented enigma. After Kelly, Dixon would have won the Heisman Trophy had he not torn his ACL late in the season.

3. As long as Oregon has Nike founder Phil Knight as a sugar daddy—Knight has donated more than $150 million to the athletic department where he once ran track—Oregon will be a Pac-10 player.

4. Most important, no one outside of USC in this league knows how to play defense. The Trojans finished second in the nation in scoring defense (16.0 points per game) in 2007. The next Pac-10 team, UCLA, finished 29th (22.3 points). Between the two schools were seven ACC schools, five Mountain West schools, and four each from the Big Ten and the SEC.

Washington, UCLA, and Arizona State have a tradition of success that is receding in the rearview mirror. The Huskies have the excuse of the NCAA mess created during former coach Rick Neuheisel's firing. Neuheisel participated in a March Madness pool and got canned for it. Then the NCAA piled on. Washington and the NCAA handled the case so poorly that Neuheisel won a seven-figure settlement. Add to that recruiting nightmare the ineffective Band-Aid applied when the university replaced Neuheisel with Keith Gilbertson, and the bottom fell out of a program with a winning tradition. Coach Ty Willingham has shored up the foundation of the program but that work has yet to produce success on the field.

Neuheisel, meanwhile, left Washington under a cloud that only an alma mater could ignore. He has resurfaced at UCLA, which he led to a Rose Bowl victory as a quarterback 25 years ago. Neuheisel knows how to win as a college coach, and his specialty at both Colorado and Washington has been quick turnarounds followed by nearly as quick declines.

He has his work cut out for him in Westwood, because UCLA has been the biggest disappointment. The Bruins' inability to mount a challenge to Carroll is the reason that Karl Dorrell is now a Miami Dolphins assistant coach. The one season in which the Bruins threatened the Trojans, 2005, their game said everything about the state of the two programs. In the fourth quarter, with USC sitting on a 59–6 lead, some players spent their time on the sideline mingling with hip-hop star The Game. Plenty of other luminaries hovered nearby. The final score: 66–19.

The following year, UCLA's 13–9 upset knocked USC out of the BCS Championship Game and reminded everyone what the rivalry should be. But the rivalry isn't that at all. The Bruins fish out of the same recruiting pond as the Trojans, but they don't get nearly as many bites. It has been only a decade since UCLA owned this rivalry and the Pac-10. Seems like it has been a lot longer.

If Neuheisel doesn't bring UCLA within sight of USC, then the challenger may be Arizona State under veteran coach Dennis Erickson. The Sun Devils appeared as if they had made up ground on the Trojans in the first two-plus months of the 2007 season. Erickson took over for Dirk Koetter, a nice-enough guy who struggled with the public duties of being a head coach. Erickson knows how to find matchups that work for him on the field, and he has a knack for unearthing talent that other coaches overlook.

The latter won't help him until Erickson and his staff have recruited more players. The former made Arizona State into a midseason power. The Sun Devils reached 8–0 by overcoming second-quarter deficits of 14, 19, and 13 points and two other halftime deficits. Erickson and his staff adjusted to what they saw and took over control of the games. The streak ended with late-season losses to Oregon and USC, both more talented than the Sun Devils. Based on Erickson's 158 career victories and the two national championships (Miami 1989, 1991), Arizona State will challenge USC. Based on the 12 senior starters that the Sun Devils lost from their 10–3 team, it may not be in 2008.

That leaves California, and as I state in the chapter on active coaches, coach Jeff Tedford revitalized the Golden Bears. They even tied USC for the 2006 Pac-10 championship. But as far as threatening USC's surpremacy, Cal has left some chicken on that bone. The 2007 team, in particular, seemed like a bad mix. The Bears reached No. 2 in the nation and promptly fell apart. They needed a come-from-behind victory over Air Force in the Armed Forces Bowl to salvage a winning season.

Going into 2008, the momentum in the league rests with USC and with Oregon, which reached 8–1 and No. 2 in the country before quarterback Dennis Dixon tore his ACL. The Ducks limped home with three consecutive losses, only to show some promise in the 56–21 rout of South Florida in the Sun Bowl. Justin Roper, who as a redshirt freshman began the season so far down the depth chart he needed scuba gear for practice, threw four touchdown passes against the Bulls.

If you hadn't already heard of offensive coordinator Chip Kelly, that should give an idea of what he can do. Oregon will be the latest to make a run at USC's crown.

The Most Underrated Conference in College Football

THE SOUTHEASTERN CONFERENCE

Saying the SEC is underrated is like saying that George Clooney is more handsome than most women think. It is difficult to underrate the league that has won the last two national championships. It isn't exactly breaking new ground to say that the SEC has great players. Last season, four SEC players combined to win 10 national awards, including the Heisman (Florida quarterback Tim Tebow, the first sophomore ever to win the Heisman), the Outland (LSU defensive tackle Glenn Dorsey), the Doak Walker (Arkansas running back Darren McFadden), and the Rimington (Arkansas center Jonathan Luigs).

Before you nominate me to portray Captain Obvious, Defender of the Already Known, hear me out. The examples above speak only to the last two seasons. Once you step back and measure the breadth and depth of the league's dominance, you realize how much distance separates the SEC from the rest of college football. The SEC:

- Had 263 players on NFL rosters on Opening Day of the 2007 season, 25 more than any other league.
- Had five teams in the final AP top 15 for the second time in three seasons.
- Has five coaches who have won a national championship, and a sixth who went 13–0 and didn't get a chance to play for one (Tommy Tuberville, Auburn, 2004).
- Averaged more than 75,000 fans per game in 2007. Six of the top 11 schools in attendance in 2006 are SEC members.

That last number has nothing to do with the quality of play. In 1998, when South Carolina went 1–10 in the final year of Brad Scott's tenure as coach—lame-duck coach, lame team—the Gamecocks averaged 74,744 fans a game. SEC attendance has everything to do with what makes the league different from the other conferences. People who don't live in the South don't understand the degree to which college football is integrated into daily life. Warren St. John chronicled life among the fans who attend Alabama games around the country in their trailers and motor homes in his 2004 book *Rammer Jammer Yellow Hammer.* Sure, not all of them had their tires fully inflated, if you get my drift, but St. John wanted to get under the hood of that devotion. That he did it without ridiculing those fans is a miracle of modern reporting.

That says a lot about why SEC football is underrated by outsiders. Another reason is the question that I receive regularly from readers: what is my favorite stadium?

It's a difficult question to answer, because I have covered games or practices on more than 80 campuses across the country, from Hawaii to Miami, Boston College to Washington, Houston to Wisconsin. The best way for me to respond is to say that my favorite moment on any given Saturday is 30 seconds before kickoff. It is a sweet spot in time when both special teams run onto the field from their sidelines, when every fan in the stadium is standing and yelling, when both teams are convinced that this day will belong to them, when the tension and the excitement and the noise come together to create a feeling that no other substance created by God or BALCO can duplicate.

And when that moment occurs in a sold-out SEC stadium, no other league can duplicate it, either. The sheer amount of noise generated in these stadiums would be ear-shattering even without the sound systems that blast in concert with the end-zone video boards. When SEC teams prepare to run out onto their home fields, the video boards play a historical pastiche that touches on the school's great moments in history. I have seen many, and I have never heard a single one. From the time the first picture appears, the crowds roar with such zeal that the words and music are overrun.

What separates college football from pro football is passion. The attachment that college football fans have to their university is set in the wet concrete of youth. A student leaves home in search of himself and begins to create that identity on a college campus. For the rest of his life, he feels at peace when he sets foot back on campus. There's a reason that universities are called alma maters, Latin for "nourishing mother."

Your school represents you—the place where you grew up, or where you live, or who you are. That notion of rivalry—Us vs. Them—is hardwired in our brains. Nowhere does that passion come more alive than in the SEC.

There are theories dating back to the 1920s that explain the rise of Southern football both as an offshoot of the region's love of all things military dating back to the Civil War, or as a way of reasserting itself against the North as a result of the Civil War. One of the most famous pep talks in the history of the game came from Vanderbilt coach Dan McGugin in 1922, before the Commodores took on Michigan in the first game at Dudley Field. As Tim Cohane wrote in a biographical sketch of McGugin, the coach pointed out the window of the locker room at a nearby military cemetery.

"In that cemetery sleep your grandfathers," McGugin said, "and down on that field are the grandsons of the Damn Yankees who put them there."

Final score: Vandy 0, favored Michigan 0.

McGugin, by the way, came from Iowa and his father had been a Union officer who marched with General William Tecumseh Sherman through Georgia. That didn't come up in the locker room oratory.

The secret of Southern football is that it means more. It means more to the players, to the fans, to the culture. That's why the SEC is underrated, and will be until exchange programs are established to bring fans from other regions to the South so that they may experience it for themselves. They might need translators, but we can work that out.

That's why CBS and ESPN got weak-kneed in 2007 when the SEC began to explore its TV options, which included not only overtures from Fox but the possibility of establishing an SEC network. The networks understand what kind of show they will get from an SEC stadium in the

Great players, successful coaches, millions of rabid fans—what's not to love about the SEC?

fall. The quality of the football is high. There are All-Americans and future NFL heroes, and those football measurements that declare the SEC as special. But the networks know that the color and pageantry will be vivid. TV loves a good show, and the SEC knows how to stage one.

2. THE BIG 12 CONFERENCE

We don't have the Big 12 to kick around anymore, and I did it for so long that I sprained every tendon in my foot. The league rebounded in 2007, thanks largely to the North Division, which pulled a Rip Van Winkle about the time that Tom Osborne went to Congress.

A decade ago, when Nebraska knew how to win football games, and Colorado and Kansas State took turns nipping at the Huskers' ankles, the North more than held its own. Funny thing, though—when the Big Eight merged with the money-making portion of the Southwest Conference to form the Big 12, Osborne, on the verge of coaching Nebraska to three national championships in four seasons, warned that the balance of power in the league would tilt south. About four years after he retired, it did.

A lot of it had to do with coaching hires. South Division powers Texas and Oklahoma traded head coaches John Mackovic and John Blake for Mack Brown and Bob Stoops, respectively. Nebraska began to wobble under Frank Solich. The university fired him just as Bill Snyder began to wobble at Kansas State, and as Gary Barnett ran into a morass of problems at Colorado.

Oklahoma and Texas started winning championships. The North stopped winning anything. For five seasons, from 2002 to 2006, the North had a record of 29–66 against the South, with nine of the victories coming against Baylor. Coming out of 2006, the North gave little reason to believe that it would not only awaken but roar. Gary Pinkel had been coach of Missouri for six mediocre seasons, winning two more games than he lost (37–35). Mark Mangino, after going 2–10 in his first season at Kansas, had spent four seasons losing two more games than he won. Nebraska and Kansas State showed no signs of rising above average. Iowa State had begun a rebuilding period. And Colorado had just gone 2–10 in its first season under Dan Hawkins.

Yet there they were Thanksgiving Saturday night, playing to a national television audience, No. 2 Kansas (11–0), with the last unbeaten record on the mainland, playing No. 3 Missouri (10–1). You could have knocked most of America over with a Jayhawk feather. But both schools got there the way that the Missouris and Kansases of the world always get there: they let their opponent make the mistakes, they scheduled well, and they made smart gambles in recruiting.

Mistakes: the Jayhawks, anchored by All-American cornerback Aqib Talib, led the Big 12 by creating 35 turnovers. The Tigers finished second with 33.

Scheduling: Kansas "scheduled well" in terms of padding their win total. It's become a tradition in Lawrence: since the creation of the Big 12 in 1996, Kansas has played four (four!) nonconference opponents from the group of original BCS automatic-bid partners: a 1999 game at Notre Dame, a 2001 home game against UCLA, and a home-and-home with Northwestern. The Jayhawks lost all four. In 2007, Kansas played Central Michigan, Southeastern Louisiana, Toledo, and Florida International. In the long run, I think the Jayhawks sacrificed credibility for success. It took them a long time to climb into the rankings. How, then, does that make them underrated? The 24–21 Orange Bowl victory over Virginia Tech should have quelled all doubts.

Recruiting: Missouri and Kansas aren't going to take Oklahoma and Texas head-on and win many living-room battles, at least not until the Tigers and the Jayhawks prove themselves over a longer period of time. So they break the recruiting mold. They recruit players who aren't 6'3". They recruit players who might be a step slow but still get there faster than the other guy because they know where to go.

The Tigers ran a spread offense with a quarterback who had been running it since seventh grade. Chase Daniel led Southlake (Texas) Carroll High to about 400 victories. *Parade* magazine named him a high school All-American. But Daniel couldn't get Texas or Oklahoma to pull the trigger on recruiting him. Why? He's listed at 6'0", 225 pounds, and he's a cheese-burger short of burly.

But man, Daniel gets rid of that ball in a hurry, and he puts it on the receivers' numbers.

The same can be said for Kansas quarterback Todd Reesing, an Austin native rejected by the hometown school because of his size. The Jayhawks list him at 5'10" and 200 pounds, which may be right if Adidas starts putting cleats on heels.

Missouri and Kansas shouldn't always have to take chances on recruits. Once a school starts winning, recruits have a way of finding it. But the fact remains that Missouri and Kansas took chances that paid off. The Jayhawks got a BCS bid without winning the Big 12 North. Missouri would have gotten one if the BCS didn't have a limit of two bids per conference. And here's one of my favorite statistics from the 2007 season: Kansas won more games than Alabama and Notre Dame.

Combined.

Kansas went 12–1, Alabama went 7–6, and Notre Dame went 3–9.

Colorado also showed some life, improving to 6–7. But the most important evidence of life in the North is the final tally against the South. The North won 10 games. The South won nine. That didn't mean that Texas and Oklahoma took a step back. The Sooners won their second consecutive Big 12 championship and fourth under Stoops. The Longhorns lost three conference games for the first time in 10 seasons, but still won 10 games for the seventh consecutive season. And there's Texas Tech, which remains an offensive mother lode under coach Mike Leach, whose spread offense showcased freshman Michael Crabtree so well that he became an All-American.

There's another reason to expect that the Big 12 will get better from here. Nebraska and Texas A&M pulled the plug on coaches who had shown they couldn't get the traction to get out of mediocrity. While there's no guarantee that Bo Pelini, the highly regarded defensive coordinator of national champion LSU, will win with the Huskers, or that former Green Bay Packers coach Mike Sherman will turn around the Aggies, schools with tradition and resources (money and the willingness to spend it) will always have the opportunity to get better.

3. THE WESTERN ATHLETIC CONFERENCE

Yeah, yeah, you say, the WAC is the last league that should be underrated. As underdogs go, the league has gotten more publicity than the 2007 New

York Giants. It got so bad that Boise State coach Chris Petersen begged off answering questions about the Broncos' 43–42 overtime victory over Oklahoma in the 2007 Fiesta Bowl. That victory finished a 13–0 season. It made Boise State a national phenomenon. For months afterward, anyone who wore a Boise State sweatshirt anywhere in the nation got a smile of appreciation.

When Hawaii followed suit by finishing the 2007 regular season as the only undefeated team in the nation, it only added to the league's reputation. But when Georgia humiliated Hawaii 41–10 in the Sugar Bowl—and trust me, it wasn't that close—the talk about the WAC screeched to a halt. Hawaii going to New Orleans was a little suspect because of a schedule that included two I-AA teams, although the Warriors got stuck playing Northern Colorado (who knew Colorado had a directional school?) and Charleston Southern (who knew this was a school and not a railroad?) because, in the era of 12-game schedules, schools on the mainland would rather stay home and play a I-AA school than go all the way to Honolulu.

Hawaii had the weak schedule and it won two games in overtime and a third by two points. But the Warriors finished the regular season No. 10 in the nation, so they qualified for an automatic bid to a BCS bowl. Hawaii came all the way to New Orleans and won the coin toss and just about nothing else. The question after the game was whether Hawaii frittered away all the goodwill that Boise State created.

Here's why the WAC really is better than you think:

Hawaii went 12–0, and that should be rewarded, even if the Warriors laid an egg in the Sugar Bowl. Hawaii wasn't the only team to have an easy schedule. But if only one team goes undefeated, it must be pretty difficult to do.

It is true that neither Boise State nor Hawaii would have been granted a BCS berth if it were up to the BCS bowls and the conferences that get automatic bids. Both schools got bids because Congress leaned on college football poobahs to make more room at the feeding trough for the have-nots. The bowls' refusal to invite them was not a reflection of the quality of the teams. It reflected the money those schools could bring with them to those bowl games.

Bowls might be football games, but their primary task in life is to drive the economic engine of their host city for at least four days. Bowls are interested in putting butts in stadium seats, hotel beds, and restaurant chairs. Bowls want a competitive game because it will keep the TV network happy. The bowls believed that when you get a WAC team, you may have a harder time selling tickets, and you may not get a competitive game.

Neither worry proved true with Boise State. And although Hawaii was competitive right up to the opening kickoff, a surprising amount of Warrior green could be seen in the French Quarter leading up to the game and in the Superdome on New Year's. It may be a long way from the islands to Poydras Street, but it seemed like every Hawaii native who lived on the mainland dropped what he was doing to come to New Orleans and see his Warriors make the big time. There's a message there regarding the viability of WAC teams in the BCS. Invite them, and they will come.

The WAC is a business-school casebook for showing how to use available media to overcome its schools' disadvantages in the recruiting marketplace. WAC members have been willing to play whenever and wherever ESPN suggests in order to maximize the number of TV cameras pointed at their teams. Those weeknight games, plus the decision by schools to allow streaming of their games on the Internet, have made WAC football more accessible to potential recruits.

The biggest reason that the WAC has been underrated is coaching. For three years, it had the only active member of the College Football Hall of Fame. Nevada coach Chris Ault retired from coaching in 1995, got inducted into the Hall in 2002, and returned to coaching in 2004.

(Active coaches weren't eligible at the time; in 2006, the Hall changed its rules to say, hey, if you're 75 and still coaching, you're eligible. It's known as the Let's-Figure-Out-How-To-Induct-Bobby-Bowden-And-Joe-Paterno-Together-While-They're-Still-Vibrant Rule.)

Ault is fifth in victories among active coaches with 191. Dick Tomey of San Jose State is seventh with 175. Boise State's Petersen is 23–3 in two seasons. Pat Hill's philosophy of Play Anybody Anywhere has made Fresno State, as they say in baseball, a tough out. Hill, 85–55 in 12 seasons, has coached teams that beat Kansas State, Washington, Oregon State,

Programs like Hawaii and Boise State have made the WAC a conference to be reckoned with. (Photo courtesy of AP Images)

Wisconsin, and Colorado—and all of them on the road. Hill also has shown a knack for developing tough secondaries: the Bulldogs have had seven defensive backs drafted by the NFL with Hill as head coach.

Hill, like Petersen and June Jones, the coach who dug Hawaii out of a ditch when he arrived in 1999, is considered an excellent judge of talent. Finding the right recruits is doubly difficult at WAC schools, which have to calibrate a) which players they like, b) which players they like that they can sign, and c) which players they like that no one else wants. Boise State tailback Ian Johnson rushed for 1,713 yards and 25 touchdowns during the 2006 season. He became a folk hero when he proposed to his girlfriend, Broncos cheerleader Chrissy Popadics, on the field after the Fiesta Bowl while on national television. Johnson signed with the Broncos because they made him an offer. No big schools did.

Jones took a chance on quarterback Colt Brennan. The quarterback had pled guilty to first-degree criminal trespass and second-degree burglary over an incident in a female student's room in January 2004 during his freshman year at Colorado. Brennan not only turned his life around off the field—he spoke to inmates at a juvenile detention center near his Honolulu apartment—he blossomed on the field under the tutelage of Jones. The coach has gambled and won on players who have had problems with the law. Those aren't gambles he will have to take at SMU. Jones, unable to withstand the lure of a bigger salary and better facilities, left Hawaii for Dallas in January 2008.

That's a blow to the WAC, and the conference will suffer again when men such as Ault and Tomey retire. In the meantime, if the WAC makes the BCS in January 2009 and you're still surprised, you're just not paying attention.

CHAPTER 3

Rivalries

The Most Overrated Rivalry in College Football

USC-UCLA

As a native of Alabama who has lived in California, Texas, and now New England, I've got a pretty good grip on regional biases. They have in common the trait of ignorance. People dismiss what they don't know.

But as someone who has covered college football for more than 20 years, and as someone who has covered Alabama-Auburn, Ohio State–Michigan, Texas-Oklahoma, USC–Notre Dame, Florida-Georgia, etc., etc., I want to pre-empt criticism of what I am about to say. I might be wrong, but it's not from ignorance.

The USC-UCLA rivalry is the most overrated in college football. There is a rivalry. There is some emotion. There is some dislike.

But, c'mon. It's in L.A.

There are the sellout crowds at the Los Angeles Memorial Coliseum and the Rose Bowl. There's the delight the Bruins took in ending the Trojans' national championship hopes in 2006 with a 13–9 upset. There's the 1967 game, in which the No. 4 Trojans and their Heisman Trophy candidate, tailback O.J. Simpson, defeated the No. 1 Bruins and their Heisman Trophy

The laidback attitude of most Californians makes for a lukewarm rivalry between USC and UCLA.

winner, quarterback Gary Beban, 21–20. The game turned on Simpson's 64-yard, gravity-defying touchdown sprint in the fourth quarter. Dan Jenkins, the best college football writer since Grantland Rice, has that '67 game on his short list of all-time greats.

But, c'mon. It's still in L.A. These people don't know how to hate a college football opponent. The weather's too nice. There's too much else to do. College football is just not important enough.

The lifeblood of a college rivalry is the identity that alumni and fans invest in their school. It is oxygen. It is all there is. UCLA may have lost eight of the last nine to USC by an average of 21 points, but the typical Bruin doesn't feel a sliver of the angst that has taken up residence in the gut of every Alabama fan. The Crimson Tide faithful awaken every day knowing that they have to go into the office and face Auburn fans who will let them know—every day—that the Tigers have won six straight Iron Bowls.

College football does not do well in urban markets, largely because of the arrival over the last 50 years of NFL fever. Los Angeles is an exception because there's no NFL team, and because USC and UCLA have healthy fan bases. But L.A. college fans don't have the same allegiance to these two schools that college fans around the country have. L.A. people are more than their school. When their teams lose, they don't riot. They just don't show up.

USC and UCLA fans say that they work together uneasily. They say that marriages between alums of the two schools are "mixed." But you could generate a healthy debate regarding whether UCLA is even USC's biggest rival. The Trojan players, and probably the fans, may tell you that they would rather beat the Bruins than anyone else. They do have to live there. The rest of the country pays more attention to USC–Notre Dame (which, by the way, began in 1926, three years before the USC-UCLA rivalry).

If there is any doubt about the identity of your biggest rival, then by definition your rivalry is overrated. The only place that doubt is allowed in any rivalry regards the outcome. UCLA and USC are lacking here, too. UCLA's 2006 upset of USC prevented the Trojans from playing for No. 1. But one of the reasons that the upset made the earth move is that it was so, so unexpected. When one team consistently loses to the other by an average of three touchdowns, that's not a rivalry.

Bruin fans may counter that the rivalry's heartbeat has slowed, not stopped—UCLA trails USC 42–28–7 in the all-time series. In their defense, the rivalry does possess one of the trademarks of any great rivalry: pranks. Bruin fans traditionally defaced the Tommy Trojan statue on the USC campus until the arrival of the Trojan Knights, 24-hour volunteer guards during the week of the game, who annually encase bronzed Tommy in—we kid you not—duct tape. This may be a case of the cure being worse than the illness.

The rivalry's trophy, the Victory Bell, once belonged to UCLA. USC frat boys stole the bell and hid it, and after the administrations of the schools negotiated, they agreed that the winner would keep it for the following year. The team that wins the Victory Bell paints it the appropriate color: UCLA's "true blue" or USC's cardinal.

Not bad, although trophies themselves, while fun, aren't necessary. Many of the top rivalries don't play for trophies, and if they do, the most ardent fans couldn't tell you what they are. In most top rivalries, the trophy is the scalp of the losing coach. There is a hint of that in UCLA-USC. Karl Dorrell went 1–4 against USC and 34–23 against the rest of the competition. UCLA fired him. John Robinson, in his USC sequel, went 0–5 against UCLA, but neither athletic director Mike Garrett nor Robinson listed that among the reasons he was fired.

Ask Texas coach Mack Brown about winning 10 games and being castigated for not beating Oklahoma. Not until the national championship season of 2005, when junior quarterback Vince Young had matured and the Sooners were rebuilding, did a 45–12 Longhorns victory calm the faithful.

It is entirely possible that new Bruins coach Rick Neuheisel will do a Dr. Frankenstein on the USC-UCLA rivalry and make it compelling again. It is entirely possible that USC coach Pete Carroll will get bored with dominating the Pac-10 and begin his third attempt to climb the NFL mountain. I think Carroll is smarter than that and would rather continue being the King of Los Angeles. But never discount the power of ego among head coaches. Until one of those things happens, until this rivalry becomes competitive, and until the schools move it to a smaller place where it will consume every molecule of air for the week leading up to the game, you're going to have to find me a better rivalry than this one.

The Rest of the Most Overrated

2. NOTRE DAME–MICHIGAN

They may have the two greatest fight songs in college football. They may rank 1-2 in all-time victories (Michigan 869, Notre Dame 824) and 1-2 in all-time winning percentage (Michigan .745, Notre Dame .739). They may have national fan bases, which means that even if they ranked 1-2 in all-time losses, the television networks would beat down their doors.

They also have a dramatic history, on and off the field. When Notre Dame wanted to join the Western Conference, the Big Ten's original name, Michigan blocked the doorway.

Michigan and Notre Dame have played 26 times since the birth of the Associated Press poll, and in every game, at least one of the teams was ranked. In eight of the games, both teams were ranked in the top 10. That's quality stuff.

The Fighting Irish and the Wolverines have given us great moments: Irish kicker Harry Oliver, who had never made a kick longer than 38 yards, makes a 51-yarder to win the game 29–27 in 1980; little-known Raghib Ismail returns two kickoffs for touchdowns in a 24–19 Irish victory in 1989; and Remy Hamilton's 42-yard field goal with :02 to play to give the Wolverines a 26–24 victory in 1994, a kick that lost some luster after Michigan lost its next game, the 27–26 Hail Mary shocker pulled off by Colorado.

Good memories all, but they're not enough.

For one thing, both have bigger rivals (and if I have to spell out that Notre Dame has USC and Michigan has Ohio State, you have my permission to put this book down and pick up a romance novel).

For another, any rivalry that pretends to be serious has to play every year. This seems as basic as making fun of the other team's fight song/mascot/cheerleaders/you name it. But it proved difficult for Michigan and Notre Dame to grasp. They didn't begin to play regularly until 1978. Before that, they didn't play largely because of ego. Michigan coach Fielding Yost, embarrassed by an 11–3 loss to Notre Dame in 1909, cancelled the 1910 game. Knute Rockne always believed Yost had it in for the Irish because of anti-Catholic bias.

Whatever the reason, Yost and Michigan led the opposition to Notre Dame joining the Big Ten in 1926. They played twice during World War II, when travel restrictions trumped ego, but the schools didn't begin playing regularly until 1978. Even then, Notre Dame and Michigan took two-year hiatuses from each other in 1983–84, 1995–96, and 2000–01. It wasn't until August 2007 that the two schools guaranteed that will play each other every year by signing a 20-year extension that will take them through 2031.

I hope they move the game to later in the season. It's hard to take any rivalry seriously that is played in September. How big can the stakes be?

3. TENNESSEE-FLORIDA

Tennessee and Florida play a game with championship ramifications most every September. In 14 of 16 seasons since the Southeastern Conference adopted the two-division format, the Volunteers or the Gators have won at least a share of the East championship. That made it pretty easy for the schools' fans to learn how to loathe the other guys' shade of orange. Former Gators coach Steve Spurrier relished beating the Volunteers every season, and given the nature of Steve Spurrier, he made sure that the Vols knew how much he relished it. The Gators beat the Vols and everyone else in the 1990s, of course, but beating Tennessee and its Heisman candidate, quarterback Peyton Manning, in three consecutive seasons drove the entire Vol Nation to distraction—and usually to the Citrus Bowl.

In 1998, the year after Manning graduated, Tennessee ignited its national championship run with a 20–17 overtime victory over Florida. In 2001, when the 9/11 tragedy forced the schools to postpone their game until December, the fifth-ranked Vols made their season by upsetting the second-ranked Gators 34–32 to knock them out of the national championship hunt. The game meant so much to Tennessee that, when all it had to do to play Miami for the national championship was beat LSU in the SEC Championship Game, the Vols had nothing left. The No. 21 Tigers beat them 31–20.

But there's a difference between a rivalry based on hatred and a rivalry based on results. In the former, it doesn't matter what the teams' records are. Stanford finished the 2007 season 4–8, but by finishing 4–8 with an upset of California, the Cardinal had a good season. If the price of beating Army meant losing the previous 11 games, most Navy players would say, "Aye, aye, sir," faster than you could say "Annapolis."

In the latter, the goal is to win a championship, not to win the rivalry. If Tennessee and Florida fell to the bottom of the SEC East, would anyone at either school care who won the game? No. And don't snicker. It could happen. If you don't believe me, ask Nebraska. In the 1980s and 1990s, the Huskers developed some friction with Colorado. From 1990 through 1997, Nebraska and Colorado won or shared four of the eight national championships. The road to No. 1 for each school led them to the other.

But when Nebraska and Colorado both fell off the championship rails in recent years, the rivalry lost its urgency. The rivalry didn't have deep roots. These days, the Huskers and Buffaloes don't care about beating each other as much as they care about beating anybody.

Clemson coach Tommy Bowden and his father, Florida State coach Bobby Bowden, have created an overrated, made-for-TV rivalry between the two ACC foes.

4. CLEMSON–FLORIDA STATE

Clemson and Florida State is a rivalry the way that *Survivor* is a competition. They are both made-for-TV events. To quote a TV star from the last decade, and to defend my employer, let me be the first to say, "Not that there's anything wrong with that."

But the Tigers and the Seminoles don't play in prime time on ESPN every year because they have a history. They play in prime time on ESPN every year because their coaches have a history. TV can't get enough of emotion, and what could be more emotional than having the winningest coach in the history of the game on one sideline and his oldest son on the other? If that's not made-for-TV drama, then *Law & Order* has never been shown in reruns.

It's nice that both schools are in the Atlantic Coast Conference, and it's nice that both are in the same division, which could be the Atlantic, unless it's the Coastal—or the Pacific—and it really doesn't matter. Outside of the guys in the ACC office who split 12 teams from Boston to Miami into divisions, and maybe the league's coaches, no one can tell you which ACC team is in which division.

But I digress.

Clemson and Florida State didn't have much history before the Seminoles joined the ACC, but what's there is "cherce," as Spencer Tracy said of Katharine Hepburn in one of the most underrated sports movies of all-time, *Pat and Mike*. In 1988, Florida State, trying to recover its balance after opening the season at No. 1 and losing to Miami 31–0, trailed at Clemson for nearly the entire game.

In the fourth quarter, with the score tied at 21–21 and less than 2:00 to play, the Seminoles had a fourth down at their own 20. Clemson would have good field position after a punt, and Florida State would have a good chance of losing another heartbreaker. But Seminoles coach Bobby Bowden called not just any fake punt in the shadow of his own goal line. He called the puntrooskie. Blocking back Dayne Williams took the snap and handed the ball forward between the legs of LeRoy Butler, who stood like a statue until the Seminoles drew the Tigers to the right side of the field. Butler then took off left. He ran 78 yards to the 1, and Florida State won 24–21.

Nothing that Clemson and Florida State have played since Tommy Bowden arrived in Death Valley in 1999 has remotely compared to that, and no game that the two teams have played under father and son has compared in drama to the first one. Tommy's 3–3 team nearly upset Bobby's No. 1, undefeated team before falling 17–14. The Seminoles won the first four father-son games, but the Tigers have surged, and the rivalry now stands at Bobby 5, Tommy 4. And the minute one of the Bowdens retires, this rivalry won't be rated enough to be overrated. It will carry all the excitement of that other traditional ACC clash, Wake Forest–Boston College.

5. PITTSBURGH–WEST VIRGINIA

If only this rivalry reached the standard of its name—the Backyard Brawl. The name speaks to passion and uninhibited battle. It implies a lack of sophistication that flatlanders associate with the land of the Hatfields and

McCoys. Hah-vahd and Yale do not brawl, dear Reginald, and they would never hold such an engagement in the backyard. On the veranda, perhaps.

Pitt and West Virginia are each other's oldest rival, and there is merit there. They are separated by 75 miles of I-79, so proximity, and all that it means in recruiting out of the same pool, counts for something. It has been 12 years since either team won more than two consecutive games. And the Panthers reminded everyone of the enmity this rivalry has held in the past in 2007. In the 100th game between the two schools, Pitt not only upset 11–1, third-ranked WVU 13–9 on the last Saturday of the regular season, but the Panthers knocked the Mountaineers out of the BCS Championship Game.

But that game crystallized in my mind what has been missing from this game—relevance. A rivalry doesn't have to mean something to be great. But if it wants to avoid being overrated, it should mean as much as it promises. The Backyard Brawl's reputation exceeds its performance. It may have something to do with both schools joining the Big East. Once they became charter members of the league in 1991, winning the Brawl no longer meant as much on its own merits. What did it mean for the Big East race?

Usually, not much. Only once in the 17 seasons of conference play have both teams been ranked—in 2002, when No. 24 WVU upset No. 17 Pitt 24–17. In fact, it's been rare throughout the history of this rivalry that both teams have been good. The Panthers dominated through World War II, winning 15 in a row beginning in 1929. The 1930s remain the glory years of Pitt football. The Panthers claim four national championships in that decade. By no coincidence, they shut out the Mountaineers in eight of their 10 games.

The upset by the Panthers in 2007 has given the Backyard Brawl some momentum. The loss of Rich Rodriguez and promotion of Bill Stewart at WVU has made the skeptical among us—that would be yours truly—believe the Mountaineers' hold on the Big East in recent years is coming to an end. As Panthers coach Dave Wannstedt enters his fourth season with expectations of greatness, he could continue to rebuild the relevance of the Brawl. Playing for bragging rights is fine. But if the Panthers begin to play for the Big East championship, the Brawl will reassert its primacy among the nation's top rivalries.

The Most Underrated Rivalry in College Football

CLEMSON–SOUTH CAROLINA

Lord knows there are rivalries that have made more history than Clemson vs. South Carolina.

Through 2007, the schools had played more than 200 seasons combined and have eight 10-win seasons and one national championship (Clemson, 1981) to show for it. In seven decades of rankings, only seven times did Clemson and South Carolina take the field when both were ranked.

There are rivalries that regularly provide more goose bumps per snap than the Tigers and the Gamecocks. Only 33 of the first 105 games have been decided by fewer than seven points, and the ratio is that high only because the last three games have been decided by four, three, and two points, respectively. Clemson has won 64, South Carolina only 37 (with four ties). That is by a long shot the greatest disparity of any of the major rivalries.

There are rivalries that have made a larger impression on the football public. The average football fan couldn't place Clemson in the state of South Carolina any more than he or she could remember Frank Howard. The state only produces about 10 to 15 Division I-A–worthy players per season, including those—such as recent All-Americans Peter Boulware of Florida State, Courtney Brown of Penn State, and Joe Hamilton of Georgia Tech—who made their names without attending either school.

But if ever someone creates a machine to measure the passion generated by a rivalry, Clemson and South Carolina will make that machine tap dance.

As early as 1946, when the South Carolina stadium seated only 26,000, some 10,000 counterfeit tickets were sold. So many people took the field that Howard, the legendary Clemson coach, recalled fans standing on the sideline next to him suggesting play calls. That may be a big reason why South Carolina won 26–14.

The Gamecock faithful are a study in determination. The school has epitomized mediocrity in football, yet the 80,000 seats in Williams-Brice Stadium are filled every Saturday night. Three football coaches who won

national championships came to South Carolina with great hopes of repli-
cating their success. Both Paul Dietzel and Lou Holtz left the school with
losing records. Steve Spurrier is barely above .500.

None of that frustration, however, has ever lessened the feeling that
South Carolina fans have for Clemson, and vice versa. It would be polite to
use gloved adjectives such as "fierce" or "relentless" to describe Clemson and
South Carolina. But the gloves have always come off in this one. South
Carolinians play for keeps, on the field and off. Whether the tools used are
physical, verbal, or merely humorous, the edges are always sharp.

Thus the phone message I once received from wide receiver Jerry Butler,
a former Pro Bowl player with the Buffalo Bills, the player development
director with the Cleveland Browns, and nearly 30 years removed from his
collegiate career: "This is Jerry Butler of the Clemson Tigers and the
Cleveland Browns, and I hate the Cocks!"

Thus the infamous stunt by the Sigma Nu fraternity at South Carolina
in 1961. The frat boys dressed as Clemson players, ran onto the field and
lined up for warm-ups. After a couple of exercises, that newfangled rock
music blared through the stadium speakers and the fans went slack-jawed as
the Tigers broke into dance steps.

A clever prank, worthy of the finest card stunts pulled by Harvard and
Yale, or the scientific shenanigans pulled by Cal Tech students at the Rose
Bowl. But the butts of those practical jokes didn't run onto the field and ini-
tiate a brawl. Clemson fans did, and it took the South Carolina state
troopers to restore order.

"When I was at Auburn," said Iowa State defensive coordinator Wayne
Bolt, a veteran coach who has worked at Clemson as well, "everybody
thought Auburn-Alabama was the only rivalry in the world. That's true in
the state of Alabama. When you go to South Carolina, Clemson–South
Carolina is just as big as any rivalry in the country. There was a lot of ill
feeling. The ill feeling was among the fans, not the coaches and the players."

What it lacks in size—South Carolina is the smallest state in the
South—it makes up for in a feistiness that stretches from the present day
back into the 19th century. The Civil War began at Fort Sumter, in the
Charleston harbor, in 1861. No one personified the spirit of South Carolina

more so than John C. Calhoun, the "Lion of the Senate," the man who defended his state's rights with fervor.

When Calhoun died in 1850, he left his plantation near Greenville to his daughter and her husband, Thomas Green Clemson. When Clemson died in 1888, he willed his plantation to the state, on the condition that it create an institution of higher learning. He saw it as a way to ratchet the state out of the poverty of Reconstruction.

Not only that, Clemson demanded that admission to the college be made available to the sons of agriculture, the farmers and mechanics looked down upon by the gentry in the cities of Charleston and Columbia, the latter the state capital and the home of the state university.

The governor elected in 1890, "Pitchfork Ben" Tillman, championed the sons of the soil. Tillman rose to power as a populist and a virulent racist. Pitchfork Ben wanted to provide education for the working man, as long as he was white, and Tillman considered the University of South Carolina an elitist institution.

Before Clemson University even existed, in other words, the seeds of the rivalry had been planted. Clemson began as a military school, which only heightened the esprit de corps generated by its status as poor country cousin.

"Clemson was founded in 1889, and it was only 12 years later when they started playing South Carolina in football," former Clemson president Phil Prince said. "A lot of that animosity existed between people who supported Clemson—there were no graduates to speak of—and thousands of South Carolina graduates, and wealthy planters, and legislators."

A near-riot after South Carolina's 12–6 victory in 1902 resulted in a seven-year suspension of the football rivalry. At that point, the schools decided to play the game during the annual State Fair on a Thursday. The rivalry soon became known as Big Thursday.

"This rivalry is really a humdinger," Prince said. "It was even more so in the days of Big Thursday. It was the only thing happening in college football on a Thursday in October. It got a lot of attention nationally. The women all dressed up and wore big hats, and men wore coats and ties. The [South Carolina] governor always started on one side of the field and at half, he ceremoniously walked over to the other side."

After years of complaints, seething, and quiet negotiation, Clemson's resentment over playing in Columbia every year came to a head following the 1956 season. Cooler heads at Carolina prevailed. On January 29, 1957, the schools announced that they would cancel Big Thursday and play home-and-home.

Tradition being what it is in the Deep South, this announcement went over as if the schools had announced they had banned the use of the word "y'all." But in 1960, South Carolina came to Clemson. The Tigers won 12–2, and the next day, the sun defied the predictions of Gamecock fans and did, in fact, rise.

The passions generated by the rivalry have deepened, if anything, over the ensuing half-century. Sometimes, they electrify, as Butler did with his last-minute, 20-yard touchdown catch that beat South Carolina in 1977. Sometimes, they go too far, as they did in the brawl in 2004, after which both

While their meetings often take place outside of the top 10, no rivalry stirs more passion than Clemson–South Carolina. (Photo courtesy of AP Images)

schools penalized themselves by not accepting bowl invitations. But always, there is more passion within than is known outside the state. That's why this rivalry is the most underrated in college football.

The Rest of the Most Underrated

2. WASHINGTON–WASHINGTON STATE

The rivalry between Washington and Washington State, tucked in the upper left corner of our nation, has had trouble gaining attention for decades. It is not the most prominent rivalry in the Pac-10. It is not the most prominent rivalry in the Northwest, having been overtaken by the Civil War between Oregon and Oregon State (blame that on the name "Apple Cup": one sounds like a battleground and one sounds like it belongs in a Happy Meal).

All of that is too bad, because what the Huskies and the Cougars do offer is plenty of what makes other rivalries tick. There is the State U–Ag School relationship. There is the urban-rural component. Washington is in Seattle, which is to the left on your map and to the left on your political spectrum. Washington State is in Pullman, which is several hours from most of civilization.

"I've always felt being a Cougar prepares you well for life," former Washington head coach Don James once said. "You learn not to expect too much."

There is also grand history. They have played 100 times, and they have played for the Apple Cup—the actual trophy—since 1962. But the rivalry came of age in 1982. Washington came into the game 9–1 and ranked fifth in the nation. Washington State had a 2–7–1 record. James had a 7–0 record against the Cougars and a victory would send the Huskies to their third consecutive Rose Bowl.

However, Washington State had brought the game back to Pullman instead of playing its "home" game in Spokane. The Cougars' 21–20, fourth-quarter lead teetered on the possibility that the Huskies' All-American kicker Chuck Nelson, who had made 30 consecutive field goals, would miss a 33-yarder. He missed it—narrowly, as if that mattered.

"Those are good at home," Nelson said, "but we weren't at home."

The upset sent the Huskies to the Aloha Bowl and, all of a sudden, the Apple Cup had a national reputation. A year later, the Cougars upset the Huskies again, this time by a score of 17–6, denying Washington yet another Rose Bowl and, in 1992, No. 25 Washington State stunned No. 5 Washington 42–23.

The acerbic tongue of James, and the never-resting tongue of Washington State coach Jim Walden, added some bite to the rivalry.

"Nothing in my job—not the Rose Bowls, not the Holiday Bowls, nothing—is more important than beating the University of Washington," Walden said.

"I'm a 2000-word underdog," James said, referring to Walden's inactive mute button.

Beginning with that 1982 game, the rivalry has tilted much less toward Seattle. Washington leads 16–10, with two of those victories coming in overtime. Nothing makes a rivalry like annual doubt about the outcome.

3. FLORIDA STATE–FLORIDA

Florida has Tennessee and Georgia to climb over in the SEC East. Florida State has Miami, both as an archrival and, since 2004, as an ACC rival. The Florida State–Miami rivalry has the headlines and the national relevance. Florida State and Florida have the one quality that every rivalry needs— hatred. The emotions at the nexus of the of the Seminole-Gator rivalry are rooted in the history of the rivalry. Florida is *The* University of Florida. It expects the attention and the resources because it once got all of them.

Florida State started out as a women's college. It didn't begin playing football until after World War II. Florida State had to play football for 11 seasons before the game with Florida was scheduled, and it happened the way that most such games are scheduled—at the point of a legislative gun. In 1958, after Governor LeRoy Collins "suggested" the teams should play and Seminole-loving state legislators "suggested" that they might get involved, Florida deigned to play the newcomer.

The Seminoles needed seven years to beat the Gators (16–7 in 1964). When Bobby Bowden arrived in 1976, the Gators had won 14 of 17 games, with one tie.

And that's when the rivalry began.

"I don't know what a big-time coach is," Bowden said when he was hired, as quoted in *The Book of Bowden*. "But I know if I beat Florida, I'll be a big-time coach."

Bowden immediately put the Seminoles on an equal footing. Florida State beat Florida 37–9 in 1977, Bowden's second season. When Florida State won the next three, going to the Orange Bowl in the 1979 and 1980 seasons, the victories proved that the Gators would have to deal with the Seminoles for good.

Miami became a national power in the early 1980s. Florida State joined the Hurricanes at the top in 1987. Their rivalry produced games that have been pressed into the sport's family bible. In every season from 1987 through 1993, Miami and Florida State went into their game ranked in the top 10. As feverish as the rivalry became, a mutual respect existed between the two schools. They remembered their humble beginnings. Now that Miami has joined Florida State in the ACC, the bonds between the schools will grow. That doesn't mean they will be lovey-dovey. Plenty of rivals are in the same conference. But there will be a better understanding of each other.

But back to the 1980s: as Miami rose to the big time, Florida dropped it from its schedule. Florida didn't try that with Florida State.

Steve Spurrier lost only 27 games in 12 seasons at Florida. He lost eight of them to Florida State. Bowden, in 32 seasons, is 17–16–1 against the Gators (including two bowl games). *That's* a rivalry. Florida State has earned respect from Florida. But they remain two public universities going after the same public resources. They remain two schools in separate leagues. More separates Florida State and Florida than unites them. That is what makes a rivalry tick.

4. KANSAS-MISSOURI

When Missouri and Kansas played in November 2007 at Arrowhead Stadium in Kansas City, college football fans across the nation reveled in the discovery of two teams new to the top of the rankings. The No. 4 Tigers (10–1) played the No. 2 Jayhawks (11–0), the last team east of Hawaii to remain undefeated.

Missouri won the game 36–28, clinched the Big 12 North championship, and rose all the way to No. 1.

Emotions run high whenever Kansas and Missouri renew their border rivalry on the football field.

Most of all, the ferocity of the game revealed what people who live outside of a 200-mile radius of Arthur Bryant's Barbeque did not know: Kansas-Missouri is one mean rivalry. Fans outside the two schools don't know it because both schools have stunk in football for—let's be completely accurate here—eons.

The Kansas-Missouri rivalry is the oldest west of the Mississippi, but that doesn't explain the enmity. Suffice it to say that when the schools agreed a few years back to change the nickname of the rivalry from Border War to Border Showdown, most old-time fans didn't like it.

The reason is that the rivalry transcends football. It dates to the nation's oldest, fiercest debate, when North and South argued about slavery. Guerillas from the slave state of Missouri raided Lawrence, Kansas, site of the University of Kansas, and killed Jayhawk settlers. Bushwhackers from Kansas traveled into Missouri and responded in kind.

The Civil War didn't do much to ameliorate the hatred between the two states. The football field provided a healthy outlet, beginning in 1891 and proceeding uninterrupted for 116 games. Kansas dominated the early rivalry. As the late Bob Broeg wrote in his history of Tiger football, *Ol' Mizzou*, the university got serious about beating the football Jayhawks in 1909. A Missouri professor lured Princeton coach William W. Roper to Columbia. When he got off the train, Broeg wrote, Roper addressed the 400 students who greeted him with words sweet to their ears: "I understand you want to beat Kansas."

Those Tigers beat the Jayhawks 12–6 to finish the season 7–0–1.

Of course, Roper up and returned to Princeton because Missouri could not double his salary to $5,000. That may be the story of Missouri football right there.

In 2000, 91 years after Missouri hired Roper, it hired Gary Pinkel. "I went to a reception at one of the hotels here," Pinkel said the week of the 2007 game. "I think the first 10 people came up to me and said, 'Coach Pinkel, great to have you here, uh, but we better beat Kansas.'"

The more things change….

The enmity runs in both directions, of course, and so do the victories. Officially, Missouri leads, 54–53–9. In Kansas, the Jayhawks lead, 54–53–9. The school claims a 23–7 victory in 1960 that the NCAA later demanded that it forfeit. When two institutions of higher learning can't agree on math or the meaning of the word "forfeit," that's a rivalry we all need to know better.

5. BOSTON COLLEGE–NOTRE DAME

When Notre Dame became a national football power in the 1920s, the university did so in spite of the blatant religious prejudices of the day. That's why the Western Conference, which evolved into the Big Ten, blackballed Notre Dame. Somehow, the Irish survived not joining the league. Instead, it decided to become the most recognizable name in college football for the rest of the century.

This country is long past the day when fans would greet the Fighting Irish with the chant, "Mackerel Snappers Go Home." The last time I recall the subject of Catholicism being noticeable came at the height of the Notre Dame–Miami rivalry in the late 1980s, when T-shirts promoting "Catholics vs. Convicts" became big sellers. If there's any prejudice there, it's not against the Catholics.

But religion lies at the heart of the on-again, off-again rivalry between Boston College and Notre Dame. It's not anti-Catholicism. This is a family battle. Boston College is a Jesuit institution. Notre Dame is run by the Congregation of the Holy Cross. Family battles can be vicious, which is why, despite the fact that they have played only 17 times, this rivalry never disappoints.

Notre Dame and Boston College didn't play until 1975. Knute Rockne didn't believe in playing Catholic schools. He wanted Notre Dame to be every Catholic's favorite team (mission pretty well accomplished). The 1975 game was only the second against a Catholic institution since the Rockne Era.

If that had been the only reason for Boston College to dislike Notre Dame, that would have been sufficient. In 1941, however, the Irish hired away coach Frank Leahy, who had just taken the Eagles to an 11–0 record, including a 19–13 upset of Tennessee in the Sugar Bowl. Leahy, of course, became one of the greatest coaches in the history of the game.

In 17 games since 1975, Notre Dame holds a 9–8 advantage. However, the Eagles have won the last five, including a 14–7 upset of the 8–0, fourth-ranked Irish in 2002, when Notre Dame, under first-year coach Tyrone Willingham, came out in their famed green jerseys.

Not one of the all-time great motivational ploys.

Even that game pales before the 1993 game, when No. 17 Boston College knocked off Notre Dame, which had just ascended to No. 1 after stunning Florida State 31–24 in the Game of the Century. After a week of celebration, the Irish fell behind the Eagles 38–17 in the fourth quarter, only to rally with 22 of the most dramatic points in the school's very dramatic history.

With 1:09 to play, Boston College quarterback Glenn Foley drove the Eagles to the Irish 24, from where David Gordon nailed a 41-yard field goal. Okay, "nailed" is inaccurate. Gordon kicked a ball that only Tim Wakefield could love, a wobbly, floaty, left-footed effort that didn't exactly soar over the crossbar.

And the kicker, as they say, is that the kicker was raised neither Jesuit nor in the Congregation of the Holy Cross. Gordon is Jewish.

CHAPTER 4

Heisman Trophy Winners

The Most Overrated Heisman Trophy Winner in College Football History

CHARLES WOODSON (1997)

Peyton Manning has won a Super Bowl. He has made every television commercial in the last three years that Tiger Woods didn't make first. He has hosted *Saturday Night Live*. And the only person who feels more vindicated than Colts president Bill Polian, who drafted Manning with the first pick instead of Ryan Leaf, is me. I think Manning is the best passing quarterback I have covered in college football. The only quarterback I would rank above him is Tommie Frazier of Nebraska, who led the Huskers to consecutive national championships and gave a primer on how to run the option offense just as the option offense headed for the exits.

I understand how good Michigan corner Charles Woodson was. He began the season as a returning All-American. He occasionally played wide receiver. He finished second in the nation with eight interceptions. But did he achieve more than Manning? No. What Woodson did was play on a team that won the national championship. His 1997 Heisman Trophy victory reflected the Wolverines' drive through an undefeated season.

Players often say that the Heisman is a "team" award, and, in the ultimate team sport, they have a point. But in rewarding Woodson, the voters held Manning to too high of a standard. Voters penalized Manning because he had a career oh-fer against Florida. Manning couldn't lead the Volunteers past the Gators; therefore, the thinking went, Manning couldn't be the most outstanding player in the nation. It didn't matter that he threw for 3,819 yards, 36 touchdowns against just 11 interceptions, or that he completed 60.2 percent of his passes (287-of-477). And it didn't help that Florida coach Steve Spurrier, always quick with the needle, predicted that Manning could become the first three-time MVP of the Citrus Bowl, then and now the home of the best SEC team not to make a BCS game.

The bottom line on Manning vs. Woodson: the Volunteers lost a game. The Wolverines didn't.

Manning isn't the first candidate to be held to a higher standard. That's what the media does. It demands more of the front-runner than it does the underdog. Ask Senator Barack Obama, who, on Super Tuesday in February 2008, won more state contests and more delegates than Senator Hillary Clinton, yet had to answer questions about not meeting the expectations that had arisen from his campaigning the previous week.

Don't you just hate the media? Oh, wait. That's me.

The demands are obvious in college football, which uses votes to decide not only its major awards but the two teams that will play for the national championship. Every season, the No. 1 teams are judged not by whether they won but whether they won like a No. 1 team should win. The same has gone for the top Heisman candidates, although I feel that in recent years they have been judged more on their performance and less on expectation than even in Manning's time.

Manning played well against Florida as a sophomore. As a junior, he threw for a school-record 492 yards against the Gators, although he also threw four first-half interceptions against the national-champions-to-be. In 1997, the teams played early in the season, and the hype got so big that *Sports Illustrated* put the game *preview* on the cover. And the Vols lost

Charles Woodson rode the Michigan Wolverines' undefeated season in 1997 all the way to the Heisman Trophy. (Photo courtesy of AP Images)

33–20. Manning took the heat for the loss, despite completing 29 of 51 passes for 353 yards and three touchdowns. He threw two interceptions, one of which Tony George returned for an 89-yard touchdown. He got sacked twice and hurried any number of times because Tennessee couldn't handle the Gators' pressure.

And he lost the Heisman Trophy.

Point of information: in the team's three victories over Tennessee when Manning started, Florida scored 130 points. Does that sound like an issue that could be laid at the foot of Manning's locker?

Hey, as one of the leading practitioners of giving quarterbacks more credit than they deserve, I understand that Manning got what's good for the gander. But still....

Manning did have one bad game as a senior. He completed eight of 25 passes for 126 yards and an interception in the Vols' 22–7 defeat of South Carolina. A week later, he gave one of the best performances I've ever seen from a college quarterback. Tennessee played Southern Mississippi, a good Southern Mississippi team with a defense that included corner Patrick Surtain, now a 10-year NFL veteran. Manning picked the Eagles apart, throwing for 399 yards, then the second-highest single-game total in Tennessee history. The Vols won 44–20.

But on that same day, on national television, undefeated No. 4 Michigan humiliated undefeated No. 2 Penn State 34–8. Woodson caught a 37-yard touchdown pass from Brian Griese. Manning has said that he believed ABC and ESPN promoted Woodson because the network would be televising the Rose Bowl with the Wolverines in it. I don't know if there was a vast, single-wing conspiracy. I'm not a great believer in the power of Brent Musburger and Chris Fowler to deliver Heisman votes.

In the end, Manning couldn't do anything to overcome the momentum behind Woodson. On the day that Manning threw for a school-record 523 yards and five touchdowns in a 59–31 defeat of Kentucky, Woodson returned a punt 78 yards for a touchdown, intercepted a pass in the Wolverine end zone, and caught a 37-yard pass in a 20–14 defeat of No. 4 Ohio State. He became the first defensive player to win the Heisman.

Manning did all right in the award department. He won the Draddy Trophy, the "Academic Heisman" awarded to the most outstanding scholar-athlete in college football. He won the O'Brien and Unitas awards, given to quarterbacks, and he became only the fourth football player in 68 years to win the Sullivan Award, given to the most outstanding amateur athlete in the nation. Yet somehow, he didn't win the Heisman.

(Manning didn't become a three-time winner of the Citrus Bowl MVP, either. Tennessee got invited to the Orange Bowl to play Nebraska. However, Manning, slowed by a leg injury so severe he scarcely practiced, played like a shell of himself in a 42–17 loss to the Huskers).

As it turned out, Manning didn't even break any ground there. Another Manning, his dad Archie, also lost to an overrated Heisman winner.

The Rest of the Most Overrated

2. PAUL HORNUNG (1956)

When you start to describe the power of those two little words—"Notre Dame"—in the history of college football, save the 1956 Heisman for your closing argument.

Paul Hornung gets as much attention today for winning the Heisman on the worst Irish team in history as he does for his Hall of Fame career with the Green Bay Packers or his one-year NFL suspension for gambling.

Yes, the '56 Irish, at 2–8, finished with a worse record than the 2007 Irish, who rallied to finish 3–9. Hornung finished second in the nation in total offense with 1,337 yards, and in a late-season game against North Carolina, he scored every point (three touchdowns, three extra points) in a 21–14 victory.

But the news that he won the Heisman Trophy stunned even him. Credit the Lady on the Dome and a little bit of luck. Oklahoma extended its winning streak to 40 games and won yet another national championship. The Sooners, who finished No. 1 ahead of the Vols, had shut down Hornung, intercepting four of his passes, in a 40–0 nationally televised humiliation in South Bend. For the season, Hornung threw 13 interceptions and three touchdowns.

Hornung's luck, Part I: the Sooners had a Heisman problem. Halfback Tommy McDonald may have been the best back in the nation. Center-linebacker Jerry Tubbs may have been the best lineman. In many cases, if a team has two Heisman candidates, it has none. McDonald won the Maxwell Award, and Tubbs won the Walter Camp. Between them, they received nearly 1,700 points in the Heisman vote that Hornung won with 1,066. Separately, they received enough points only to finish third and fourth, respectively.

Hornung's luck, Part II: Tennessee also finished the season undefeated. Volunteer tailback Johnny Majors separated his right shoulder, missed one game, then suffered a rib injury and missed all but one play of another. He still finished second to Hornung, with 994 points.

Hornung's luck, Part III: the other prominent candidate, Syracuse half-back Jim Brown, rushed for 986 yards and led the nation with an average per carry of 6.2 yards. But Brown, an African American, could have proba-bly rushed for 3,000 yards and still wouldn't have gotten a single vote south of the Mason-Dixon line back in 1956.

It may be better to be lucky than good; Hornung proved it's best to be lucky *and* good. When Notre Dame publicist Charlie Callahan summoned

Hornung to his office at the end of the season, the last thing that Hornung expected was for Callahan to hand him the phone and say, "Tell your mother you won the Heisman Trophy."

Notre Dame players have won seven Heisman trophies, a total that has them tied with Ohio State and USC for the most from any one school. It says here that at least two, and probably three, Irish Heisman winners are overrated. That is a debate for another time. About Hornung's Heisman, there isn't much debate.

3. STEVE OWENS (1969)

It is entirely possible that calling Oklahoma back Steve Owens overrated is judging him by modern-day football standards, like ripping Junior Johnson for winning the 1960 Daytona 500 when he averaged only 125 mph. He still went faster than everyone else.

Owens may have led the nation with 1,523 rushing yards, but he did it in bruising, old-school fashion. He didn't go faster than everyone else. Owens carried the ball 358 times in 10 games, which hurts just to type. He finished with 81 more rushes than any of the other top-10 backs in the nation.

Well, that's old-school football. Three yards and a cloud of dust. To be more accurate, it was 4.3 yards per carry, which ranked ninth among those same top-10 backs. Owens did what every other back would have been asked to do in those pre-wishbone offenses: he ground it out.

It is entirely possible that Owens is not overrated. It could be that he stood out as an example of a vanishing breed—the running back who didn't need speed to succeed. They have a phrase for those backs in modern football. That phrase is "tight end."

So perhaps we are judging by different criteria. It wouldn't be fair to ask why Owens didn't break outside and turn the corner with a sprinter's gait. If Owens ran outside the tackles, he usually needed directions to get back to the huddle. At 6'2", 215 pounds, still big for a back today, Owens rarely strayed from between the tackles.

It wouldn't be fair except for one thing. The passing game looked pretty good by modern standards. In choosing Owens, the Heisman voters chose against one of the best group of quarterbacks in any one season up to that time.

Purdue senior Mike Phipps, at 6'3", 206 pounds, represented the new breed of passer. He threw for 2,527 yards and 23 touchdowns, both school records, and led the Boilermakers to an 8–2 record. The week after leading Purdue past No. 9 Notre Dame 28–14, Phipps outdueled Stanford junior Jim Plunkett in a 36–35 victory over the No. 16 Indians. Phipps threw for 429 yards and all five touchdowns the Boilermakers scored that day. That's what made him the consensus All-American quarterback. Plunkett finished eighth in the Heisman voting (he won it the following year).

Ole Miss junior Archie Manning electrified the nation in a nationally televised night game at Legion Field in Birmingham. Manning accounted for 540 yards of total offense and five touchdowns in a 33–32 loss. He led the Rebels with 502 yards rushing, threw for 1,762 yards, and threw or rushed for 23 touchdowns. He finished fourth, behind Owens, Phipps, and Ohio State junior quarterback Rex Kern.

Neither Phipps nor Manning led their teams to conference championships, but Owens didn't win because of the Sooners' success, either. The 1969 Sooners went 6–4, which in those days—gasp!—didn't even get you to a bowl game. It appears as if the voters looked at the rushing stats, saw who led the nation, and wrote in "Owens" on their ballots.

4. GEORGE ROGERS (1980)

In most seasons, a tailback with George Rogers's resume not only runs to the Heisman, he runs away with it. Rogers came into the 1980 season as the odds-on favorite, a senior who had finished second in the nation in rushing as a junior. As a senior, he indeed led the nation in rushing with 1,781 yards.

So maybe the fans in Heisman Stadium wouldn't be chanting "OH-ver-RAY-ted" if Rogers came out of the locker room tunnel. Maybe Rogers is only slightly overrated. You can make a case, even in hindsight, that Rogers should have won.

Just don't ask me to argue it for you. Not in the 1980 race, not in the South, and not anywhere near Georgia, where a freshman tailback named Hush-ul changed the face of college football in one fell swoop.

Herschel Walker stood 6'1", 215 pounds, had a sprinter's speed and a body-builder's physique. He had been the subject of a legendary recruiting battle between Clemson and Georgia, but the native of Wrightsville, Georgia, chose to stay home. Much was expected of Walker as opposed to his team, coming off a 6–5 season that included a 31–0 home loss to Virginia.

Former Tennessee coach Johnny Majors, with tongue in cheek, used to blame himself for the rise of Walker. The Volunteers took a 15–0 lead against the Bulldogs in the season opener. Georgia coach Vince Dooley, who had intended to ease his star recruit into the lineup, turned that plan into confetti and threw Walker out there. His first touchdown is such an iconic moment in the state of Georgia that I think it's taught to first-graders. Walker ran 16 yards, the last few right over Tennessee senior safety Bill Bates. Bates, who would go on to a long NFL career, looked like Wile E. Coyote expecting the Road Runner and getting the 18-wheeler instead.

Walker rushed for 1,616 yards and scored 15 touchdowns, five of them on rushes of more than 50 yards. He sat out the equivalent of nearly three games because of either injury or because Dooley called in the Dawgs, which he did a lot. With Walker leading the offense, Georgia went 12–0, including a 17–10 defeat of Notre Dame in the Sugar Bowl that clinched the national championship.

In the eighth game of the season, Walker and the Dawgs played Rogers and the Gamecocks. Rogers seized the opportunity, rushing for 168 yards. Not bad—he finished only 51 yards short of Walker's 219, which included a 76-yard touchdown.

In the end, it shouldn't have mattered that Rogers finished ahead of Walker in statistics. If the Heisman is to be awarded to the statistical rushing or passing champion, then why vote at all? There would be no romance left in the sport.

The main reason that Walker didn't win the Heisman is simple. Voters held a latent skepticism about freshmen, who had been eligible for varsity play for only a decade or so. Walker helped make the college football landscape safe for freshmen, just as, in the spring of 1983, he made the professional football landscape safe for juniors. Once Herschel left for the USFL, the NFL relaxed its rules for signing underclassmen.

Walker finished third behind Rogers and Pittsburgh defensive tackle Hugh Green, the Lombardi Award winner. These days, underclassmen win the Heisman more often than not. Although the prejudice against freshmen isn't completely erased, Oklahoma tailback Adrian Peterson finished second to USC quarterback Matt Leinart in 2004.

Given how Walker performed, and what he meant to the national champions, he should have won the Heisman. Two years later, he did.

5. TIM BROWN (1987)

On the night of September 19, 1987, the networks televised two coronations across America. On NBC, Miss Michigan, Kaye Lani Rae Rafko, was crowned Miss America. On ESPN, Notre Dame wide receiver/kick returner Tim Brown was crowned Mr. Heisman, largely by crowning Michigan State upside the head.

It took only two first-quarter snaps, four plays apart, for Brown to end the Heisman race. He returned a punt 71 yards for a touchdown. The Irish

Tim Brown's big plays on national television won him the Heisman Trophy over a more deserving Don McPherson in 1987. (Photo courtesy of AP Images)

kicked off to the Spartans, held them, and forced another punt, which Brown took 66 yards for a touchdown. After the second touchdown, a member of the Notre Dame band leapt into Brown's arms, becoming the first person in uniform to get close enough to Brown to touch him.

And that was that. As long as Brown didn't cost Notre Dame any games and didn't show any signs of moral turpitude, he had won. Brown benefited from having a sunny personality, from the resurgence of Notre Dame under second-year coach Lou Holtz, and from the university's long association with the award. It had been 23 seasons since the last Irish player, quarterback John Huarte, won under similar conditions. Huarte led a resurgent Notre Dame team into the top 10 before it faded at season's end.

In the meantime, a few hundred miles to the east, a much more vibrant renaissance was taking place. Syracuse hadn't won more than seven games in six seasons under coach Dick MacPherson. In fact, Syracuse had won eight games only once in the last 20 years, a period in which the Indians/Orangemen had an average record of 5–6.

And all of a sudden, Syracuse exploded. Senior quarterback Don McPherson executed the option with silky smoothness. The Orangemen began the season 5–0 and rose to No. 13 in the AP poll when into the Carrier Dome strutted No. 10 Penn State, the defending national champions, 5–1, and most important, winners of 16 straight games over their hosts.

On the first play from scrimmage, McPherson, Mr. Option, threw an 80-yard touchdown pass to freshman wide receiver Rob Moore. Bedlam. Chaos. Jet Engines. Syracuse fans released two decades of frustration with a roar that didn't subside for the rest of the 48–21 rout. McPherson completed 15 of 20 passes for a school-record 336 yards and three touchdowns. He ran for two more.

The Orangemen finished 11–0, including a 32–31 thriller against West Virginia. McPherson led the nation in passing efficiency (164.3), threw for 22 touchdowns, and ran for six more.

And Brown won by nearly a two-to-one margin in Heisman points. Syracuse never rose above fourth in the polls, trailing the equally undefeated Oklahoma and Miami as well as Florida State, which lost 26–25 to Miami during the season.

Ask yourself this: if the uniforms had been on the other backs, and McPherson had led Notre Dame to an unbeaten season, who would have won the Heisman?

6. GINO TORRETTA (1992)

It's been 16 years, and I still don't know what to make of Gino Torretta.

He came to Miami a lightly recruited quarterback from Pinole, California, a guy who didn't have the strongest arm or the quickest feet. Miami listed him at 6'3", but he hasn't gotten there yet.

Former Hurricanes coach Dennis Erickson prides himself on being a good judge of talent. Torretta will always be one of his prize specimens. Torretta had a quick mind and a way of being on the team with the most points at the end of the game. Torretta started five games as a redshirt freshman in 1989 because of an injury to starter Craig Erickson. He won four of them.

When he took over as the starter in 1991, he didn't lose a game. And when the Hurricanes started the 1992 season as defending national champions, Torretta led them to 11 consecutive wins, right through the regular season. That team scuffled, winning three consecutive early-season games by a total of seven points, but Miami kept winning. When Dennis Erickson referred to how smart Torretta was, he meant something like the 123 consecutive passes without an interception as a senior.

Torretta threw for 3,060 yards in that Heisman season, and his passing efficiency rating of 132.0 fell just out of the national top 10. But Miami started the season at No. 1 and remained there through the Heisman vote, which raises the debate of the role of the team in an individual award. The only rule seems to be that the winner must play on a very good, but not necessarily great, team.

Once that parameter is established, the direct relationship between "we" and "me" fluctuates every season.

(That "me" is meant to connote not selfishness but what the individual player achieves as opposed to the "we" accomplishments, or lack thereof, of his team.)

In 1992, the Heisman scale swung toward the "we" of Torretta as opposed to the "me" of San Diego State sophomore tailback Marshall Faulk, who led the nation in rushing for the second consecutive season. Faulk rushed for 1,630 yards and 15 touchdowns for the Aztecs, who went 5–5–1. That won-loss record is what bit him in the Heisman behind—that and the general suspicion that national voters had over the strength of the schedule of a team, like San Diego State, in the Western Athletic Conference. Faulk may have been dealing with a little Detmer backlash. The voters awarded BYU junior quarterback Ty Detmer the 1990 Heisman, only to have his team lose its last regular-season game at Hawaii 59–28, followed by a 65–14 loss to Texas A&M in the Holiday Bowl. Detmer's chance of the repeating as the Heisman winner in 1991 pretty much ended there.

Faulk finished second to Torretta in the 1992 Heisman vote, barely ahead of Georgia tailback Garrison Hearst. Though the we-me relationship is recalibrated in every Heisman race, the questioning of credentials of players from the WAC or the Mountain West, where San Diego State now plays, continues unabated.

Hindsight, without the glare of that Miami winning streak in my eyes, says that Faulk should have won the Heisman. I didn't vote for Torretta in 1992, and I remember feeling pretty smug about it when Alabama disman-tled Miami and its quarterback 34–13 in the Sugar Bowl game for the national championship. But the allure of a successful quarterback on a national championship contender will never go away. Football and the media's reporting of it are built for that kind of player.

7. EDDIE GEORGE (1995)

I take the Heisman personally. When the identity of the most outstanding player in college football is as obvious as the face mask on your helmet, and that player doesn't win, I don't understand. The reason that Eddie George is an overrated Heisman winner is not because I didn't even have him on my 1995 ballot. That season had more choices than a Starbucks menu.

Florida quarterback Danny Wuerffel led the Gators to an undefeated regular season, led the nation in passing efficiency, threw 35 touchdown passes, and finished third. Northwestern sophomore Darnell Autry led the Big Ten in rushing (152.3 yards per game) and starred on the Cinderella team of our generation. Iowa State sophomore Troy Davis became only the fifth rusher to crack 2,000 yards in a single season. They didn't win the Heisman, but they're not the reason that George is overrated.

No, the reason that George is overrated is that Tommie Frazier of Nebraska is the best college football quarterback I have ever covered.

Frazier made coach Tom Osborne's option offense flow. Frazier ran like a tailback and threw well enough to keep defenses honest. He won the starting job midway through the 1992 season as a freshman. Though most Husker historians say that Osborne revitalized his program by recruiting more speed and switching his 5-2 defense to a 4-3, it is merely stating fact to point out that the rise of the Huskers mirrors the rise of Frazier.

In three-plus seasons as a starter, Frazier had a record of 33–3. He missed seven games of his junior season with blood clots in his leg but came back to start the Orange Bowl, a 24–17 victory over Miami that gave Osborne his first national championship in 22 seasons as the Huskers' head coach.

In 1995, the senior directed an offense that averaged 399.8 rushing yards, 556.3 total yards, and 52.4 points per game. Frazier rushed for 803 yards, averaging more than seven yards per carry, and 16 touchdowns. He threw for 1,467 yards and 18 touchdowns, with a passing efficiency of 156.14.

His numbers tell the story about as well as the height and width of a painting capture its beauty. His numbers say nothing of his ability and willingness to throw a block. His personal stats don't explain how, when Nebraska beat No. 7 Colorado 44–21, the Huskers committed no turnovers and no offensive penalties.

This was one of the best teams that ever played college football, and Frazier served as the conductor. Only one opponent came within 23 points of the Huskers—Washington State stayed "close" to Nebraska and lost 35–21. Frazier should have won the Heisman. Instead, he had to content himself with being the quarterback of the first team to win consecutive national championships in 24 seasons. That Nebraska did so by humiliating Florida 62–24, with Frazier contributing a 75-yard touchdown run on which he broke seven tackles, made a statement more compelling than anything written.

8. ANDRE WARE (1989)

Andre Ware has become the poster child for bad Heisman decisions, which is unfair to him and to history. The best way to look at the Houston quarterback is as the quarterback equivalent of *Miami Vice* fashion. No one wears T-shirts under Armani blazers anymore, and no one falls for passing numbers in and of themselves anymore.

The run-and-shoot offense that John Jenkins installed at Houston in the late 1980s caught the rest of the Southwest Conference wholly unprepared. No one had seen anything like it, if you couldn't tell by the scores that Houston ran up on its way to a 9–2 season. The Cougars' point totals in their nine victories ranged from a low of 36–7 at Arizona State to a high of 95–21, an ugly victory over an SMU team in Year Two after its death penalty. Ware played only 13 minutes but still threw for 517 yards and six touchdowns.

Ware threw for 4,699 yards and did so in one fewer game (11) than did the previous NCAA record-holder for season passing yards, BYU's Jim McMahon in 1980. No one had ever seen anything like the Cougar offense before. In fact, no one saw it in 1989, either. Houston, under NCAA probation, couldn't appear on TV.

So Ware won the Heisman despite going unseen. He won despite Houston losing to Arkansas, the only ranked team that the Cougars played all season. He won because it took a few years for both defenses and voters to figure out that the run-and-shoot could embarrass a bad defense but couldn't overcome greater size and speed.

When Ware flamed out with the Detroit Lions in the NFL, he helped neither his legacy nor the cause of run-and-shoot quarterbacks. Some of the skepticism that greeted Hawaii quarterback Colt Brennan's remarkable 2007 performance emanated from doubts that remained about Ware.

I voted for Ware, and I did it because of the numbers. Not to quote Senator Hillary Clinton on the current war in Iraq, but if I knew then what I know now, I might have voted differently.

Ware won because of the traditional prejudice of Heisman voters against losing teams. Indiana tailback Anthony Thompson, who set an NCAA single-game rushing record (377 yards against Wisconsin) and led the nation with 1,793 yards and 24 touchdowns on the ground, won the Walter Camp and the Maxwell awards. But Indiana went 5–6, losing its last two games, and Paul Hornung of Notre Dame remained the only Heisman winner to play for a team with a losing record.

Unlike Senator Clinton, I declare that my vote was a mistake.

9. PETE DAWKINS (1958)

Pete Dawkins is an American hero. He starred at West Point, where he became the first Cadet to be class president, First Captain (leader of the Corps of Cadets), team captain, and rank in the top 5 percent of his class academically. He would become a Rhodes Scholar, at the time the youngest (36) inductee into the College Football Hall of Fame, and the youngest (45) brigadier general in the U.S. Army.

I'm just not convinced he was the best player in college football in 1958.

Dawkins was an All-American in that year of The Lonely End, as Army's offense became known. Coach Red Blaik stationed flanker Bob Carpenter wide on every play. Think of it as the ancient version of the spread offense. With the defense having to account for Carpenter, Army had to deal with one fewer defender in the box, and the Cadets capitalized. They went 8–0–1, and Dawkins, who played halfback and safety, was the biggest reason why. He rushed for 428 yards, caught 16 passes for 491 yards (the 30.7-yard average led the nation), and scored 12 touchdowns.

And he accomplished all of that despite missing one game and all but one play of another because of a hamstring injury.

The appeal of Dawkins went far beyond his unceasing attributes. Army football had come out of its grave. The team had been decimated in 1951 when the Academy dismissed 37 football players for honor code violations. Blaik rebuilt the program over the length of the decade, and when he did so with a young man as sterling of character as Dawkins, voting for him served as a way to recognize not only his achievement but to celebrate the entire Army team as well.

It's hard to argue against any of that, except that Iowa quarterback Randy Duncan had an incredible year for a team that went 8–1–1 and finished second in the nation to LSU. Duncan led the nation in passing yards

(1,347), touchdown passes (11), and completion percentage (58.7). That's pretty much the Triple Crown of passing. When the NCAA developed its passing efficiency formula in 1979 and applied it retroactively to the 1958 season, Duncan won that, too (135.1).

Duncan won the Walter Camp, awarded out of New Haven, which is close enough to West Point that it makes you wonder how they saw past the glow coming off of Dawkins to reward a player way out in the Midwest.

If I'm being completely honest with you, I might have fallen for the Dawkins saga and voted for him over Duncan. On the other hand, the guy who won the 2007 Heisman is, like Dawkins, every bit as impressive off the field as he is on, and I didn't vote for him at all. Which leads us to the 10th guy on this list.

10. TIM TEBOW (2007)

Take a talented quarterback with a great backstory. Stir in a heartthrob smile. Add an offense designed to take advantage of his skills. Add healthy doses of viral marketing. Heat and serve.

Meet Tim Tebow of Florida, who in 2007 became the first sophomore to win the Heisman. The 6'3", 235-pound Tebow finished second in the nation in passing efficiency (172.5) and accounted for more than 4,000 yards of total offense and 55 touchdowns. That's five more than any *team* in the Atlantic Coast Conference.

It's hard to be skeptical about a player with those numbers, much less a player who is a devout Christian, a summer missionary, and an example who would make any parent beam. Tebow fans believe that he is a freak of nature—an issue that the website TimTebowFacts.com addresses with equal helpings of wit and devotion:

> "Tim Tebow has counted to infinity…twice."
> "Superman wears Tim Tebow pajamas."
> "If tapped, a Tim Tebow rush could power the country of Australia for 44 minutes."

The question that I wrestle with regarding Tebow is to what extent his numbers were built on HSH—Human Stat Hormone. Late in the season,

Florida quarterback Tim Tebow is a fine player—just not as fine a player as Dennis Dixon was in 2007.

Tebow's numbers really began to benefit him at the polls. In the last six games, Florida scored 18 rushing touchdowns. Tebow scored 13 of them, nine of them from three yards or closer. That he did this after sustaining a cracked bone in his right (non-throwing) hand in the eighth game says volumes about Tebow's toughness.

It could be that he is what's next in quarterbacks, the stage beyond Vince Young.

But every player's role has a context within the team. I can't remember an offense that depended so heavily on one player to pass and run. That's what bothered me. The numbers indicated not just his talent but the fact that he dominated the ball.

I don't doubt that Florida coach Urban Meyer's first goal was to win games, not Heismans. But even he questioned the wisdom of using Tebow the way he did. At the end of the 2007 season, Meyer said he wanted to use two quarterbacks in 2008 to save the wear and tear on Tebow. That's why Tebow's season is overrated. Even his own coach wants him to have the ball less.

As Tebow made his salary drive for the Heisman, his toughest competition for the trophy limped out of the competition. Oregon quarterback Dennis Dixon, whose grasp of new offensive coordinator Chip Kelly's offense propelled the Ducks into the No. 2 ranking, tore his ACL in the ninth game of the season. Dixon played one quarter of Game 10, crumpled to the ground, and the Ducks crumpled with him. They went from 8–1 to 9–4.

Me? I thought that proved without a doubt that Dixon was the most out-standing player in college football and I voted for him. But only 16 other voters agreed with me. Arkansas tailback Darren McFadden proved himself to be the best tailback in the nation when he lined up in traditional sets. But when the junior took the shotgun snap in the Wild Hog offense, he made NFL teams want to lose games just so they could draft him. The 206 yards he gained against No. 1 LSU in the Razorbacks' 50–48, triple-overtime upset victory nearly tripled what the Tigers had been allowing on the ground (78.0 yards per game). McFadden had to settle for becoming the first player in almost 60 years to finish second in consecutive Heisman races.

CHAPTER 5

National Champions

The notion that a No. 1 team may not be the best team is as much a part of college football as popcorn and cheerleaders. It's what makes America great and what drives LSU fans crazy every four years.

In trying to figure out which No. 1s are overrated and underrated, I tended not to delve deeply into comparisons of national champions with the other overrated and underrated champions. In some cases of the overrated champions, of course, the comparisons are not only obvious, they remain disputed. What I didn't do is compare the teams the way that the media compares teams today; i.e., this champion's secondary vs. that champion's wide receivers. I'm not sure what the relevance of such comparisons would be, and I don't trust the materials available to me to make an accurate comparison.

I limited the field to the poll era, which began when the Associated Press released its first poll in 1936. Obviously, for the last 21 seasons, which I have covered, I have a better feel for what happened.

The Fighting Irish took the easy way out, playing for the tie against Michigan State to win the national championship in 1966.

The Most Overrated National Champion in College Football History

THE 1966 NOTRE DAME FIGHTING IRISH

Four decades later, it remains a tie more controversial than the one Monica Lewinsky gave Bill Clinton, more characteristic than the bow ties worn by Groucho Marx and George F. Will, more famous than any tie in history. No. 1 Notre Dame won the 1966 national championship by accepting a 10–10 deadlock with No. 2 Michigan State and preserving its place atop the polls.

Notre Dame head coach Ara Parseghian went to the College Football Hall of Fame based on his success as a head coach over 24 seasons at Miami (Ohio), Northwestern, and Notre Dame. But the game for which he is best known is neither one of his 170 victories nor one of his 58 losses. It is for the fourth of his six ties.

In case you've forgotten: with the score 10–10, the Fighting Irish took possession of the ball at their 30-yard line with 1:24 to play. Head coach

Ara Parseghian ordered quarterback Coley O'Brien to run the ball into the line. The plays produced befuddlement from the fans, followed by ardent booing, which pretty much continues to this day.

It would not be fair to apply modern football standards to Parseghian's decision. Forty years later, teams are much better prepared to go great distances quickly than they were in 1966. But still.

Notre Dame endured a great deal of mockery for the tie. It began on the field from the Spartan players. It continued in the press in the days after the game. *Sports Illustrated* senior writer Dan Jenkins's parody of the Notre Dame fight song enshrined the very un-John-Wayne-ness of it all:

> "Cheer, cheer for old Notre Dame,
> *Equal* the echoes, *deadlock* her name,
> *Draw* a volley cheer on high,
> *Level* the thunder from the sky.
> What though the odds be *even* or small?
> Old Notre Dame will tie over all,
> While her loyal sons are marching
> Onward to victory."

You have to admit that Parseghian's decision not to try to win proved to be a shrewd one. It's not merely because his calculation proved correct and the Fighting Irish hung on to No. 1. Notre Dame had another game, against USC, in which to impress the voters. But Parseghian's decision exploited Notre Dame's fame and the politics of the time.

No. 3 Alabama began that weekend undefeated and untied and ended the season the same way. The Crimson Tide had two things working against it. First of all, Alabama had won the last two AP national championships. In those cases, voters, consciously or not, look for a reason to vote for another team. Second, the national image of Alabama in 1966 couldn't have been any lower. Much of what the nation came to abhor about the South and the way it treated its African American citizens emanated from Alabama, from the church bombing in Birmingham in 1963 to the bloody march over the Pettus Bridge in Selma in 1965. As author Keith Dunnavant pointed out in his 2007 book about the 1966 team, *The Missing Ring*, when fans and poll voters across the country looked at Alabama, they didn't see Bear Bryant—they saw the bigoted governor, George Wallace.

Alabama never rose above third. The Crimson Tide shut out six of its 10 regular-season opponents, including the last four, obliterated Nebraska 34–7 in the Sugar Bowl, and never budged.

The Irish, meanwhile, had fallen behind the Spartans in the coaches' poll. Michigan State had no more games. Notre Dame, however, had to play its archrival, No. 10 USC. After a week of enduring taunts, the Irish unleashed their anger upon the Trojans, winning 51–0. The rout restored them to No. 1 in the coaches' poll and bolstered their standing in the AP poll.

Michigan State coach Duffy Daugherty hoped aloud that the teams would be co-champions. But Notre Dame's victory over USC pretty much ended the debate. Three more seasons would pass before Notre Dame would accept a bowl bid. The Irish, 9–0–1 with no more games to play, finished at No. 1. Bryant pointed out that many of players would be going to Vietnam and he hoped that they wouldn't play for a tie.

I don't know if the voters had a predilection to pick Notre Dame or not. I do know that in the postwar era up to 1996, when the NCAA introduced overtime and ended ties, on only two other occasions did an unbeaten team with a tie finish ahead of an unbeaten team without a tie. In 1970, when Nebraska (11–0–1) won the national championship, Arizona State (11–0) finished only sixth. The Sun Devils, then in the Western Athletic Conference, couldn't overcome the prejudicial judgment that WAC teams didn't measure up to the rest of the world.

In 1946, No. 1 Notre Dame (8–0–1) and No. 2 Army (9–0–1) played a 0–0 tie late in the season, yet both finished ahead of Georgia (10–0). No one complained about that Irish team—considered one of the greatest college football teams ever—because that Irish team took advantage of every opportunity it had to try and defeat the Black Knights.

The irony is that the 1966 Irish may have been the best of Parseghian's 11 Notre Dame teams. The Irish, like Alabama, shut out six opponents. They beat two ranked teams (Oklahoma and USC) and the average final score of their nine victories was 39–3. But this team goes down in history as overrated because it left a question unanswered.

Had Parseghian made an attempt to win the game and failed, Notre Dame's reputation wouldn't have acquired a taint. If Notre Dame had turned the ball over and lost, the Irish might have been remembered for their failure to protect the tie, but I doubt it. Though Parseghian and the Irish can argue that he made the correct decision because the Irish finished No. 1, they must come up with an answer for the decision Nebraska coach Tom Osborne made in the 1984 Orange Bowl. The No. 1 Huskers could have kicked an extra point in the final minute of play to tie No. 2 Miami and secure the national championship. Osborne chose to go for two points and the victory. The pass fell incomplete and Miami won 31–30. Instead of tarnishing Osborne's reputation, the decision to go for two made it.

If you buy into the belief that it doesn't matter what people say as long as they spell your name right—and if your name is Parseghian, you might— then the decision to play for the tie has paid royalties as if it were a Texas gusher.

More than four decades later, the game is not a settled piece of history. Like any controversial subject, perspectives may change, but the controversy never quiets. Parseghian's failure to go for the win has left a doubt about the team that time will never erase.

The Rest of the Most Overrated

2. THE 1997 NEBRASKA CORNHUSKERS

When Tom Osborne announced at the end of the 1997 regular season that he would retire after 25 seasons as head coach at Nebraska, you had to figure that he would get plenty of recognition. Osborne had won two national championships and 254 games, and he had given the Huskers and their fans much to treasure for a generation.

So let's see: the National Football Foundation waived the customary three-year waiting period and elected Osborne to the College Football Hall of Fame in 1998. The Third Congressional District in Nebraska elected Osborne to three terms in the U.S. House of Representatives. The university completed the Tom and Nancy Osborne Football Complex in 2006.

And there's the first big present that Osborne received, courtesy of the American Football Coaches Association: the 1997 national championship in the coaches' poll.

Game shows used to call the presents they gave to departing players "lovely parting gifts." The "gold watch" became shorthand for sending a retiring worker out the door. The AFCA's board of voters in the ESPN/*USA Today* poll gave Osborne a gift neither he nor the Huskers—nor the Michigan Wolverines—would ever forget.

The Huskers rose to No. 1 in mid-October, overtaking Penn State after the Nittany Lions barely defeated Minnesota 16–15. Three weeks later, the Huskers used a play out of the Cirque du Soleil playbook to get into over-time at unranked Missouri. Trailing the Tigers 38–31 with :07 to play, Husker quarterback Scott Frost threw a 12-yard pass into the end zone that wingback Shevin Wiggins couldn't handle. The ball bounced off Wiggins, and as Missouri's Harold Piersey went down to intercept it, Wiggins's right foot lifted the ball high into the air. Out of nowhere, third-string freshman Matt Davison dived flat out and grabbed the ball inches off the ground.

Davison went on to a nice career at Nebraska. He could have converted to quarterback and won three Heisman Trophies, but for the rest of his life he would be known for one play. He'll never have to buy a drink in the state of Nebraska again.

The Huskers won the game in overtime 45–38, but as polls go, they didn't win. They fell to third behind Michigan and Florida State. The Seminoles would lose their last regular-season game to Florida. But Michigan not only didn't lose, the Wolverines finished the season by beating No. 23 Wisconsin, No. 4 Ohio State, and, in the Rose Bowl, No. 8 Washington State.

Nebraska beat unranked Iowa State, unranked Colorado, No. 14 Texas A&M, and, in the Orange Bowl, No. 3 Tennessee. You can make the case that the Huskers' 42–17 rout of the Volunteers warranted a share of the championship. However, Vols quarterback Peyton Manning, playing despite a leg injury he suffered in the SEC Championship Game, looked like a guy who hadn't practiced or worked out for a month.

The writers and broadcasters in the AP poll ignored the sentiment attached to Osborne's final game and stayed with Michigan. Though no one will ever know how the coaches would have voted if Osborne had waited until after the Orange Bowl to announce his retirement, I've got a pretty good hunch. Given the nature of how they won their third and final national championship under Osborne, these Huskers belong on the list of overrated national champions.

3. THE 1984 BYU COUGARS

Speaking as someone who supported the expansion of the BCS, as someone who welcomed the victory by Utah in 2005 Fiesta Bowl, who praised Boise State's upset of Oklahoma in the 2007 Fiesta Bowl as one of the best college football games ever, and who supported Hawaii's bid to the 2008 Sugar Bowl—okay, two out of three ain't bad—Brigham Young shouldn't have won the 1984 national championship.

In a year when every other I-A team lost a game, the Cougars got an award for finishing undefeated. Couldn't we just give them a plaque and move on?

BYU did have a good team that year, and I don't say that only because center Trevor Matich has been a colleague of mine at ESPN. It is no small feat to say that this may have been coach LaVell Edwards's best team. Edwards, in 29 seasons, won 257 games and won or shared 18 Western Athletic Conference championships. Edwards took so many teams to the Holiday Bowl, then the postseason home of the WAC champion, that he should have paid taxes in San Diego.

Quarterback Robbie Bosco came out of the Norm Chow School of Quarterbacking and proved a worthy successor to All-Americans Jim McMahon (1981) and Steve Young (1983). In his first year as a starter, Bosco threw for 3,875 yards, or exactly 27 fewer than Young had the previous season, led the nation in total offense (3,932 yards), and finished second nationally in passing efficiency (151.8 rating). Vai Sikahema led the WAC in kickoff returns (25.1-yard average), a skill he displayed for eight seasons in the NFL.

The biggest problem that BYU had is the biggest problem that all schools from the second-tier conferences have on the subject of national championships: strength of schedule. BYU opened the season by beating No. 3

Pittsburgh 20–14. That appeared to be a great win at the time, but the Panthers went on to finish just 3–7–1. The Cougars did not play another ranked team all season.

BYU faced only two teams that won seven games—Hawaii and Air Force—and beat each of them by five points. The Holiday Bowl proved anticlimactic when the game's organizers invited Michigan. They got the winged helmets, the fiery Bo Schembechler, and the fight song, but they didn't get much else. The Wolverines, only 6–5, gave the Cougars a run before succumbing 24–17.

And that was that. No. 4 Washington (10–1) and No. 2 Oklahoma (9–1–1) played in the Orange Bowl, where the Huskies defeated the Sooners 28–17. The voters remained unmoved. Between those teams stood No. 3 Florida, which went 9–1–1 but didn't go to a bowl game because of an impending NCAA investigation. It might be that the voters really believed that BYU was better than everyone else. More likely, they held their nose and voted for the only undefeated team.

4. THE 1998 TENNESSEE VOLUNTEERS

If they ever turn Tennessee's run to the 1998 national championship into a musical, I've got just the title: *Guys and Vols.* I don't know whether Phil Fulmer can sing and dance the way that Marlon Brando did in the 1955 movie. What I do know is that no one in and out of any crap game, be it in a Salvation Army storefront or in Las Vegas, has had the die fall their way more than did Fulmer and the 1998 Vols.

General Robert Neyland, the legendary coach of the Vols from the late 1920s into the early 1950s, prophesized "game maxims" that would lead to success on the field. One of the most prominent: "Make and play for the breaks. One comes your way, score."

Give credit to the Volunteers: they played well enough that when the breaks came their way, they scored. But most teams don't get half the breaks that fell Tennessee's way. Here's a quick list of the Vols' biggest breaks, ranked on a scale of 1–10 horseshoes:

- Game One: No. 10 Tennessee beat No. 17 Syracuse 34–33 on the road, thanks to a controversial pass interference call on the

The Tennessee Volunteers needed good timing and a lot of lucky calls to bring the national championship to Knoxville in 1999.

final drive. On fourth and seven at the Tennessee 35, Orange corner Will Allen hit Vol wide receiver Cedric Wilson as he went to catch a pass from Tee Martin. The Southeastern Conference crew made the call, Tennessee kept the drive going, and Jeff Hall kicked a 27-yard field goal as time expired.

Horseshoes: Two. When I covered the game, I thought Syracuse got robbed. When I saw a replay several years later, I thought the SEC guys got the call right.

- Game Two: No. 6 Tennessee broke a five-game losing streak to No. 2 Florida, defeating its archrival 20–17 in overtime when Gator kicker Collins Cooper yanked a 32-yard field goal wide left.

Horseshoes: Four. Cooper wasn't an outstanding kicker—he missed six extra points that season. During regulation, two Gator drives inside the Vol 5-yard line resulted in a total of only three points.

- Game Nine: In its first week at No. 1, Tennessee defeats unbeaten, No. 10 Arkansas 28–24. Razorback quarterback Clint Stoerner, trying to nurse a 24–22 lead with 1:43 to play, trips over the foot of his guard, Brandon Burlsworth. Stoerner breaks his fall with the hand that, unfortunately, held the football. Tennessee recovers the fumble at the Arkansas 43 with 1:43 to play and drives to score.

  Horseshoes: Twelve. That play will never happen again. Ever.

- Game 13: On Championship Saturday, while Tennessee beats Mississippi State 24–14, No. 2 Kansas State blows a 15-point, fourth-quarter lead and loses in double overtime to Texas A&M 36–33, while No. 3 UCLA loses at Miami 49–45. The Bruins play the game in December because of a September postponement due to a hurricane that ended up veering away from Miami. If the game had been played in September, UCLA wins by two touchdowns. No. 4 Florida State moves into the Fiesta Bowl, the first BCS Championship Game, but without starting quarterback Chris Weinke, who suffered a neck injury. The Vols throttle Weinke's backup, Marcus Outzen, win the game 23–16, and claim their first national championship since 1951.

  Horseshoes: Eight. The team Tennessee should have played, Ohio State, finished the regular season at No. 3 after pounding—you guessed it—Texas A&M 24–14 in the Sugar Bowl.

Tennessee won the national championship with a Hand-of-God fumble and a sequence of upsets that removed their toughest competition. The Vols may have won it anyway, but they didn't get tested in the championship game.

5. THE 1939 TEXAS A&M AGGIES

These Aggies seem like a tough team. On defense, they allowed a total of eight points in their last six games. On offense, big, bruising fullback John Kimbrough led the Southwest Conference with 10 touchdowns. Those scores, and not his grand total of 475 rushing yards, help to explain why he finished fifth in the Heisman Trophy voting. He averaged just 3.3 yards per carry, nearly a first down per play less than the 12.2-yard average of the national leader, UCLA's Jackie Robinson. Yes, *that* Jackie Robinson, the man who would break the color barrier in Major League Baseball eight years hence.

The other reason that Kimbrough helped the Aggies capture the imagination was his size. At 6'2", 210 pounds, Kimbrough weighed more than all but three of his fellow All-Americans that season, including the linemen. Think of the Internet bandwidth that would be devoted to a 300-pound tailback today and you get the idea.

So the Aggies had a star, and they went undefeated. What's not to like? Nothing. They were a good team. But they weren't the best team in the 1939 regular season. The Tennessee Vols also went undefeated in that regular season. They also had an All-American back, who happened to have one of the greatest nicknames in college football history: George "Bad News" Cafego. What separated the Volunteers from the Aggies and everyone else is simple math: Tennessee didn't give up a point in 10 regular-season games. No. 1 Tennessee beat No. 8 Alabama 21–0 in a game that attracted writers, broadcasters, and newsreel cameras from across the country.

As Bob Gilbert recounted in his biography of General Robert Neyland, the Vols' coach, Henry McLemore of the United Press asked, "Isn't it time that Tennessee was broken up along with the Yankees?"

For some reason, after the games of November 18, when Tennessee defeated Vanderbilt 13–0 and Texas A&M beat Rice 19–0, the voters flip-flopped the two teams and moved the Aggies to No. 1. Both teams had byes the following week, and in the November 27 poll, Tennessee had fallen to No. 4 behind USC and Cornell. The fall may have had something to do with a knee injury to Cafego. Still, Tennessee won every game by at least 13 points until the season finale, when, without Cafego, they edged Auburn 7–0.

Still, Tennessee went undefeated and unscored upon until the Rose Bowl, when USC won a 14–0 upset. But that had no impact on the poll. In those days, and well into the 1960s, the AP published its final poll at the conclusion of the regular season. Tennessee did what no team has done since, and likely will never do again: they threw a 10-game shutout. The Volunteers should have been No. 1.

The Most Underrated National Champion in College Football History

THE 2003 USC TROJANS

There are two surefire ways to start an argument in Louisiana: 1) use "coonass" as a term of endearment (ask former Louisianan Nick Saban); 2) use the phrase "national champion" to describe the 2003 USC Trojans.

USC finished No. 1 in the final AP poll, which for the previous 66 seasons had been an accepted measure of identifying the national champion. The Football Writers Association of America and *The Sporting News*, two organizations that can claim they know what they're talking about, also picked the Trojans.

But if you say as much in Louisiana, get ready for a verbal throwdown. Never mind that split national champions have been a part of college football for more than 50 years, and the sport not only survived but thrived. The Tiger fans see it as a slur on their beloved team, which won LSU's first national championship in 45 years.

If anyone is slurred in this discussion, it is the Trojans. They finished the regular season No. 1 in the polls, only to have the computer rankings boot them out of the BCS Championship Game in favor of LSU and Oklahoma.

USC had lost to California 34–31 in triple overtime in September. LSU had lost to Florida 19–7 in October. Oklahoma lost 35–7 to Kansas State in December. The Trojans lost earlier than the other two teams, had the smallest margin of defeat, and did not lose in regulation. Five years later, I'm still trying to figure out what I missed.

The AP voters supported the Trojans, which is why I include USC on this list of underrated *national champions*. Now that five seasons have passed, five seasons in which USC has gone a cumulative 59–6 (.908), all of college football takes for granted that the Trojans will be in the national championship race. It's worth taking a step back to recall the excitement that USC engendered in that 2003 season.

USC had gone 11–2 in 2002 but had lost Heisman-winning quarterback Carson Palmer to the NFL. At tailback, the Trojans began 2003 with little experience and a lot of curiosity about two freshmen, Reggie Bush and

LenDale White. The preseason speculation at quarterback focused on Matt Cassel and Purdue transfer Brandon Hance. Third-year sophomore Matt Leinart attracted little outside attention. Yet in spring practice, offensive coordinator Norm Chow saw a spark he liked in Leinart, whose game experience amounted to four handoffs and no passes. Leinart secured the starting job in August. Before the opener at No. 6 Auburn, Chow verbally threw his palms up at the lack of experience on his offense.

Regarding Leinart, said Chow, "What can you do? You go play them. If you don't see a wet spot down his leg, you're okay."

On the road before 86,000 hostile fans, Leinart completed 17 of 30 passes for 192 yards and a touchdown. USC won 23–0 and showed that instead of slowing down, the Trojans merely shifted gears.

After the loss at Berkeley, USC won its last eight regular games by at least 20 points. They beat teams every way there is to beat teams. White, though a freshman, led the Trojans in rushing. Bush, in a part-time role, averaged six yards a rush, 20 yards a catch, and led USC with an average of 27.3 yards per kickoff return. Leinart threw for 3,556 yards, 38 touchdowns, and only nine interceptions, numbers that might have stood out more if Leinart himself hadn't eclipsed them the following season, when he won the Heisman.

The defensive line featured two All-Americans in end Kenichi Udeze and tackle Mike Patterson. At the end opposite Udezi, Shaun Cody merely made All-Pac-10, one of nine Trojans who did so.

They rose to No. 2 in the polls, and on the last day of the season, a couple of hours before the Sooners got shocked by the Wildcats, USC overran Oregon State 52–28. After the game, as Beavers coach Mike Riley walked off the field, I suggested to him that the Trojans might not make it to the BCS Championship Game ahead of Oklahoma and LSU. Riley looked like I had told him the sun would be rising over the Pacific.

"Are you serious?" Riley said. "I would think they are No. 2. If you make any mistake, they come down hard. It's hard for me to imagine they wouldn't be in there."

And this was before the Sooners lost. Yet USC did not reach the BCS Championship Game, done in by the computer rankings in a BCS formula that didn't give enough weight to human voters. That's not my opinion. After

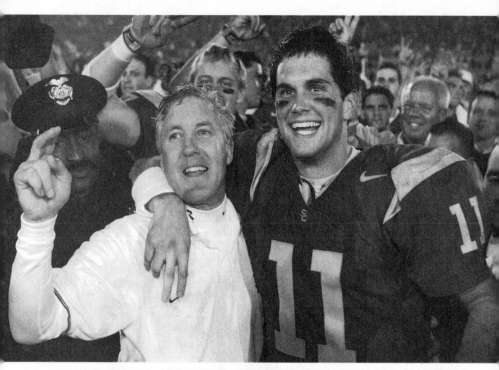

Despite being left out of the BCS Championship Game, the 2003 USC Trojans are still the most underrated "national champion" of all time.

the season, the commissioners who run the BCS changed the formula, a tacit acknowledgment that USC should have been in the BCS Championship Game, presumably against LSU.

The Trojans instead went to the Rose Bowl, 15 minutes up the Harbor Freeway from campus, to play No. 4 Michigan. The Wolverines, 10–2, had won six consecutive games and, of course, the Big Ten championship, and they were hopelessly outclassed. The speed of the USC defense caught the Wolverines unawares. The Trojans sacked quarterback John Navarre nine times, only six fewer than Michigan had allowed during the regular season.

On defense, Michigan, which had given up five touchdown passes all season, gave up four, including a flea flicker in which Leinart pitched to tail-back Hershel Dennis, who pitched to wide receiver Mike Williams, who threw a 15-yard touchdown pass to Leinart.

After the game, Michigan coach Lloyd Carr, alluding to the ludicrous contractual commitment of the AFCA, which guaranteed that its poll voters would select the winner of the BCS Championship Game No. 1 no matter what they actually thought, said, "I'm committed to vote the winner of the Sugar Bowl as the national champion. If I was a member of the media or the press, you could certainly make a case for Southern Cal. You could make me an honorary member."

So it is that USC and LSU, rather than meeting on the field in the Sugar Bowl and deciding who was No. 1, will play in the minds of their fans in perpetuity, or until the Internet shuts down, whichever comes first.

The Rest of the Most Underrated

2. THE 1991 WASHINGTON HUSKIES

Washington split the national championship with Miami in 1991, chiefly because the Huskies made the mistake of starting out the season ranked fourth to the Hurricanes' third. Neither team ever lost; the Huskies and the Hurricanes each defeated three top-10 teams, including one on the road. Washington won at No. 7 California 24–17, the only game that the Huskies won by fewer than 11 points. The Bears went on to finish 10–2. Miami solidified its standing atop the AP poll by knocking off No. 1 Florida State 17–16, a game you know by the phrase on every Seminole fan's door to hell, "Wide Right." Seminole kicker Gerry Thomas missed a 34-yard field goal in the waning seconds.

That game remains one of the seminal moments in the sport's biggest rivalry of the 1990s, and its legacy has contributed to the overshadowing/underrating of Washington. On the one hand, no argument here: if Florida State hadn't lost, Seminoles head coach Bobby Bowden never would have uttered one of college football's great quotes. At a press conference on the morning after the game, Bowden, masking his devastation with humor, said, "On my tombstone, they'll put, 'But he played Miami.'"

On the other hand, I remain convinced now, as I was at the time, that Washington would have gotten the better of Miami. Washington had the better defense. Though the Huskies finished second to the Hurricanes in scoring defense (Miami allowed 100 points in 11 games to Washington's

101), the Huskies also finished second in rushing and total defense and third in passing defense.

The week after the emotional, last-second victory over its biggest rival, Miami had to play at Boston College. It would prove to be a stunning welcome to the Big East Conference. The Hurricanes, in their first season in the league, had been able to schedule only two conference games. Playing in cold Northeastern weather, Miami hung on to win 19–14.

Meanwhile, across the country, Washington blasted its Apple Cup rival, Washington State, 56–21. The coaches responded by flipping the top two teams in the CNN/ *USA Today* poll. Washington remained No. 1 through the Rose Bowl, in which it dominated Michigan 34–14. Wolverine wide receiver Desmond Howard, whose 640 first-place votes broke a record for a Heisman Trophy winner, made only one catch against the Huskies. Score one for Washington defensive tackle Steve Emtman, the Outland Trophy winner and fourth-place Heisman finisher. The Wolverines became the seventh team to have its lowest point total of the season against the Huskies.

My vote for Washington didn't carry as much weight in the AP poll as it did on the five-man Football Writers Association of America panel (Washington won that one, as well as the coaches' vote). It may be that the teams were separated by one continent and not much else. But the legacies of the two have diverged, perhaps because Miami returned to greatness a decade later, while the Huskies hit the bottom of the Pac-10 and have climbed barely halfway back. Washington has won 10 games or more only once (11–1 in 2000) since that 1991 season. Trust me: the 1991 Huskies could have beaten anyone.

3. THE 1947 NOTRE DAME FIGHTING IRISH

What is a team considered one of the greatest in history doing on this list? The Fighting Irish began the season with a nine-game unbeaten streak and doubled it. They won eight of their nine games in 1947 by 15 points or more. They never trailed in a single game. Forty-two players from this national championship team went on to play professional football. Johnny Lujack won the 1947 Heisman and joined four other Notre Dame starters as All-Americans.

This is an underrated team?

Well, in one sense, yes. The Irish weren't the only team to go 9–0 in 1947. Michigan and Penn State also went 9–0. While the Nittany Lions didn't rise higher than fourth in the polls, the Wolverines gained a lot of support. They had only two victories decided by fewer than 21 points and shut out four opponents in the regular season. Backs Bob Chappuis, Bump Elliot, and Jack Weisenburger led the most prolific offense in the nation (412.7 yards and 38.3 points per game).

What Michigan did not do—would not, if you ask the Notre Dame faithful—is play the Irish. When the season ended, the AP voters gave a narrow victory to Notre Dame, its second consecutive national championship and fourth in the last five seasons.

Notre Dame, in those days, did not accept invitations to bowl games. Michigan most certainly did. The Wolverines returned to the Rose Bowl for the first time since the first Rose Bowl in 1901. In that game, Michigan humiliated Stanford 49–0, a game so lopsided that not only did the team captains agree to end the game with eight minutes left to play, but the Tournament of Roses chose not to stage another football game for 14 years.

In the 1947 season, the Rose Bowl made a deal with the Big Ten and Pacific Coast conferences for their champions to play in Pasadena on January 1, a deal that continues to this day, give or take a BCS-caused interruption. On January 1, 1948, Michigan played No. 8 USC and won by the same score that the Wolverines had won by in the inaugural game played 46 years earlier. The 49–0 final caused an epidemic of buyer's remorse among AP voters across the nation.

The AP, petitioned to hold a post-bowl vote, did so. Michigan, with its rout of USC, surged past idle Notre Dame. The AP declared the vote unofficial and Notre Dame remains the 1947 champion. However, the post-bowl straw vote has, in the modern day, left a Maize-and-Blue smudge on the Irish's trophy.

But here, as radio legend Paul Harvey would say, is the rest of the story: in Notre Dame's last game, they also beat USC, and beat the then-No. 3 Trojans at Los Angeles Memorial Coliseum, and beat them 38–7. That's pretty much equal to 49–0 and serves as an Irish antidote to the Wolverines' strongest argument.

Michigan gained a measure of revenge in 1948, when both teams again finished 9–0. The AP voted the Wolverines ahead of Notre Dame. But make no mistake—1947 belonged to the Irish.

4. THE 1961 ALABAMA CRIMSON TIDE

In 25 seasons at Alabama, Bear Bryant won five Associated Press national championships. He won passing the ball with Joe Namath and Steve Sloan in 1964–65. He won running the wishbone with a cast of thousands in 1978–79. He won when the final poll came out before the bowls and when it came out afterward. He won with two-platoon football and with one-platoon football.

But the best of Bryant's national champions were not the teams that won after he had become a legend. The best, and least known, of his teams was the 1961 Crimson Tide, a team that won it all when Bryant was known as a coach who could win games but hadn't yet won it all.

Bryant came close with Kentucky in 1950. The No. 7 Wildcats stunned No. 1 Oklahoma 13–7 in the Sugar Bowl, but the polls had already closed. In 1957, behind Heisman Trophy-winning back John David Crow, the Aggies reached No. 1. But with an 8–0 record, on the day before playing No. 20 Rice, the headline hit the papers: "Bear Goes to Bama." The Aggies lost to the Owls 7–6 and lost two weeks later to archrival Texas 9–7.

Bryant called the Crimson Tide players he took over in 1958 "a fat, raggedy bunch." But he loved the freshman class he signed, and that class formed the core of the team that won the 1961 championship. It included All-American tackle Billy Neighbors and quarterback Pat Trammell, the fifth-place finisher in the Heisman vote whom Bryant called his greatest leader. The juniors on the 1961 team included future coaches Charley Pell, Bill "Brother" Oliver, and Richard Williamson, as well as Lee Roy Jordan, whom Bryant considered the best linebacker he ever coached.

The Crimson Tide didn't just beat teams—it suffocated them. North Carolina State, which lost 26–7, outscored every other opponent. Alabama allowed only 22 points in 10 regular-season games, and didn't give up a touchdown in the last seven games. The game has changed, of course. Football is a two-platoon sport now, and nearly every rule that has been changed in the last 50 years has been to benefit the offense. Still, no defense has come within shouting distance of the 1961 Tide.

The knock against this team has been that, until it met No. 9 Arkansas in the Sugar Bowl, Alabama didn't play a ranked team or one that would win more than seven games. But the Tide won that game in the same way it won the rest: in a 10–3 final, Arkansas twice had a first down at Alabama's 10-yard line and only got a field goal. The Razorbacks missed another, and had a third blocked.

Defense is not sexy, and Bryant's first national champion has been lost in the celebration of all the national champions Bryant coached afterward. But it just might have been his best.

5. THE 1993 FLORIDA STATE SEMINOLES

The popular stance is to declare that Bobby Bowden's best team in 32 years as Florida State head coach is his 1999 national champion Seminoles. That team began the season at No. 1, beat five ranked teams, never fell out of first, and closed out with an electrifying 46–29 defeat of No. 2, unbeaten Virginia Tech in the Sugar Bowl.

That team did what Bowden's 1993 national champions couldn't do— namely, close off debate. The '93 Seminoles lost at No. 2 Notre Dame 31–24 in the 10th game of the season—the game that also should be remembered for giving birth to ESPN *College GameDay* on campus—yet finished ahead of the Fighting Irish in the final poll. Why? Notre Dame, the week after defeating Florida State, lost at home to No. 17 Boston College 41–39. Here's how poll voters think: Florida State lost on the road to the No. 2 team in the nation. Notre Dame lost at home to the No. 17 team, and lost a week later than Florida State.

(Advocates of a playoff recoil at the notion that Notre Dame should have been ranked below Florida State after beating the Seminoles, but the fact is playoffs are about who is hot at the end. Ask the 2007 New York Giants.)

The 1993 Seminoles dominated in ways that many national champions never do. They won their 11 regular-season victories, including five against ranked teams, by an average margin of 37 points.

Quarterback Charlie Ward and the 1993 Florida State Seminoles won 11 regular season games by an average of 37 points. (Photo courtesy of AP Images)

To get to the Orange Bowl to play No. 2 Nebraska, Florida State had to win on the road against their most-hated rival, No. 7 Florida. Crowd noise at "The Swamp," as Florida Field became known under Steve Spurrier, is similar to four hours of an iPod fully cranked. The Gators mounted a fourth-quarter comeback to pull within 27–21. They shut down the Seminoles on first down, and again on second. It's third-and-10, Florida State is on its 21-yard line, and the Gators are one play away from forcing a punt and getting the ball back.

It is the single loudest moment I have ever witnessed in my career. Jet engines? Led Zeppelin? Screaming baby in 36B when you're trying to sleep in 35B? No comparison. And then, suddenly, as Seminole quarterback Charlie Ward threw a swing pass to freshman tailback Warrick Dunn, who made one fake to get to the left sideline and sprinted for the game-clinching touchdown, it got so quiet you could hear 85,000 hearts drop.

That's how good this Florida State team was. The backfield included a Heisman Trophy winner at quarterback (Ward) and first-round picks at fullback (William Floyd) and tailback (Dunn). Florida State also had All-Americans at linebacker (Derrick Brooks) and in the secondary (Corey Sawyer), as well as, for the first time in about 400 years, a dependable kicker. After consecutive years of Wide Right, freshman Scott Bentley arrived from Colorado and made the field goal that won the national championship, clinching an 18–16 victory in the Orange Bowl.

In February 1994, Lou Holtz spoke at a Notre Dame function in Dallas, with your intrepid reporter covering it for *The Dallas Morning News*. As we ate lunch together, the topic of the national championship came up. I explained my vote. Holtz countered my arguments, and I would have to say he ended lunch a lot more pissed off than he began.

I just have a way with people.

CHAPTER 6

Moments

If you don't want to find that there's no Santa Claus, don't read the rest of this chapter. Separating fact from legend is no fun. Put it this way: the legends aren't overrated, just the facts.

The Most Overrated Moment in College Football History

SAM CUNNINGHAM RUNS OVER ALABAMA

The story of the performance of USC fullback Sam Cunningham at Legion Field in Birmingham in 1970 long ago passed from journalism to hagiography. The African American sophomore rushed for 135 yards and two touchdowns—on only 12 carries—as the No. 3 Trojans overpowered No. 16, lily-white Alabama 42–21.

Long before the game was played, so the story went, Crimson Tide coach Paul "Bear" Bryant had gone to his good friend, USC coach John McKay, and asked him to play in Birmingham in order to hasten the day when Alabama fans would cheer on an integrated team.

After the game, so the story went, Bryant said, "Cunningham did more for integration in Alabama in 60 minutes than Martin Luther King Jr."

The performance of USC's Sam Cunningham against Alabama in 1970 has gone from legitimate historical event to overrated myth. (Photo courtesy of WireImages)

Then, the story continues, Bryant took Cunningham through the Alabama locker room, introducing him to the team he ran over, saying, "Gentlemen, this is what a football player looks like."

It is a great story, one that serves many masters. It is one more validation of the errors of segregation. It is an example of Bryant being proactive regarding an issue on which he had been dragging his feet.

Veteran sports journalist Don Yaeger has written a book about the game, and the many histories written about Alabama and USC football in recent years discuss the importance of Cunningham to the integration of the Crimson Tide. It would be easy, nearly 40 years later, to try to deny what that integration meant. But that's not the intent of proposing that the Cunningham story is overrated. I don't deny the impact of the performance. The next year, Alabama put its first African American players—back Wilbur Jackson and defensive end John Mitchell—on the field. It is not entirely a coincidence that Alabama improved from 6–5–1 in all-white 1970 to 11–1 in 1971.

But Cunningham is the most overrated story in college football because of one simple reason, one that children, comedians, and novelists all learn: people never let the facts get in the way of a good story. Most of the details that I listed above are myths that have grown unencumbered by the truth, myths with motives assigned in hindsight.

It is true that Bryant planned the game that spring, which became possible because the NCAA passed legislation at its 1970 convention to increase the schedule from 10 to 11 games. But if Bryant adhered to the idea of scheduling the game to soften opposition to integration, he never said it publicly. In fact, he had signed Jackson to a scholarship before he scheduled the game.

It is also true that playing the game in "Bombingham," only seven years removed from Bull Connor and his fire hoses, carried some significance for the Trojans' black players, some of whom carried weapons on the road trip for self-protection. One of USC's best players, running back Clarence Davis, grew up in Birmingham. His presence alone illustrated the handicap under which Bryant operated. It makes sense that after a 6–5 season, no one would have been more aware than Bryant of a need to infuse the Crimson Tide with better talent.

But there's no evidence that Bryant believed he needed to prepare his fans for the inevitability of integration. Allen Barra, in his 2005 biography, *The Last Coach*, quoted longtime assistant Clem Gryska scoffing at the idea that Bryant would schedule any game he didn't intend his team to win. Gryska believed that Bryant leapt at the idea of playing USC for the money and national exposure it would generate. At any rate, using the USC game as a weapon against segregation is an idea that came from the newspapers, and only in retrospect.

The quote regarding Cunningham and Dr. King has been attributed to Bryant by journalists through the years, including at least once by yours truly. That's sloppy. As Bryant said in his autobiography, "When USC came in here and beat us so bad in the opening game in 1970, [longtime Bryant assistant] Jerry Claiborne made the remark that their big black fullback,

Sam Cunningham, did more for integration in the South in sixty minutes than Martin Luther King did in twenty years."

Claiborne, of course, played for Bryant at Kentucky and went on to become a College Football Hall of Fame head coach at Virginia Tech, Maryland, and his alma mater. It's a good line, though, and the least potent of the myths.

As for the episode in which Bryant brought Cunningham into the Alabama locker room, it's awfully hard to find anyone who was there who remembers it. Neal McCready of the *Mobile Register* wrote a story in August of 2003, days before USC made its first trip back to the state (and beat Auburn 23–0), and couldn't find a single Crimson Tide player or coach who remembered it. Barra quotes both Trojans coach John McKay and one of his assistants, Craig Fertig, recalling that Bryant came to get Cunningham, and quotes a third man, the late sportswriter Al Browning, remembering that Bryant showed Cunningham off to some boosters.

Cunningham, the guy who should remember it most clearly of all, gave McCready a convoluted answer that sounded like a man tiptoeing around a myth so that it doesn't collapse under the weight of the truth.

"For the sake of history, I was taken in," Cunningham said. "I kind of think it didn't happen. I think I would remember, but I don't want to be the guy who said it didn't happen."

That may explain the answer I got from Cunningham when I interviewed him at Jordan-Hare Stadium at Auburn, where he watched his Trojans from the sideline. When I interviewed Cunningham, I was unaware of McCready's story. When I asked him about the locker room visit, Cunningham said, "If I had been on the losing end, I'm not sure I would appreciate it. It was pretty intimidating. I'm not one to be thrown up there. But one icon [McKay] passed me to another [Bryant]. What do you do?"

Perhaps his memory kicked in after he spoke to McCready. More likely, Cunningham gave an answer to perpetuate a myth that no one wanted to die.

The postscript to the Cunningham tale is that in the spring of 1971, Bryant and McKay met in Houston, and McKay made the mistake of bragging to his friend that USC was about to sign an African American prospect from Mobile who had played at an Arizona junior college. Evidently,

McKay had no idea that Bryant already had signed Jackson. Bryant excused himself, called his office, and instructed his staff to get after defensive end John Mitchell. It just so happened that Mitchell was in Mobile on break, and within a couple of hours Bryant had him on the phone. Mitchell signed with Alabama and started in the 1971 season opener—against USC. The Crimson Tide sprung the wishbone on the Trojans, jumped out to a 17–0 lead, and held USC scoreless in the second half to win 17–10. As a senior in 1972, Mitchell became the first black All-American at Alabama.

The Rest of the Most Overrated

2. JOHNNY RODGERS'S PUNT RETURN

There may have been other Games of the Century, but the first one in the modern era of televised college football took place in Norman, Oklahoma, on Thanksgiving Day 1971. No. 1 Nebraska edged No. 2 Oklahoma 35–31. The most recognizable play from that game is the 72-yard punt return for a touchdown by Huskers junior Johnny Rodgers. The junior caught the punt, got hit by Sooner star Greg Pruitt, stumbled, righted himself, angled to the left sideline with the help of either a great block or a clip, depending on what shade of red you prefer, and raced to the end zone.

"Take me now, Lord. I've seen it all," Nebraska play-by-play man Lyle Bremser said.

The touchdown came too late for Rodgers to win the 1971 Heisman, awarded that very day—remember, this was the year 8 B.E. (Before ESPN); Heisman ceremonies that looked like the Academy Awards in shoulder pads were a generation away—to Auburn quarterback Pat Sullivan. But the return established Rodgers as a star to the nation, and, in 1972, he won everybody's favorite bronze doorstop handily.

At 5'9", 173 pounds, Rodgers didn't intimidate anyone with his size—he didn't have to. His speed and quickness were such that few tacklers could lay a helmet on him anyway. In the years before Tom Osborne brought the option to Lincoln, coach Bob Devaney knew what he had in Rodgers, and he opened up the offense to take advantage of him. In 1971,

Rodgers caught 53 passes, two fewer than he caught the following year; those two seasons ranked 1-2 for season receptions in school history until 2007, when Marlon Lucky (75 catches) and Maurice Purify (57) both surpassed them.

The legend that has surrounded Rodgers's punt return has made it the winning play in a close-fought game between undefeated archrivals ranked 1-2 in the nation. However, Rodgers didn't score the winning touchdown for the Huskers. He scored the first one. It may be one of the few plays anyone remembers from one of the all-time greatest college games, but Rodgers made the return for a touchdown in the first quarter of a scoreless game. Rodgers may have been the game breaker, but that ignores the eight touchdowns and field goal that came after him.

In fact, the Huskers' Jeff Kinney scored the winning touchdown from two yards out with 1:38 to play, an achievement recalled by few outside the Cornhusker State or the Kinney family. That shouldn't diminish the play itself, only its effect on the outcome. I'm sure there has been a first-quarter play that has received more attention than this one. Just don't ask me what it is.

3. "WRONG WAY" RIEGELS

As bonehead plays are measured, what California center Roy Riegels did in the 1929 Rose Bowl has stood tall against the test of eight decades. Riegels picked up a Georgia Tech fumble and eluded a couple of tacklers. In doing so, however, he spun around and raced toward his own end zone. You could blame it on the fact that Riegels played the line and didn't often carry the ball. However, most linemen generally understand that the end zone in front of them scores points for their team, and the end zone behind them scores points for the other team.

Georgia Tech, as you may imagine, didn't exactly sprint to catch him. Riegels's teammate Benny Lom did, however, and turned Riegels around near the Cal goal line. According to the *Chicago Tribune's* account of the game ("Blunder Defeats California: Captain Elect Runs 69 1/2 Yards to Wrong Goal"), "Riegels was grasping at the stuff of which heroes are made. He sprinted like one possessed. Benny Lom was among the first to see the bottom had fallen out of the world—and Benny is the fastest of California's speedsters. He tried to overtake Riegels, shouting frantically the while."

Lom got Riegels turned around, but Tech immediately tackled him. Cal tried to punt its way out of trouble, but the "Golden Tornado"—that's what Georgia Tech went by in those days—blocked the punt. Cal fell on it in the end zone, and Georgia Tech led 2–0. But here's where the overrated came in: as with Rodgers, Georgia Tech scored the points in the first half. An entire half of football awaited them. To blame Riegels for losing the Rose Bowl would be like blaming the loss on the Bears' Stanley Barr, who dropped a pass standing alone on the Tech goal line—in the first quarter.

The difference is that ends drop passes every Saturday. The number of linemen who pick up a fumble and run the wrong way with it is pretty short. Jim Marshall did it for (to?) the Minnesota Vikings in 1964. He shares top billing for this type of play with "Wrong Way" Riegels, whose play served as a cherry on top of the Roaring Twenties. Riegels initially took the play and the infamy that came with it hard, in part because the public didn't want to let it go. *Time* magazine ran this item in January 1939:

"Last week, on the tenth anniversary of his wrong-way run, Roy Riegels's wife filed suit for divorce. Reason: moroseness."

The respect that his teammates had for him is evident by his captaincy as a senior in 1929. And he eventually made his peace with celebrity. Reporters called him whenever a similar play happened, from high school to Marshall's run. In 1991, the Rose Bowl named him to its Hall of Fame. He died in 1993, a week before his 85th birthday. A goat? Yes. Caused the loss of a Rose Bowl? Not guilty.

4. THE BUSH PUSH

In 2005, Notre Dame fans spilled onto the field to celebrate a 31–28 victory over No. 1 USC, which would snap the Trojans' 27-game winning streak. The USC drive appeared to peter out inside the Irish 1-yard line. However, the officials put seven seconds back on the clock. USC quarterback Matt Leinart signaled to his offense that he would spike the ball to give the offense time to figure out one more play. The Trojan linemen's instructions

Reggie Bush gave quarterback Matt Leinart a nudge across the goal line to help beat Notre Dame 34–31 in 2005. (Photo courtesy of AP Images)

on such a play are to surge forward. Leinart has the option of spiking or going for the quarterback sneak.

Tailback Reggie Bush walked up to Leinart and asked, "You going to go for it or you going to stop the clock?"

"What do you think?" Leinart asked.

"Yeah," Bush said.

After the game, Leinart said he already had made up his mind.

"I was going to do it anyway," he said. "You're on the 1. It's really now or never. It's get in the end zone or go home."

Leinart took the snap and spun to his left. Here's what Notre Dame fans still scream about—Bush ran into Leinart and shoved him over the goal line to seal a 34–31 win, the Trojans' 28th-straight victory.

Is it against the NCAA rule book? Yes.

Is it done everywhere? Yes.

Is it the play that should be remembered from that final drive? Not a chance.

Notre Dame had scored a touchdown to take a 31–28 lead with 2:04 to play. The Irish sacked Leinart on second down, giving him a third-and-19, and, after a 10-yard run by Bush, a fourth-and-nine at their own 26. Leinart, a senior in his third year as a starter, coolly checked off at the line of scrimmage and called a new play.

He took a three-step drop, trusting sophomore wideout Dwayne Jarrett to get a step on Irish corner Ambrose Wooden. Jarrett sprinted inside of Wooden, and Leinart delivered a fastball right into his hands, one All-American to another. It remains one of those rare plays of skill, timing, and import that should tower over every other snap in the game, especially because Jarrett made the catch despite dealing with double vision out of his right eye after his helmet came down hard on his head earlier in the game.

Wooden, to his credit, dove to stop Jarrett at the Notre Dame 13, which set up the heroics and the illegal push at the end of the game. But to the 80,795 who saw the game live, the Bush Push will never be the play of the game. Jarrett and Leinart made theirs a play for the ages.

5. HOWARD'S HEISMAN POSE

It has become known as the pose that won Michigan wideout Desmond Howard the 1991 Heisman. Howard returned a punt 93 yards for a touchdown against archrival Ohio State, capping a 17-point rally in a 2:21 span of the second quarter, to give the Wolverines a 24–3 lead. They cruised to a 31–3 victory, their fourth straight over the Buckeyes.

But a punt return for a touchdown, even one that extended nearly the entire length of Michigan Stadium, does not make a memory on its own—not when the final margin is 28 points. It is what Howard did at the end of the punt return that cemented this play in college football history. As he came to a stop in the Big House end zone, Howard assumed the Heisman pose, replete with straight arm.

Howard, who has been a colleague of mine at ESPN, held the pose as a way to have fun with the enormity of being the Heisman front-runner. The audacity of the gesture sent the sport's Aunt Minnies racing for their smelling salts. It also opened a door on Heisman marketing and showmanship that will never be closed.

The one thing that Howard's pose did not do was win him the award. There is a long history of All-Americans having outstanding years and fighting for the Heisman; 1991 is not in that history. Take a look at the final standings. The runner-up, Florida State quarterback Casey Weldon, had one-quarter of the points that Howard received in the 3-2-1 Heisman vote. Weldon faded after he suffered strained knee ligaments in the seventh game of the season. BYU's Ty Detmer, trying to become the first Heisman winner to repeat, never had a chance after the Cougars began the season 0–3. He finished third.

The guy who should have had a chance, the nation's leading rusher, finished ninth. The voters didn't warm to him, largely because he was a freshman at a school in the WAC, a league not known for its rush defense. The voters must feel pretty good about that assessment. After all, the freshman,

Desmond Howard's Heisman pose overshadowed his stellar season for the Wolverines in 1991.

Marshall Faulk of San Diego State, ran for 4,589 yards and 57 touchdowns in three collegiate seasons before rushing for 12,279 yards and 100 touchdowns in 12 seasons in the NFL. No, no, don't want to take a freshman Heisman candidate seriously.

Faulk scored 23 touchdowns as a freshman, which tied him for first that season with, yes, Desmond Howard. But Faulk being underestimated is not the point. Howard's Heisman pose is overrated because of the hagiography, developed over nearly two decades, that his showmanship won him the Heisman. Howard won because he caught 61 passes, 19 of them for touchdowns, at an average of 15.6 yards per catch. He became the most dangerous player on a team that lost only to Florida State 51–31, and in the Rose Bowl to national co-champion Washington 34–14. Howard would have won the Heisman whether he posed or not.

* * *

The definition of an underrated moment? It's finishing a paper in high school English and realizing, "Hey, I like to write." It's sitting in the coffeehouse at the end of your third date and thinking, "I want there to be a fourth date—and a 40th." It's seeing your child—any one of them—set the dinner table without being asked.

All right, that last one veered into Jim Nabors singing "The Impossible Dream," but you get my point. An underrated moment is the pebble that never stops rippling the pond. Only with the benefit of hindsight can you see that it represented not just a shift but a sea change in college football.

The Most Underrated Moment in College Football History

JOHNNY BRIGHT'S BROKEN JAW

The story of the integration of college football focuses, as most integration stories do, on the South and the existence of the color line at major universities into the 1970s. The struggles of African American players at schools outside the South began long before Sam Cunningham and USC traveled to Legion Field in Birmingham in 1970 to play Alabama.

Paul Robeson, the Rutgers All-American in 1918, went on to gain world renown for his singing and national opprobrium for his politics. The Downtown Athletic Club awarded the Heisman 26 times before the trophy went to an African American, Ernie Davis of Syracuse. The name Johnny Bright doesn't carry the same emotional or historical heft as either Robeson or Davis. But Bright, a star African American back at Drake University in 1951, is owed a debt that history has yet to repay.

Bright, big for his day at 6'0", 195 pounds, led the NCAA in total offense as a sophomore (1,950 yards) and again as a junior (2,400). He ran and threw with equal skill, accounting for 30 touchdowns as an All-American junior in 1950.

When 1951 began, Bright picked up where he had left off. Through five games, he again led the nation in rushing and scoring. Bright already had broken the NCAA career total offense record, set by North Carolina back Charlie "Choo-Choo" Justice, when he led Drake into a road game against Missouri Valley Conference foe Oklahoma A&M (now Oklahoma State).

Top offensive players are sometimes called "marked men" in the same sort of breathless vernacular that applies war metaphors to football games. Before the game, stories emanating from Stillwater labeled Bright as a "marked man." Little did anyone know. Two years earlier, Bright had been the first African American to play at Lewis Field in Stillwater. The Aggies won 28–0 without incident.

In this game, the incident began on the first play from scrimmage.

Bright handed off to fullback Gene Macomber and, as quarterbacks do to this day, stood, out of the play several steps behind the line, facing down-field. Aggies tackle Wilbanks Smith ran at Bright from his right. Without pause, Smith swung his right forearm into Bright's jaw and broke it. Here, from Maury White's story in the *The Des Moines Register* the following day:

> "Trainer Ben Mankowski was out on the field for several minutes, working over the prostrate Bright, and it wasn't long before Coach Warren Gaer joined him.
>
> "Bright finally got up, rubbing the left side of his face, *and lined up with the Drake offense.*" (Italics added)

On the next play, Bright rolled out and threw a 61-yard touchdown pass. Bright played one more series. According to White's story, he took seven snaps and was knocked unconscious by Smith three times before being helped to the Bulldogs' bench. X-rays taken during the second half confirmed that Bright had suffered a broken jaw.

Oklahoma A&M won the game 27–14, and under normal circumstances, the incident would have closed there. After all, Jim Crow was alive and well in Oklahoma. As recently as 1937, the state had passed a law requiring public carriers to be segregated. Bright might have claimed that he took a cheap shot, but Oklahoma A&M could have denied it. In fact, after the game, the college's interim president, Oliver Willham, denied that anything untoward had taken place, according to a 2005 story in the Oklahoma State campus paper.

It might have died there, except that *The Des Moines Register* had sent photographers Don Ultang and John Robinson to Stillwater. Transportation being what it was, if Ultang and Robinson wanted their photos in the Sunday paper, they would have little time to shoot the game before they had to send the film to the nearest airport. When Bright took the first snap, Robinson clicked off nine photos, apparently from a photo deck above the field.

The first one showed Bright turning to hand the ball off.

The third one showed Macomber running away from him with the ball.

In the next six, Smith closes in on Bright and coldcocks him.

The following morning, the *Register* published a series of six of the nine photos above the fold in its sports section. If that wasn't damning enough, *Life* magazine, as powerful in 1951 as today's CNN, MSNBC, and YouTube are combined, purchased the sequence of nine photos and published them.

After *Life* published the photos, Smith tearfully apologized, Oklahoma A&M forfeited the game, and Oklahoma rescinded its Jim Crow laws.

Or not.

In truth, Oklahoma A&M did nothing. The Missouri Valley Conference did nothing, and did nothing so thoroughly that it refused to launch an investigation. Drake, the league's oldest member, withdrew its membership in protest, severed ties with Oklahoma A&M, and never played the Aggies— or the Oklahoma State Cowboys—in football again. *The Des Moines Register* won the 1952 Pulitzer Prize for photography. The NCAA Football Rules Committee adopted a measure that called for disqualification of any player striking an opposing player with his forearm, elbow, or locked hands. But not until 2005 did Oklahoma State issue a formal apology. In a letter to Drake president David Maxwell, Oklahoma State president David J. Schmidly said, "The incident was an ugly mark on Oklahoma State University and college football and we regret the harm it caused Johnny Bright, your university, and many others."

Bright, jaw wired, recovered well enough to play in the Bulldogs' last two games of the season and still finished fifth in the 1951 Heisman voting. Taken with the fifth pick of the 1952 draft by the Philadelphia Eagles, Bright chose instead to take a better financial offer from the Canadian Football League. In 13 seasons with Calgary and Edmonton, he rushed for 10,909 yards, still third-best in CFL history. He became a junior high school principal in Edmonton and died at age 53 when he suffered a heart attack during knee surgery.

Wilbanks Smith's attack on Drake quarterback Johnny Bright was a pivotal moment in the integration of college football. (Photo courtesy of The Des Moines Register)

Three years before he died, Bright told *The Des Moines Register,* "What I like about the whole deal now, and what I am smug enough to say, is that getting a broken jaw somehow has made college football better. It made the NCAA take a hard look and clean up some things that were bad."

Bright said that with the benefit of 30 years' hindsight. Whatever reason he had for making his life in Canada, his name and his story receded from the American consciousness. The truth is, integration moved slowly on the college football field, and acceptance of it across large parts of the country moved even slower. Few have ever sacrificed more on the football field and with lesser acclaim. In 2005, Drake University renamed its stadium in honor of Johnny Bright.

The Rest of the Most Underrated

2. MICHIGAN 10, OHIO STATE 10

Bo Schembechler would have complained about how Michigan got screwed by the Big Ten in 1973 to the day he died, if anyone had asked. I can vouch that he was asked four days before he died, and that the banked fire in this sick, elderly man caught a fresh draft and blazed again.

In 2006, the matchup between No. 1 Ohio State and No. 2 Michigan held the attention of the entire nation. It's rare that a Monday press conference in Ann Arbor during the regular season attracts writers from across the country. But that's how big the game had become—undefeated archrivals playing for a place in the BCS Championship Game. Michigan brought out players, head coach Lloyd Carr—and Bo, the man who won the Ten-Year War against the Buckeyes and his mentor, Woody Hayes.

In the decade that spanned from Schembechler's arrival in Ann Arbor (1969) to Hayes's firing (1978) in Columbus, either Michigan or Ohio State played in the Rose Bowl every year. In nine of those years, they played for the right to visit Pasadena. Michigan won five games, Ohio State four, and, in 1973, the No. 4 Wolverines tied the No. 1 Buckeyes 10–10. The Wolverines dominated the second half, yet failed to win the game because of two missed field goals. Schembechler called the game his "greatest disappointment," not because of the field goals, but because of what happened the following day. With Michigan and Ohio State as co-champions, the Big Ten athletic directors voted to award the Rose Bowl bid to the Buckeyes. Wolverine quarterback Dennis Franklin had suffered a broken collarbone late in the Ohio State game. The athletic directors, anxious about losing a fifth consecutive New Year's Day game to the Pacific-10 Conference, sent the team with the healthy quarterback, not the team that had knocked No. 1 off its perch. The Wolverines, as did all Big Ten runners-up in those days, stayed home.

In his autobiography, written in 1989 with Mitch Albom, Schembecher called the vote "only maybe the dumbest football decision of all time." On that November day in 2006, 33 years removed, Schembechler may have forgiven. He hadn't forgotten.

"They literally screwed us out of the Rose Bowl—and I mean it just exactly the way I said it," Schembechler said.

The controversy over the decision didn't die down. In 1974, the conference responded by voting to allow its non-champions to go to bowl games. From that tie, from that vote, from Schembechler's "greatest disappointment" came the explosion of bowl games that we know and love to this day. In 1973, college football had 11 bowls. But with Big Ten teams and their massive alumni bases suddenly available for your ticket- and hotel-room-buying pleasure, the number of bowls began to increase. College football has never been the same: the sport has 33 bowls and the reality of a playoff has never been farther away.

"You know," Schembechler said, four days before he died, "the thing finally fades away. If anything, there was some good that came out of it. The number one thing it did was take the athletic directors out of there and all their political bullshit."

There will never be another Bo.

3. LUJACK'S TACKLE

The 1946 game between No. 1 Army and No. 2 Notre Dame featured one Heisman Trophy winner and three Heisman winners-to-be: the Cadets' Doc Blanchard (1945) and Glenn Davis (1946) and the Irish's Johnny Lujack (1947) and Leon Hart (1949). It featured two of the best teams in the history of the sport, thanks to rosters bulging with eight years' worth of the best players in the country, many of them returning to college after serving their nation on the battlefields of World War II. The game included green teenagers like Hart as well as 26-year-old veterans with years of combat experience. There has never been an era with so much talent concentrated in so little time (and let's hope there is never another war to cause another one).

West Point didn't suffer from the talent drain that caused some major schools to shut down football for a year or two. That's why Army dominated football during World War II. When the war ended, Army didn't have to gin up its football program; it had remained at full speed. Notre Dame coach Frank Leahy not only attracted the best players through normal recruiting, he had his stars from the 1941-43 teams return to play for him again.

When the teams met at Yankee Stadium on November 9, the city of New York had passed frenzy and moved toward mania. For a nation aching to return to normalcy after four years of war and sacrifice, college football provided a release for that pent-up energy. One newspaper said that scalpers got $200 for end zone seats and $400 to sit at midfield—this when a salary of $50 a week qualified as a princely sum. Notre Dame and its depth came into the game as a two-touchdown favorite over a team that had won 25 consecutive games.

The greatest play in this greatest game came near the end of the third quarter, when Blanchard found a lane to the right sideline and looked to be gone. Only Lujack, as good on defense as at quarterback in those one-platoon days, had a chance of stopping him. With an ankle tackle, Lujack cut Blanchard down at the Notre Dame 37. The game ended as it began, at 0–0.

"Maybe two great unstoppable teams went out there and proved there is no such thing," wrote Bill Leiser of the *San Francisco Chronicle*.

In his autobiography, Army coach Red Blaik thought that perhaps he and Leahy had been too conservative. The fans, expecting an offensive showcase, left disappointed. That two of the greatest teams in history tied, and a scoreless tie at that, overshadowed the great plays that occurred within. When you go back and examine the game, it's easy to see why Lujack's tackle of Blanchard should be remembered. For one thing, Lujack threw three interceptions and only caught one of his own. For another, when one Heisman winner saves a touchdown in the biggest game of his career by stopping another Heisman winner from scoring, that's a moment that shouldn't be lost to history. In fact, a moment like that might never happen again.

4. GOGOLAK CHANGES THE GAME

Cornell sophomore Pete Gogolak may not have been the first collegian to kick a football from the side. But Gogolak is the player who transformed soccer-style kicking from oddity to acceptance to, as it is today, status quo.

The funny thing is, Gogolak made only nine field goals in 27 attempts in his three seasons at Cornell, three seasons in which the Big Red went a combined 12–15. But when Gogolak made his first field goal, a 41-yarder against Princeton in the Big Red's 30–25 road loss in 1961, he began a journey that revolutionized the entire sport.

Gogolak and his family came to the United States in 1957 from Hungary, a year after the Soviet crackdown against his native land. Gogolak went out for his high school football team in Ogdensburg, New York, for the simple reason that the school had no soccer team. When the kicking tryouts began, Gogolak didn't stand directly behind the ball. That's when the fun started.

"I lined up from the side, in a 45-degree angle," Gogolak said in *Going Long*, the 2003 oral history of the AFL written by Jeff Miller. "And I had these high boots on, so everybody started laughing. 'You're going to kick the ball into the stands. You're supposed to kick it straight.' Nobody wanted to hold for me, thinking I was going to kick them, so I couldn't get the ball up in the air. The ball went about three feet off the ground. Everybody said, 'Send this guy back to the old country.' That's how it started."

Gogolak enrolled at Cornell and quickly began to draw attention, at the very least as an oddity. He kicked three field goals, one of them a 48-yarder, for the freshman team against Yale. His success on three-pointers remained erratic at best throughout his college career, as his percentage (.333) illustrates. But the form was in there somewhere. The closer to the goalposts, the more automatic Gogolak became. He closed out his Cornell career with a streak of 44 consecutive extra points, an Ivy League record (and a Cornell record until 2007).

In the war between the upstart AFL and the NFL, Gogolak looked like just the kind of attraction that might sell tickets. The Buffalo Bills signed

Pete Gogolak changed the art of kicking at Cornell and later played for the Buffalo Bills and New York Giants. (Photo courtesy of AP Images)

him, and after two seasons in which he finished second in the league in scoring, the New York Giants swiped Gogolak and brought him to the more established NFL. The AFL teams took the Gogolak signing as an act of war. After the AFL courted established NFL stars such as San Francisco quarterback John Brodie and Chicago tight end Mike Ditka, the two leagues entered into the talks that resulted in the 1970 merger. Pretty soon, straight-on kickers, like milkmen and typewriter repairmen, became tokens of a different era.

Gogolak would be named among the 100 Most Notable Cornellians. But his impact on college football has never been properly recognized. That 41-yarder he kicked in 1961 started something bigger than he or anyone else ever imagined.

5. STICHWEH SCORES—AGAIN?

Navy went into its 1963 game with archrival Army with everything to lose. The Midshipmen had climbed to No. 2 in the nation, with only a midseason 32–28 loss at SMU preventing the service academy from being No. 1.

Junior quarterback Roger Staubach already had won the Heisman Trophy. And despite all of that, if ever a stadium filled with more than 100,000 people possessed an empty feeling, it was Philadelphia Municipal Stadium on this December Saturday. The game had been postponed a week after the assassination of President John F. Kennedy, for whom the stadium would be named. Army and Navy mourned their commander-in-chief.

Navy won a game that, as is the nature of most rivalries, played closer than the teams' record should have allowed it. Army, trying to close a 21–15 deficit, ran out of time with the ball at the Navy 2-yard line. But the outcome of the game had nothing to do with this underrated moment. That occurred during the game, when Army quarterback Rollie Stichweh rolled out and scored on a two-yard touchdown run.

The day before, Tony Verna, the director of the CBS Sports telecast, casually mentioned to his play-by-play man, the legendary Lindsey Nelson, that the network had a new technological gimmick it wanted to try.

"We have a way now of playing back what has just been shown on the screen," Verna told Nelson, who recounted the anecdote in his 1985 autobiography. "We can play it right back. I don't know whether we will get to use it or not, but if we do, you will have to explain to the viewers that what they are seeing is not live, that's it's a replay of what they have just seen."

Verna decided to try it after Stichweh's touchdown. Nelson let the viewers know they would see the touchdown again. And then he went silent, watching it along with everyone else. Verna said to him in his earpiece, "Hey, what do you know, it works!"

The term "instant replay" didn't come along until 1966, according to *Merriam-Webster's 11th Collegiate Dictionary*. And as technology went, the instant replay that CBS used was something like the caveman's wheel compared to the computerized, digitized video of today. Instant replay has been taken for granted for at least a generation. The technology is so good that it now helps decide college and pro football games, as well as buzzer-beater shots in NCAA basketball and NBA games. And it got its start in football on that Saturday in December of 1963.

CHAPTER 7

Coaches

The Most Overrated Coach in College Football

CHARLIE WEIS

America loves a good comeuppance. Forget the echoes—in 2007, Notre Dame woke up the *schadenfreude*. In his first two seasons with the Fighting Irish, head coach Charlie Weis won 19 games with bluster and arrogance that he only occasionally coated with a quick wit. He took a team that had sunk into mediocrity under Ty Willingham and elevated it. Weis would solve Notre Dame's recruiting woes. Weis would solve Notre Dame's offensive woes. If he objected to being called an offensive genius, he didn't object loudly.

The university fell for him so deeply that a half-season into his tenure, Notre Dame wrote him a new contract. The private school never said what it's paying Weis, but it never denied the reports of more than $3 million per year.

No one expected Weis to achieve in his third season at Notre Dame what Frank Leahy, Ara Parseghian, Dan Devine, and Lou Holtz did in their third seasons: win the national championship. But Weis pretty much did the exact opposite. The bottom didn't fall out. It disintegrated. Notre Dame plummeted like Rudy Giuilani running for president. Weis didn't match history in his third season—he made it. Weis became the first Irish coach to lose nine games in one season.

Charlie Weis may play a genius on TV, but he's been overrated as head coach of the Fighting Irish.

Weis lost his Mensa membership when he lost quarterback Brady Quinn and wide receiver Jeff Samardzija. Quinn, a four-year starter whom Weis polished into a gem, went in the first round of the NFL Draft. Samardzija, projected as a first-round pick, instead signed a five-year, $10 million contract to pitch in the Chicago Cubs' farm system. And whaddya know, both of them were recruited by Willingham. Maybe he *could* recruit a little bit.

The 2007 offense redefined ineptitude. It took four games to score a touchdown. It took four games to finish with positive rushing yardage. Notre Dame finished fifth from the bottom in rushing (75.3 yards per game) and dead last in sacks allowed (58). Rarely is a line equally inept in both styles of blocking.

Weis changed his quarterbacks like he changed his socks. Demetrius Jones started the opener against Georgia Tech and transferred to Cincinnati before September ended. Sophomore Evan Sharpley and freshman Jimmy Clausen shared the job for the rest of the season.

Why did Weis start three different quarterbacks? Because he didn't have four.

The entire season, there were a lot of stories that included the clauses "for the first time" and "in history." Notre Dame had never begun the season 0–5, had never lost five straight at home, and had never lost to USC so one-sidedly. The 38–0 margin, in the eighth game of the season, came despite the Trojans playing with a backup quarterback, and despite the Irish wearing their famed big-game green jerseys. That Weis pulled that stunt thinking it might have made a difference indicated the desperation that the Irish felt.

The eighth loss attracted the most attention because the last time Notre Dame lost to Navy was in 1963, when the Midshipmen's quarterback Roger Staubach won the Heisman Trophy. Staubach was 65 years old on the day of Navy's 46–44, triple-overtime victory in 2007.

Notre Dame rallied at the end of the season with victories over Duke and Stanford to finish 3–9. If you're an Irish optimist, and there must be a few remaining out there, then you finished 2007 bragging that both Notre Dame and national champion LSU took two-game winning streaks into the 2008 season.

And if you're an Irish optimist, you point at the high rankings that Weis's recruiting classes continue to receive.

But it's worth noting that five sophomores transferred out of Notre Dame during or immediately after the 2007 season. And it's worth noting that the Irish often looked physically outclassed last season. And it's also worth noting that Weis's three-season record of 22–15 is a dead-on ringer for the record of, by many Irish accounts, his hopelessly overmatched predecessor, who went 21–15.

As a Notre Dame grad, Weis drew on the support of alumni he has known his entire adult life, such as Joe Montana, whose son Nathan, also a quarterback, is an invited walk-on for the 2008 season. But other Irish alumni lashed out at Weis: former offensive lineman Bob Kuechenberg called him an "ogre" in a *Boston Herald* story in 2007.

"To me," Kuechenberg said, "it's karma that he's getting his ass handed to him."

Weis is a good man, deeply involved in clarity, who also dropped everything to travel to the Middle East for a week in May 2008 to visit U.S.

military personnel. And arrogant is not a synonym for overrated. But Weis makes the top of this list because he brings to mind a story that the late Dick Schaap told in his 2001 autobiography, *Flashing Before My Eyes: 50 Years of Headlines, Deadlines & Punchlines.*

"It may be apocryphal," Schaap warned before he related an exchange between broadcaster Howard Cosell, another one who drank from the well of arrogance, and the legendary columnist Red Smith.

"You know," Cosell said, "there are fewer great sportscasters than one might think."

"Howard," Smith replied, "I know there is one fewer than you think."

The 2007 season made it clear that there is one fewer great coach than Weis thought. He didn't have the answers he thought he did. Last year, it looked like no one at Notre Dame had seen the material on the test, much less had the answers.

On the other hand, think of all those Fighting Irish haters from the shadow of USC to the shadow of Alabama legend Bear Bryant, who went 0–4 against Notre Dame and would have won at least four more national championships had the Irish not beaten the Crimson Tide on the field or at the polls. Think of all that jealousy that develops when one school wins eight Associated Press national championships and seven Heisman Trophies. Weis made those fans very, very happy, which is the definition of *schadenfreude.*

The Rest of the Most Overrated

2. DAVE WANNSTEDT

See if you've heard this profile before: head coach with middling NFL success returns to college game on a campus that fits him like Under Armour. Championships ensue.

It happened with Pete Carroll, who treaded water with the New England Patriots and the New York Jets before finding his bliss at USC. Carroll couldn't have set the stage better for Dave Wannstedt's return to the University of Pittsburgh.

In 11 seasons as head coach of the Chicago Bears (1993–98) and the Miami Dolphins (2000–04), Wannstedt went 82–87 (.485). His teams made three playoff appearances and never made it to a conference championship game. That's somewhere north of bad and south of intimidating.

Wannstedt returned with great fanfare to Pittsburgh, his alma mater, the year after he left the Dolphins. He had starred with the Panthers in the early 1970s, anchoring the 1973 offensive line that made Tony Dorsett a freshman sensation. He had been the defensive coordinator on Jimmy Johnson's last three teams at Miami (1986–88), which went 34–2 and won one national championship. The two teams that beat the Hurricanes, Penn State in the 1987 Fiesta Bowl and Notre Dame in 1988, won the national championship in those seasons.

Here was a guy who would build the proverbial recruiting fence around western Pennsylvania recruits. Here was a coach who would bring together the Panther faithful and reprise the dominant era of a generation ago. Here was Carroll East. In his first season at USC, the Trojans started out 2–5. From that point through 2007, they went 74–9.

And in three seasons, Wannstedt's Panthers have gone…5–6, 6–6, and 5–7. That's 16–19 (.457), slightly below his winning percentage as an NFL coach. And five of those victories have come at the expense of Mid-American Conference or I-AA teams. More troubling is the 9–12 record in the Big East, which hasn't exactly been the Southeastern Conference lately.

Offense has been a struggle. The Panthers scored more than 24 points only once in Big East play in 2007, and lost that game 48–37 to South Florida. The optimists point to quarterback Pat Bostick and tailback LeSean McCoy, who progressed well as freshmen in 2007. McCoy rushed for 1,328 yards and 14 touchdowns. His average of 110.2 yards per game led all freshmen in the nation.

The Panthers had the highest-ranked recruiting class in the Big East in each of the last three years. Wannstedt has built that fence. And yet the victories have yet to come. Carroll, in his third season, won the Associated Press national championship.

It reminds me of one of my favorite coaching stories. In the mid-1980s, after four seasons of struggling as head coach at Notre Dame, Gerry Faust met with his athletic director, Gene Corrigan. Faust, who had an unceasing fount of optimism, told Corrigan how much he loved the university and how much he wanted to continue to coach there. Faust wanted to know what he needed to do to remain.

Corrigan, considered one of the top collegiate athletic administrators of the last 50 years, said to Faust, "Gerry, win some [expletive] games."

Wannstedt has a reputation as a top recruiter. He has revitalized college football in a one-time hotbed of the sport. He has done everything but win some [expletive] games.

3. JEFF TEDFORD

Jeff Tedford is a great example of how success bred heightened expectations that his California teams have yet to meet.

The word "rejuvenate" is tossed around lightly. A shortstop who raises his batting average 30 points has "rejuvenated" his career. What Tedford did at Cal came right from the pages of Mary Shelley. If Cal football didn't die during the '90s (from 1992 to 2001, Cal had one winning season), it at least coded. Tedford brought it back to life. The Bears went 7–5 in 2002, his first season, and raised their victory total in each of the next two years. In 2003, Cal upset USC 34–31 for the Trojans' only loss in a national championship season. In the other two seasons, the Bears lost to the Trojans by a combined eight points.

Cal seemed like the perfect fit for a guy who would rather watch video than address the public relations side of his work. In the Bay Area, with all its sports, and in Berkeley, with its lack of interest in football, Tedford can work in peace. And does he ever like to work. During the season, he often sleeps at the office. Tedford once promised an Australian punting prospect a home visit. Tedford packed eight extra laptop batteries and flew 17 hours, working on his bowl game plan all the while. When he arrived in Brisbane, he spent fewer than four hours on the ground, returned to the airport, and flew home, using the remainder of the extra batteries to finish his bowl work.

"I was able to game plan and sit on a plane with the phone not ringing," Tedford recalled with delight.

Tedford built his reputation on his ability to develop quarterbacks. When Green Bay selected Cal's Aaron Rodgers with the 24th pick of the 2005 NFL Draft, he joined Akili Smith (1999) and Joey Harrington (2002) as first-round quarterbacks from the School of Tedford.

At that point, when Rodgers left, Tedford had a cumulative record of 25–13. More important, he had California positioned on USC's back bumper, looking for the opening to slingshot past the Trojans. In February 2005, Long Beach Poly wide receiver DeSean Jackson stunned USC and the recruiting world by saying no to the Trojans and yes to the Bears.

Which is how heightened expectations change the perception of a coach. In the last three seasons, the Bears have gone 8–4, 10–3, and 7–6, for a three-season record of 25–13, the same as the first three. In 2006, Cal tied USC for the Pac-10 Conference championship.

But here's what didn't happen: the Bears didn't break through. They didn't go to the Rose Bowl in that 2006 season because the Trojans beat them 23–9. In the last three seasons, USC beat Cal by 25, 14, and seven points.

Tedford the quarterback guru has stumbled, too. I don't take seriously the charge that Smith, Harrington, and Rodgers have been NFL busts. For one thing, Rodgers had to wait three seasons for Brett Favre to finally retire in Green Bay and will get his first real chance to play in 2008. For another, the NFL is a different game.

In the college game, however, Tedford has gone three seasons without a dominating quarterback. Neither Joe Ayoob nor Nate Longshore has reached the standard set by Tedford's previous passers. The guru gets one more shot with Longshore, who in the last two seasons has thrown for 5,601 yards and 40 touchdowns (good) but also has thrown 26 interceptions (bad).

Jackson, with all his speed, didn't have a catch longer than 44 yards in 2007. He left for the NFL after his junior season.

Last season, the Bears began the season 5–0 and reached No. 2 in the polls. And then, with the benefit of a week off, and at their own Homecoming, the Bears lost 31–28 to Oregon State. The team lost its focus and just about everything else it touched. Cal dropped five of its next six and finished the season 7–6. The point is simple—Tedford reached the Pac-10's glass ceiling and just keeps bruising his scalp. That may be enough at Cal. But Tedford promised more than he has delivered.

4. NICK SABAN

Of course, Nick Saban is overrated. No coach, alive or dead could meet the expectations of the Alabama faithful.

Of course, Nick Saban is overrated, because no college coach is worth $4 million a year. Not to go all earthy-crunchy on you—don't worry, I'm not going to list what Hurricane Katrina victims could do with that $4 million—but no college coach is worth $4 million and 119 athletic directors agree with me. However, Mal Moore of Alabama begs to differ, and it only takes one athletic director to decide that a coach is worth that salary. That's how baseball salaries skyrocketed over the last generation. It only takes one owner willing to pay an outlandish salary.

One thing you can bet on is that at some point, the other coaches' salaries will catch up.

In the meantime, let's break it down, shall we?

Pro: Saban is known as a builder. It took him five years to drag Michigan State out of mediocrity to a 10–2 record in 1999. It took him two years to

For $4 million per year, Nick Saban should be higher than 17th on the list of highest winning percentages for active coaches.

win an SEC championship at LSU (2001) and two more to win the national championship there. The guy has proven he knows what he's doing.

Con: In his first 11 seasons as a head coach, Saban won 10 games only three times. Saban, hired to pull the Crimson Tide out of the Mike Shula muck (26–23 in four seasons), improved Alabama from 6–7 all the way to...um, well, 7–6. His overall record of 98–48–1 (.670) is a B-plus, not an A. He ranks 17th among active coaches in winning percentage.

I know, I know. It's like sending the building inspector to the site while they're still pouring concrete. But, hey, I have deadlines. Count me among those who believe that Saban will win championships at Alabama. Until he does, and until the coaching marketplace catches up to him, he is a $4 million coach with a record that doesn't match.

Deconstructing Saban is a lot of work because he has a Britneyesque ability to attract attention, both good and bad. He takes responsibility for a heaping share of the latter. In a business peopled by control freaks with the concentration of a surgeon's laser, Saban is unparalleled in his ability to shut out the external. Saban sizes up most people by the following measure: can he or she help me win games? If it's yes, get on board. If it's no, get out of the way.

That includes the media, which, like his assistants, finds itself on the receiving end of Saban's brusqueness. The difference is that the media can talk back to Saban, and when he slips up, the media pounces. If a wide receiver handled passes the way that Saban handled his departure from the Miami Dolphins in favor of the Crimson Tide, Saban would yank his scholarship.

Saban not only denied interest in the Alabama job, he said that he would not take the job, period. Before the Dolphins equipment manager had finished washing the jerseys from the last game, Saban arrived in Tuscaloosa, Crimson Tide fans prostrate before him in gratitude.

Time will heal Saban's self-inflicted wound. Bobby Petrino of—wait, let me check. Is he still in Fayetteville?—Arkansas makes Saban look like the soul of stability. Alabama hired Saban for the discipline he brought and because a program steeped in tradition had wandered in the desert for 10 years that seemed like 40.

Time also will tell if $32 million over eight years will be a bargain. In the meantime, Alabama's football coach is first in salary and 17th in winning.

5. FRANK BEAMER

Frank Beamer is the Moses of Virginia Tech. He has brought the Hokies from Nowhere, or two games behind Nowhere, to the top of the Big East and, now, the top of the Atlantic Coast Conference. He has brought Virginia Tech to the border of the Promised Land.

And, like Moses, Beamer has had trouble with that final step.

He is a man singularly identified with his school, and it is his school. He played at Virginia Tech four decades ago. He has been the head coach of the Hokies for 21 seasons. Beamer went to bed one night in 2000 thinking he might be the North Carolina head coach, only to back away at morning light. He turned down overtures from Alabama to stay home, too.

The Hokies have thrived playing Beamerball, a brand of football that emphasizes the kicking game and defense. Beamer himself coaches the special teams. No team is better known for blocking kicks (117 in his tenure) and Beamer has been generous with his expertise. Coaches at all levels of football make the pilgrimage to Blacksburg to hear Beamer's tactics for wreaking havoc with special teams. Including his six seasons at Murray State, he has a record of 209–108–4 (.657), making him one of four active coaches with more than 200 victories.

So what's not to like?

The Hokies lose big games, and they have lost them regularly. I'm not talking about winning a national championship, which Virginia Tech played for in the 1999 season. Finishing No. 1 takes not only skill but luck. Factors outside of a team's control weigh on the outcome. But every team has big games and every team that wins has big games late in the season. That's when Beamer's Hokies have shown their fallibility.

The envelopes, please:

- In 2007, the Hokies, favored by 3.5 points, lost the Orange Bowl to Kansas 24–21. The Hokies have lost four of their last five bowls, three of which the oddsmakers favored them to win.
- In 2005, the 8–0, No. 3 Hokies got clobbered at home by No. 5 Miami 27–7. At the end of the regular season, Virginia Tech, two-touchdown favorites over unranked Florida State in the inaugural ACC Championship Game, lost 27–22.

- In 2003, the week after humiliating No. 2 Miami 31–7, the No. 5 Hokies lost to No. 25 Pittsburgh 31–28. Virginia Tech lost four of its last five games, the victory coming over Temple 24–23 in overtime.
- In 2002, Virginia Tech started 8–0, reached No. 3 in the polls, then lost four of its last six.
- In 1997, No. 19 Virginia Tech, 7–2, lost its last three games by 7, 14, and 39 points.

Is it talent? The Hokies did not falter down the stretch in 1999–2000, when Michael Vick played quarterback. They lost two games in Vick's two seasons: the 1999 national championship game 46–29 to a Florida State team that remains the best that Bobby Bowden has coached in his six decades in the game, and a 41–21 loss to Miami in which Vick played despite being hobbled by an ankle injury (yep, his dogs were barking).

Vick is one of only five NFL first-round draft picks under Beamer in his 21 seasons. By comparison, Ohio State, Florida State, and LSU had more than five in the three drafts from 2005-07 alone.

In other words, it might be talent. That's not meant as a criticism of Beamer's ability to recruit or judge players. In my mind, it's a plus, because it means that Beamer has won despite a lack of great players. But it may explain what happens to Virginia Tech in big, late-season games, when there's a greater chance that apples will be playing apples.

While better coaches than Beamer have had postseason problems, most of them pull out of them over the course of a career. Bear Bryant, for example, went 0–7–1 in bowl games from 1967 to 1974. But he finished his career at 15–12–2. Beamer's struggles have been persistent. The NCAA Record Book uses 11 bowl games as a minimum in calculating career winning percentage. Beamer, at 6–9, ranks 29th out of 38 coaches.

When Beamer retires, his wait to enter the College Football Hall of Fame will be short. He has won a lot of games. He just hasn't won enough of the big ones. Among the active coaches in the six major conferences who have not won a national championship—the coaches who really have a chance to finish No. 1—Beamer has 82 more victories than the runner-up, Mike Bellotti of Oregon (127).

What does that mean? It means that Beamer is a survivor in a tough business. It means that Virginia Tech may be one of the last places where winning—without winning it all—is acceptable. But for all the success that Beamer has had at Virginia Tech, it means that he has fallen short in some big games.

The Most Underrated Coach in College Football

MIKE RILEY

A decade or so ago, the schools that wallow in what used to be known as I-AA—the Appalachian States of the world—wanted to return to one, big, happy Division I. It looked like a naked push to get a bigger piece of the financial pie. Rather than squash the movement, former Southeastern Conference commissioner Roy Kramer merely shrugged.

"Thirty years ago," Kramer asked, "who were the big programs? Texas. Michigan. Alabama. Who are the big programs now?"

Kramer's point is that you can call it Division I or you can call it Burkina Faso. Tradition and history, like water, find their own levels. The NCAA exists to level a playing field that all the bulldozers in North America could never level. The NCAA could reduce the scholarship limit from 85 to 45, and Oregon State will never be USC. One school exudes tradition and winning. The other is Oregon State.

But it's because that playing field tilts so sharply away from Corvallis that Beavers coach Mike Riley is the most underrated coach in college football. No coach in Division I took over a job in a hole deeper than the one Riley climbed down into a decade ago. Given fallow land in Corvallis, Riley has made it produce wins and talented players year after year. Since he returned in 2003 for a second tour at Oregon State, Riley has gone 39–24 (.619).

More to the point, Riley has transformed Oregon State into a perennial threat in the Pac-10 Conference. Just to get an idea of how difficult that is, consider this: the Beavers went 6–3 in league games in 2006 and 2007, the first consecutive winning records in Pac-10 play by Oregon State since 1966-69.

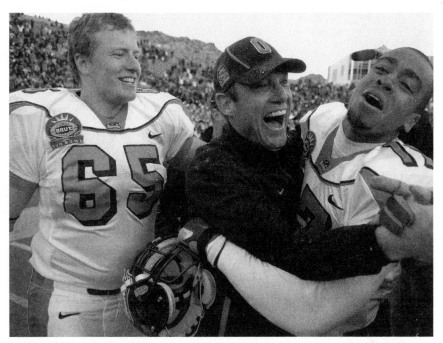

Since returning to Corvallis in 2003, Mike Riley has lead Oregon State to an impressive 39–24 record.

By the way, that's when Riley's dad, Bud, coached on the Beavers' staff for the legendary Dee Andros.

Mike Riley grew up in Corvallis, but he didn't play at Oregon State. Instead, he went across the country for a four-year tutorial from Bear Bryant at Alabama. Riley's uncle, Hayden, coached basketball for the Crimson Tide. Riley didn't play much—he lettered as a senior defensive back in 1974—but he absorbed plenty. In his four years, Alabama shared one national championship, played for another, and went 43–5.

But there's something to be said for knowing the school that you are recruiting to. No, check that. There's *everything* to be said, because there's no way a guy with Riley's resume would have been caught dead coaching in Corvallis. Oh, plenty of guys enjoyed being there, as long as they stood on the sideline opposite Oregon State. In the 25 seasons prior to Riley's arrival in 1997, the Beavers never won more than four games.

Riley coached for two seasons, going 3–8 in 1997 and 5–6 in 1998, before leaving to coach the San Diego Chargers. Dennis Erickson, upon the foundation that Riley laid, built the 2000 team that won the Fiesta Bowl and finished 11–1.

Riley lasted three seasons with the Chargers, going 14–34. Even after getting fired, he remained alluring to the people who hire college coaches. UCLA came by, and when Riley worked as assistant head coach under Jim Haslett with the New Orleans Saints in 2002, Alabama came looking.

Nearly three decades after graduating, Riley turned down his alma mater, which then hired Mike Price. Think Alabama wishes Riley had come home?

Instead, two months later, Riley replaced the guy who replaced him, Erickson. So much of success in college football is matching coach to campus. It is clear that Riley has found his home in Corvallis. In fact, Riley has proven you can go home again. And again.

Riley succeeds for a couple of reasons. The first is his ability to evaluate talent. He can find it where few others see it, or even bother to look. Tailback Ken Simonton, considered too small by most Pac-10 schools, signed with the Beavers in 1998 and as a freshman scored the winning touchdown in the two-overtime victory against Oregon. By his junior season, Simonton had "All-American" in front of his name.

Wide receiver T.J. Houshmandzadeh came into Oregon State unheralded. By the time he left—and for the last seven seasons in the NFL—everyone knew how to pronounce his name.

Matt Moore lost his starting job at UCLA as a sophomore in 2003, when he threw two touchdowns and six interceptions. Moore transferred to Oregon State, threw for 5,733 yards in 2005–06, and finished his collegiate career with a school-record 182 consecutive passes without an interception.

In February of this year, Oregon State signed tailback Jacquizz Rodgers, who broke the 19-year-old Texas high school record for career touchdowns with 136 and led Lamar Consolidated to the 4A Division I state championship. Rodgers didn't get a scholarship offer from the major schools in his home state because he stands all of 5'6" and weighs 165 pounds. If Riley gambles on him—and gamble really applies to every signee, whether they're 5'6" or 6'6"—he's a good bet.

"I always feel like they are on good players, maybe a guy who is not as hyped," said Boise State coach Chris Petersen, who has turned the Broncos into a national power by finding the players who slip through the Pac-10's fingers. "'Oregon State has that guy figured out? Aw, shoot.' We're on the right guys if Oregon State is looking at them."

Another reason that Oregon State wins under Riley is that it improves as the season goes on. In 2006 and 2007, the Beavers went a combined 15–3 in October, November, and December. Riley is 4–0 in bowl games, including the remarkable comeback victory in the 2006 Sun Bowl, when the Beavers scored 15 points in the last 6:02 of regulation, including a touchdown and two-point conversion with :22.1 to play, to beat Missouri 39–38.

Head coaches often have healthy egos. The nature of the job promotes it. They attract attention and become accustomed to the trappings of being a public figure. They come to expect microphones and cameras will record their every thought. The successful coaches have plenty of people who tell them what they want to hear.

Riley has none of those traits. He has been a head coach in the NFL, where ego reigns supreme, and, for seven seasons, at Oregon State. Yet he remains as humble as a country vicar. That may be why he's the most underrated coach in college football.

The Rest of the Most Underrated

2. JIM GROBE

Winning at Wake Forest is harder than geometry. Wake has barely more than 4,000 undergraduates, an amount less than half of what Ohio State welcomes in every freshman class. You could take the whole campus and tuck it into a corner of Penn State and no one would notice.

The same goes for Groves Stadium, which has a capacity of 31,500, or less than a third of the capacity of Neyland Stadium at Tennessee.

Yet over the last two seasons, Wake Forest has gone 11–3 and 9–4, respectively. Those records may result in a call for a coach's head at some campuses. At Wake, they describe why Jim Grobe is one of the best coaches in the business.

The secret about Grobe has begun to get out. Nebraska legend Tom Osborne met with Grobe when the Huskers needed a coach in 2007, and representatives from Arkansas and Michigan have also come knocking at the Deacon's door. Yet Grobe enjoys the low profile he keeps at Wake. He is a compact man with a warm smile and a plain manner of speaking. Grobe is not going to one-liner his way into a post-coaching TV gig. He doesn't have a unique offense the way that Rich Rodriguez does at Michigan. Grobe is not considered a defensive wizard the way that Pete Carroll is at USC.

Don't look for him at the top of the career winning percentage list. The two remarkable seasons mentioned above raised his career record to 78–72–1. Insert yawn here.

But Grobe has been driving off-the-lot stock in NASCAR races his entire career. He made a winner out of Ohio University in the 1990s, and now he has made a winner out of Wake Forest.

Before 2006, Wake Forest had won eight games only three times before— in 1944, when there was a war on, and again in 1979 and 1992. It's hardly been a coaching graveyard. Peahead Walker, Cal Stoll, John Mackovic, Al Groh, and Bill Dooley have all coached the Demon Deacons, which just goes to prove how tough it is to win there. None of them ever won nine games in season at Wake. Grobe has done it *twice.*

Grobe attempted in the 2006 season to explain how his Wake Forest team had been able to do what no Wake team had ever done.

"We've played pretty good special teams, we've played pretty good defense most of the time, and offensively we've taken care of the football. Typically when you do that, you're going to end up in the fourth quarter with a chance," Grobe said. That makes some sense on an X-and-O level. But there's something else at work. You have to see Wake play to understand it.

"We do film exchanges," Wake Forest defensive coordinator Dean Hood said. "We play somebody non-league. Everybody from that league calls. The thing they always say is, 'How do you get those kids to play so hard?' They want a drill or some kind of Vince Lombardi speech. Our kids play hard because they know the head coach cares about them. Period. End of story."

Former Wake defensive back Patrick Ghee planned to go to Stanford to play for Ty Willingham. He changed his mind when he met Jim Grobe.

"You just know he cares about you," Ghee said. "It's easy to play for someone like that, someone you respect, someone you like. When he speaks to us, it's like a fatherly love. He really cares about players. Not all coaches are like that. A lot of them are like, 'This is my job. We're going to win and I don't care what the cost is.' Coach Grobe cares about the person first, and about your character, more than he does about what happens in the game."

3. PAUL JOHNSON

There is a tendency among college football fans to dismiss a successful academy team—Army, Navy, or Air Force—with a pat on the head and condescending praise. In the case of Georgia Tech coach Paul Johnson, however, the easiest way to measure how well he did in six seasons at Navy is simple. Compare Navy to Army.

When Johnson arrived at Navy in 2002, West Point and Annapolis had a lot in common—namely, their football teams stunk. Navy had just gone winless in 2001. Army, under second-year coach Todd Berry, had gone 3–8. In 2002, when the academies played, each with 1–10 records, Navy won 58–12. It would be a sign of things to come.

In 2003, the Midshipmen went 8–5 and played in their first bowl game in seven seasons. Army went 0–13. In six seasons at Navy, Johnson went 45–29. More important, he went 6–0 against Army (average margin of victory: 28 points), the longest winning streak by either school in that storied rivalry, and 5–1 against Air Force. That adds up to five Commander-in-Chief Trophies and seven seas of happy admirals.

Johnson came to Navy from Georgia Southern, where he won two I-AA national championships (1999–2000) in five seasons while running the triple option. The offense proved an effective tonic at Navy as well. Johnson's Midshipmen led the nation in rushing in four of six seasons.

The triple-option offense works in I-AA and, like the spread, is a great equalizer. But it isn't considered a viable offense in the major conferences. Johnson has been able to adjust it and succeed with it over 20 years. From 1987 to 1994, as offensive coordinator at Hawaii, Johnson's side of the ball consistently ranked among the national leaders.

Johnson is an unusual guy. He is one of only four I-A coaches who didn't play college football. Not even Western Carolina, the I-AA school where Johnson earned a physical education degree, had use for a 135-pound center.

Among Mike Leach of Texas Tech, Charlie Weis of Notre Dame, and Mark Mangino of Kansas, Johnson has been the most consistently successful at the college level.

Yet Johnson is nothing if not confident in his competitive instinct, and he instills that confidence in his teams. For instance, in 2007, Navy succeeded in converting 19 of 29 fourth downs.

As he begins his tenure in Atlanta, there's no reason to believe he won't continue to win.

If you can recruit players to win at Navy, the academic handcuffs at Georgia Tech won't scare you. Johnson has more charisma in his little finger than half the I-A head coaches combined. That's a facet of the Georgia Tech job that went unfulfilled in the Gailey Era. In an NFL town, Georgia Tech needs a coach who can attract attention. Johnson will do that, and for the right reasons.

4. PHILLIP FULMER

Phillip Fulmer is a former offensive lineman and offensive line coach. He is not glib. Fulmer would rather stand in a stream with his custom-built fly rod in hand than represent the public face of Tennessee football.

Though he cleans up nice, as the saying goes for someone who dresses well, Fulmer has "lunch pail" written all over him. That is meant as a compliment, and among offensive linemen would be understood as such. But it works against Fulmer in the realm of image. So does the fact that he doesn't look like a sideline matinee idol. (Let's face it: who looks good dressed in orange?)

But facts are facts. Among I-A coaches with at least five years of experience, Fulmer ranks fifth in winning percentage. Raise the ante to 10 years of experience, and Fulmer is first.

Guys like Carroll, Meyer, and Stoops are rock stars in the sport. You can't type "Bowden," "Paterno," or "Spurrier" without inserting "legend" in the same sentence. Yet Fulmer gets none of that adulation. He is known as the guy who helped the NCAA take Alabama down, but not before some of the mud splashed on him. Remember Fulmer refusing to attend the SEC Media Days in 2004 to avoid being served a subpoena?

Fulmer has won a national championship, two Southeastern Conference championships, and six SEC East titles. And midway through the 2007 season, in appreciation of all that Fulmer had done for his alma mater, Tennessee fans wanted to fire him.

The Vols began the season 4–3, and had lost by margins of 14, 39, and 24 points. When Fulmer went to withdraw from the bank of goodwill, where he thought he had made deposits for 15 seasons, he found insufficient funds.

Fans. You can't live with them, you can't fire them.

Former Texas Tech head coach Spike Dykes once estimated that a coach loses about 10 percent of the fan base every season. Fulmer, who took over Tennessee in a messy coup d'etat in 1992 when Johnny Majors took ill, seemed to irritate Vol fans just by being there.

That shouldn't matter. Then again, *People* magazine shouldn't sell 3.5 million copies a week.

What Fulmer did to turn around Tennessee is what he has done throughout his long, distinguished career. He worked. Fulmer came out of the womb with a grindstone attached to his nose. What his team lacked in talent, it made up for in will. The Volunteers won their last five games, including overtime victories over South Carolina and Kentucky and a frantic fourth-quarter comeback against Vanderbilt. They won the SEC East for the sixth time.

And they made the Tennessee fans, at least the ones who wanted Fulmer gone, look foolish.

It is no coincidence that Tennessee is 7–1 in overtime games under Fulmer. Overtime is about making a play—one play—when you're dog tired, when want-to is more important than talent. The Volunteers are 6–2 in one-point games under Fulmer. One-point games bring coaching decisions to a finer point. Fulmer and Tennessee don't fold in tight games.

Have the Volunteers taken a step back over the last five years? Yes. Does the college football public have any idea that Fulmer is among the most successful coaches in the sport? None. Does he belong there? Absolutely.

5. HOWARD SCHNELLENBERGER

You can make a good case for Howard Schnellenberger to be on the overrated list. For all the attention that Schnellenberger has attracted, his career record is only 124–98–3. Yes, he's one of only 13 active coaches to have won

Howard Schnellenberger has built Florida Atlantic into a Sun Belt champion, the third time in his career he's turned around the fortunes of a struggling program.

a national championship, but he won it 25 years ago, when dinosaurs roamed the AstroTurf.

(If you're under the age of 25, you have no idea what AstroTurf is. Picture green indoor/outdoor shag carpeting. With no padding.)

Schnellenberger has been around so long that he recruited Pennsylvania prep star Joe Namath to play for Bear Bryant at Alabama. That's the same Namath whose college graduation in December 2007, *at the age of 64,* generated headlines across the country.

And Schnellenberger is not only still coaching. He's developing programs. Winning percentage is not the way to judge him. Schnellenberger has a unique talent and he has been smart enough to figure out how to use it at three different universities.

At Miami, Schnellenberger took a program left for dead—the university discussed dropping football in the late 1970s—and built it into a national champion. On the foundation he laid, the Hurricanes became the program that dominated college football from 1987 to 1992, and again from 2000 to 2002.

At Louisville, Schnellenberger took over a program that pretty much had been dropped off at a nursing home. When he arrived in 1985, the Cardinals had suffered six consecutive losing seasons. Not only did Schnellenberger revive Louisville, he took the Cardinals to their first major bowl, the 1991 Fiesta Bowl. Schnellenberger amassed a pedestrian 54–56–2 record in 10 seasons. Yet when he left after the 1994 season, Louisville knew it could thrive among the big boys. Eleven years later, Louisville joined the Big East.

And at Florida Atlantic, Schnellenberger built a program from scratch— as in, in 1998, on the to-do list was "Order footballs"—and seven seasons later, that program not only won the Sun Belt Conference, but played in the New Orleans Bowl as well. It's an amazing season when two Florida schools win conference championships (UCF won Conference USA) and neither of them are Florida, Florida State, or Miami.

"We're several years ahead of where I thought we would be," Schnellenberger said after winning the Sun Belt.

Granted, Schnellenberger has built two of those programs in the Miami area, home of one of the deepest wellsprings of football talent in the country. But building a winner from the ground up isn't easy anywhere. Ask Southeastern Louisiana, which has yet to leave a cleat print on the sport in five seasons. Better yet, ask Florida International, just a few miles away from Schnellenberger and Florida Atlantic. Florida International, which started football one season later than Florida Atlantic, lost 23 consecutive games before closing 2007 with a 38–19 victory over North Texas.

What Schnellenberger has done at Florida Atlantic is astounding. And he's done it three times. That's an underrated coach.

The Most Overrated Retired Coach in College Football History

AMOS STAGG

Amos Alonzo Stagg is football onomatopoeia: he Staggered to his 314 victories. Spread over 57 seasons, Stagg averaged 5.5 wins per year.

The numbers don't lie: over his last 17 seasons as a head coach, Amos Stagg was 23 games under .500.

You can't diminish what Stagg did for college football. As a prominent member of the NCAA Rules Committee for more than six decades—or more than half of the NCAA's existence—Stagg helped shepherd the game into the modern era. He joined the Rules Committee in 1904, the football equivalent of 1 B.C. The following year, President Theodore Roosevelt forced the major national universities to come together and form the NCAA in order to clean up the violence in the game.

In 1933, Stagg became a Life Member of the Rules Committee and remained on it until his death in 1965.

According to the late college football writer and historian Tim Cohane, Stagg brought to the game, among other innovations, the onside kick, the man in motion, flankers, the huddle, numbers on uniforms, padded goalposts, and the blocking sled.

Okay, football wouldn't be where it is without Stagg. But the game progressed so far during Stagg's career that it left him behind. As a founding member of what would become the Big Ten Conference, the University of

Chicago stood as a power on and off the field. Stagg's Maroons won seven Big Ten championships. His favorite may have been the 1905 title, secured when Chicago snapped Michigan's 56-game unbeaten streak with a 2–0 victory.

But as football and the conference grew, Chicago refused to allow the football tail to wag the academic dog. Stagg's team dropped, first to the bottom of the conference standings, and then out of the conference altogether.

Stagg, after reaching the university's mandatory retirement age of 70, moved to the College of the Pacific—like Chicago, a have-not in a region full of haves. He coached at Pacific through the 1946 season, when, at age 84, the school forced him to retire. In 14 seasons at the Stockton, California, school, Stagg had four winning seasons and finished with a record of 60–77–7 (.441).

His defenders say that Stagg, given equal resources to what, say, Fielding Yost had at Michigan, would have continued to win as Stagg did at the outset of his career. Maybe so, but the cold numbers say only that over his last 17 seasons as a head coach, Stagg's cumulative record was 23 games below .500.

Some 15 years after Stagg died, his career enjoyed a renaissance as Bear Bryant approached his 315th victory. Bryant took the record away from Stagg in 1981. A few years later, at the urging of a biographer of Pop Warner, the NCAA decided that Warner had not received credit for six victories and boosted his career total from 313 to 319.

Talk about being overrated: Stagg got passed in total victories by a dead coach.

Seriously, Stagg remains a pioneer of the game, and a legend. Surely the men who played for him at Pacific benefited from the experience. Stagg loved his players, and they loved playing for him.

But viewing through the cold lens of history, the career victories list looks a lot better with Bobby Bowden and Joe Paterno at the top.

The Rest of Most Overrated

2. RED BLAIK

Red Blaik is a personal favorite. His memoir, *You Have to Pay the Price,* is one of the best coaching autobiographies ever written, and that is not the faint praise it resembles.

Blaik combined a steely exterior with a warm, intelligent core. He coached for 25 years at Dartmouth (1934–40) and at Army (1941–58), and his record of 166–48–14 (.75877) is roughly equal to that of Woody Hayes (.75937) and Bobby Bowden (.75604).

Blaik's greatest success at Army came between 1944 and 1950, when the Black Knights went 57–3–4 (.922). Those seven seasons included unbeaten streaks of 32 and 28 games.

From 1944 to 1946, Army went 27–0–1, the tie being the famous 0–0 game against Notre Dame at Yankee Stadium. The Black Knights' backfield featured fullback Doc (Mr. Inside) Blanchard, the 1945 Heisman Trophy winner; halfback Glenn (Mr. Outside) Davis, the 1946 Heisman Trophy winner; and quarterback Arnold Tucker, the 1946 Sullivan Award winner (given to the nation's outstanding amateur athlete).

Those won-loss numbers do Blaik a disservice. His wins in the '40s are nothing more than steroids for his coaching record. That's where the overrated comes in: Blaik's greatest success started during World War II. When most schools were struggling to field a team, Blaik rolled out the best that America had to offer. Blaik, through no fault of his own, beefed up his record on a playing field that never came close to level. West Point had all the players.

College football during the war served as entertainment and perhaps, like Major League Baseball, as a sign of life as usual. So much of the rest of daily life in the 48 states had been turned upside down.

But the ability of the players during the war slipped to levels that resembled normal college football in uniform only. The talent level diminished. So did the number of available players.

"I'll put 11 men on the field, but if anything happens to them I won't be able to do anything except start praying," Princeton coach Harry Mahnken said, according to *Ivy League Autumns,* the 1996 history by Richard Goldstein. Teams consisted mostly of some combination of 17-year-olds and 4-Fs, men classified as physically unable to serve. Other schools simply stopped playing. Among those that didn't field a team in at least one year during the war: Alabama, Florida, Kentucky, Oregon, Stanford, Syracuse, Tennessee, Virginia Tech, and Washington State.

Army has a different history to tell. Blaik not only had able-bodied men, he had some of the best players in the country transfer to West Point. Blanchard, for instance, played one season at North Carolina before coming to West Point.

At halftime of Army's game against Temple in 1943, Blaik forbid his team from scoring any more touchdowns. When guard Charlie Sampson intercepted a pass in the second half, he returned it to the Owls' 1-yard line and stopped. Final score: Army 51, Temple 0.

For three seasons, nearly every game went like the first Gulf War. Army showed up, kicked butt, and went home.

The momentum created by those teams carried Army right through 1950, when the Black Knights started 8–0, only to lose to Navy 14–2 in one of the great upsets of the sport. That remains the peak of Army football to this day. After the 1950 season, a cheating scandal forced the expulsion of 90 cadets, 37 of them players, one of them a quarterback named Bobby Blaik.

Red Blaik had a fondness for this team because of his son and his son's friends. Blaik believed in the character of the young men, many of whom had been guilty of nothing more than staying quiet. The mass expulsion actually led to Blaik's best coaching.

In 1951, the first year with a decimated roster, Army went 2–7–0. Two years later, Army went 7–1–1. Though Blaik's teams never again achieved the consistent greatness they enjoyed before the scandal, in 1958 Army went 8–0–1, and halfback Pete Dawkins won the Heisman. Blaik retired after that season.

Blaik's record, loaded as it is with junk-food victories, does him a disservice. Yeah, yeah, there was a war on, and Blaik had no control over that. Still, his record reflects an unfair advantage.

3. BILL WALSH

Bill Walsh died in 2007 at age 75 a "genius," a term he liked to hear only slightly less than "interception." Walsh won three Super Bowls as the head coach of the 49ers. As coach and general manager, he built an also-ran NFL program that had spent decades in the shadow of the Los Angeles Rams into the best team in professional football.

But the operative word in that description is "professional." Walsh's genius never came to full bloom at Stanford, where he coached two years before he went to the 49ers (1977–78), and three years after (1992–94).

In his first go-round at the Farm, Walsh lifted Stanford out of the mediocrity in which it foundered under Jack Christiansen. Walsh came close to reviving John Ralston's Rose Bowl success at the beginning of the 1970s. Stanford went 9–3 in Walsh's first season, and 8–4 in his second. Walsh gave a preview of what he could do at Stanford. The 1978 season concluded in the Bluebonnet Bowl, where Stanford spotted Georgia a 22–0 lead in the third quarter before roaring back to win 25–22.

But Walsh didn't stick around long enough to finish the job. He left for the NFL, although not before getting a Southern California phenom named John Elway to sign with Stanford. The opportunity we missed to see Walsh tutor Elway for four seasons is one of those what-ifs that historians love. Stanford grads, at least those of us in school at the time, don't love it. Mostly, we close the door and weep in privacy.

When Walsh returned to the Farm for the 1992 season, he returned with three Super Bowl rings and 102 victories earned in only 10 seasons with the 49ers. The Cardinal, led by talent recruited by Walsh's predecessor, Dennis Green, went 10–3 and tied Washington for the Pac-10 Conference championship.

Stanford finished the season in the Blockbuster Bowl against Penn State, a game billed as a confrontation between two coaching icons: Walsh and Joe Paterno. The game indeed had two icons, but only one team—the Nittany Lions failed to show up. Stanford won 24–3, and as Lowell Cohn wrote in *Rough Magic,* a tremendous account of Walsh's return to Stanford, the players couldn't believe the simplicity of the Nittany Lions' schemes and their inability to decipher what the Cardinal did.

In other words, Stanford was coached much better than Penn State.

At that point, Walsh had a three-year record of 27–10 at Stanford, and the future, even for a 61-year-old coach, couldn't have looked brighter. But as the next two seasons revealed, Walsh's Cardinal had peaked. In 1993 and 1994, Stanford went a combined 7–14–1. Walsh's teams won only four Pac-10 games in two seasons, two of them against hapless Oregon State. There was talk of Walsh favoring his recruits over the players he inherited, with the result being a split locker room. But losing teams always have excuses.

At the end of the 1994 season, Walsh knew the time had come to retire from coaching for good. After several years in the 49ers' front office, Walsh came back to Stanford in 2004 as the athletic equivalent of a scholar-in-residence. The coaches who succeeded him loved having him as a resource.

"There are days when he'll come in and walk down and watch film," Stanford coach Jim Harbaugh said in July 2007, "or sit for an hour and a half and talk offensive philosophy and start drawing plays with his left hand, and I think, 'Oh my god, I'm going to laminate this!'... You never knew when he would be in his office. I found myself walking down there to see if he was there."

A week after Harbaugh said that, Walsh died of leukemia at age 75. Stanford remembers him as a legend, and that is good enough. By objective standards, Walsh's "genius" label applied only to the NFL.

4. GRANT TEAFF

Grant Teaff served as a head coach for 30 seasons, 21 of them at Baylor (1972–92). You can say that he won more than he lost (170–151–8). You can say that Teaff won two Southwest Conference championships (1974, 1980). You can say that he is a member of the College Football Hall of Fame.

And after you say that, you can say, say what? A guy who averaged a 6–5 record for a generation is in the Hall of Fame?

Teaff has been the executive director of the American Football Coaches Association since 1994. He is a respected figure among his peers. Teaff oozes spirit and sweats motivation. He put positive spin on subjects before the phrase "positive spin" even existed. He is also living proof that cronyism seeps into the College Football Hall of Fame just as it does it in all the others.

That's why Phil Rizzuto and Richie Ashburn are in Cooperstown. The Veterans Committee selected both of them (and a few others) because they hung around and everybody liked them.

The same goes for Teaff. He gained significant mileage as a representative of the coaches on issues of the day. He hung around. Teaff became known more for his motivational ploys—pretending to eat a worm before a game against Texas, for example—than for his team's play.

When Teaff coached, teams overlooked Baylor at their own peril. The Bears could occasionally rise up and win. More indicative of their comparative strength is that in the two Cotton Bowls that Teaff's Baylor teams played, they lost by a combined score of 71–22. That Teaff won 128 games in 21 seasons with the Bears is remarkable. The runner-up to him in career victories at the small Baptist university won 83 games.

By Baylor's meager standards, Teaff is worthy of recognition. By national standards, his work barely kept its nose above average. That's what forced the National Football Foundation's Honors Court to ignore its own guidelines to elect Teaff to the College Football Hall of Fame in 2001.

(In the interest of full disclosure, I began serving a five-year term on the Honors Court in 2006.)

"Coaches that have not won 60 percent of their games," the guideline reads, "may still be eligible for consideration, by the Honors Review Committee, which examines unique cases."

Teaff's winning percentage is .529, which is a few first downs short of .600. His winning percentage, among the 45 major-college coaches who have won 170 games in their careers, ranks dead last. Honors Court members may not reveal their deliberations. One member of the 2001 court said of the election of Teaff, "There was some debate in the room."

You think?

A case can be made for the Hall to honor contributors to the game, an honor that it doles out about as often as Baylor wins a conference championship. But that is not the flag under which Teaff marched into the Hall. There is a long list of coaching candidates who have better credentials. If you're searching for a noun to describe Teaff's election, try cronyism. Adjective? Try overrated.

5. JOHN ROBINSON

John Robinson extended USC's dominance after his friend and mentor, John McKay, left abruptly for the NFL in 1976. Robinson's Trojans won a share of the 1978 national championship. That they had to share it at all was the result of poll politics and the peculiar hold that Bear Bryant had on the sport. USC defeated Alabama 24–14 on September 23 of that season, yet lost the AP vote to the Crimson Tide.

In 1979, USC went 11–0–1, only to be thwarted again by Alabama, which went 12–0. Robinson's powerful offense delivered a Heisman Trophy winner in Charles White in 1979, and another one in Marcus Allen in 1981. When Robinson followed McKay into the NFL after the 1982 season, he departed with a record of 67–14–2 (.819) and his Trojans had won three conference championships.

Robinson left with the legacy of continuing the Trojans' dominance established by McKay. He left with one of the best winning percentages in the history of college football. He left with a national championship, something Tom Osborne couldn't claim at that time, or Lou Holtz, or Bobby Bowden.

The reputation Robinson earned in those seven seasons got him rehired at USC in 1993. Robinson won two more Pac-10 titles in the next three seasons but got fired in 1997 after consecutive six-win seasons. The reputation Robinson earned in two stints at USC got him hired in 1999 at UNLV, where the administration hoped some of that national championship magic would rub off on the Rebels.

It looked as if it might in his second game, when Robinson became the beneficiary of one of the great gaffes in recent college football history. Baylor, leading UNLV 24–21 in the final seconds, had the ball on the Rebels' 8-yard line. Rather than take a knee, the Bears tried to score. UNLV corner Andre Hilliard jarred the ball loose from tailback Darrell Bush near the goal. UNLV's Kevin Thomas scooped up the fumble and ran 100 yards for the 27–24 victory.

The Rebels went 3–8 in that first season, but in 2000, it looked as if Robinson had worked his magic. UNLV won its last four games, including a 31–14 victory over Arkansas in the Las Vegas Bowl, to finish 8–5. Poised to move forward, UNLV treaded water. The Rebels went 4–7, 5–7, 6–6, and in 2004, 2–9. Robinson retired after the season.

Let the numbers do the talking:

Robinson in his first tenure at USC (1976-1982): 67–14–2.

Robinson in his second tenure at USC (1993–97) and at UNLV (1999–2004): 65–63–2.

The biggest reason for the discrepancy? A different set of numbers can do the talking here. In the 1970s, the Age of Dynasties (USC, Alabama, Ohio

State, Michigan, Oklahoma), the NCAA allowed coaches to give scholarships to 105 players. In 1978, the NCAA trimmed that limit back to 95.

The Trojans began to slide from the peak they reached in 1978–79. The slide became more slippery in April of 1982, when the NCAA put USC football on probation for three years, with no bowls and no television appearances for two years. The list of grievances read like a hit parade for the excesses of the era: academic fraud, improper employment, and abuse of complimentary tickets.

By the time Robinson returned to USC in 1993, the NCAA had reduced the scholarship limit to 85 players, where it remains to this day. There is no question that the greater spread of players across rosters is one of the reasons that schools such as West Virginia and Kansas can contend for a national championship.

But it seems fair to say that once the playing field leveled, Robinson didn't produce the same results. Other coaches of his generation adjusted to having smaller rosters. Bobby Bowden had his best years at Florida State in the 1990s, after the switch to the 85-scholarship limit, as did Tom Osborne at Nebraska.

That doesn't make Robinson a bad coach. His career total of 132–77–4 (.629) is more than respectable. But it does make him overrated.

The Most Underrated Retired Coach in College Football History

FRANK LEAHY

Just off the sidewalk on Juniper Road outside of Notre Dame Stadium, there's a statue of former coach Frank Leahy kneeling, football in hands, intently watching some long-ago practice. The statue is set alone, with little fanfare, which unintentionally provides the appropriate context in which to appraise the career of Francis William Leahy. He is the Lawn Jockey in front of The House That Rockne Built.

Leahy has the second-highest winning percentage in the history of major-college football. He won four national championships. Over a span of four seasons from 1946 through 1949, Leahy's teams went 36–0–2. Those postwar teams did not once fall below second in the Associated Press polls.

Lost in the shadow of Knute Rockne, Notre Dame head coach Frank Leahy won four national championships and has the second-highest winning percentage in college football history.

But Leahy remains a distant historical figure, virtually unknown because of the one coach in the history of the game who enjoyed more success. The shadow that Knute Rockne cast over the Fighting Irish envelops Leahy to this day.

Leahy coached the same number of seasons as Rockne and won two more games, a fact known only to his relatives and college football geeks. That's the biggest reason that Leahy deserves the title of Most Underrated Coach.

The Rock became a national icon before he died, and he became a saint the day he tragically died in a plane crash on a Kansas prairie. Rockne had a movie made about his life that is still watched nearly seven decades later. His face adorned a postage stamp, the first to honor a coach in any American sport.

Leahy, on the other hand, died in anonymity in 1973, nearly two decades after his retirement. It took another 24 years to get him a statue on the Notre Dame campus. Get this: Leahy had to wait 17 years after he retired just to be elected to the College Football Hall of Fame.

Leahy brings to mind the assessment former Texas Governor Ann Richards made of Ginger Rogers: "She did everything that Fred Astaire did, only backwards and in high heels."

Leahy did everything that Rockne did, only Leahy did it with the ghost of Rockne peering over his shoulder.

There's one other reason Leahy gets overlooked, too—personality. Rockne attracted people. He had time for everyone. Leahy, on the other hand, could be as warm as a New England Christmas. In an era when coaches and sportswriters cultivated relationships more readily than they do today, Leahy remained standoffish with the writers and resented by his peers. How else to explain why it took so long for so successful a coach to be elected to the Hall of Fame?

Oh, no one could be more polite. Leahy assumed a courtliness that bordered on affectation. He spoke with the grandiloquence of an earlier time. Check out an excerpt from Leahy's speech to the Notre Dame student body shortly after his hiring, according to the 1944 book *Frank Leahy and the Fighting Irish* by Arch Ward:

> "This may sound rather funny to you, and it may seem to hit an all-time low in the realms of pessimism, but nevertheless it is our firm conviction that a defeat at times is an asset. It may make a team rise to greater heights the following week. It may have countless other effects that will outweigh the disadvantages concomitant with defeat. Lest any of you think we are sounding too pessimistic a note, we would like to say at this time with all the optimism of one entering upon a great adventure that we welcome the challenge."

Not exactly the hey-buddy patter of Bobby Bowden. If Bowden ever used "concomitant," he was mispronouncing something else. ("Hey, buddy. How 'bout that ol' Concomitant Klink in *Hogan's Heroes*?")

Despite the lack of warmth displayed by Leahy—and toward Leahy—no one ever disputed his talent as a coach. Even as the line coach in the 1930s under Jim Crowley at Michigan State and Fordham, he became known for his ability to teach fundamentals. Fordham's famed Seven Blocks of Granite? Coached by Leahy. That means that Leahy played for Rockne, and Vince Lombardi played for Leahy.

Boston College hired Leahy as head coach for the 1939 season and found immediate success. The Eagles went 20–2 over the next two seasons and defeated Tennessee in the 1941 Sugar Bowl 19–13. Shortly afterward, when

Notre Dame coach Elmer Layden accepted an offer to become commissioner of the NFL, Leahy's alma mater called.

At Notre Dame, Leahy coached with the brilliance foreshadowed by his early seasons at Boston College. He risked abandoning Rockne's famed but outdated Notre Dame Box offense and installed the newfangled T-formation. The offense took advantage of Angelo Bertelli's ability to run and pass, and Bertelli responded by winning the 1943 Heisman Trophy. Three more Irish players would win Heismans during the Leahy Era.

Leahy spent the 1944–45 seasons in the navy. He came back to the greatest dynasty the sport has ever known. Not only did the Irish go 17–0–1 in 1946 and 1947, they never fell behind in those two seasons (the tie, 0–0 against Army, is considered one of the greatest games ever played). Get this: 42 players off the 1947 team would go on to play professional football.

Leahy may have been too successful. After the 1947 season, four schools, including Michigan and Army, dropped Notre Dame from their schedules. The university responded by cutting his scholarships from 33 to 18, but after the Irish went 4–4–1 in 1950, the university restored the scholarships.

Leahy, in turn, restored Notre Dame football, but the stress of coaching had begun to wear him down. He developed arthritis at a young age. He also had to deal with high blood pressure and pancreatitis. During the 1953 Georgia Tech game, Leahy collapsed in the locker room and his pulse registered so lightly that he had to be taken to the hospital. A Notre Dame priest who came upon the scene administered the last rites of the Catholic Church.

Leahy recovered well enough to admit to himself that he couldn't go on coaching and survive. But an incident in one of the last games of his career tarnished his stature forever.

The 1953 Irish went 9–0–1 but salvaged the 14–14 tie against Iowa because the Irish players, at Leahy's direction, feigned injury in order to stop the clock. It didn't matter that faking injuries had been a competitive tactic for years. Critics seized on Leahy and his Fainting Irish. The great coach tied the game and lost some stature.

Upon getting off the train in Iowa City, as Gordon S. White and Merv Hyman wrote in their book *Big Ten Football,* Hawkeye coach Forest Evashevski stood on a baggage cart and recited:

"When the one great scorer comes
To write against your name,
He won't write whether we won or lost,
But how we got gypped at Notre Dame."

Weeks later, the American Football Coaches Association formally condemned the practice. It has been frowned upon ever since.

In January 1954, at the age of 46, Leahy retired. A half-century ago, before the days when fired and retired coaches alike showed up at ESPN's door awaiting assignments alongside a play-by-play man, Leahy's public profile dimmed.

He flirted with replacing Bear Bryant at Texas A&M in 1958 but, wary of the old stresses returning, let the opportunity pass. Three decades later, when Notre Dame celebrated its football centennial, President Ronald Reagan, who played George Gipp in the movie *Knute Rockne All American,* came to campus to unveil the stamp with the Rock's visage. Leahy's name and career were an afterthought.

At least, until you look at the record books.

The Rest of the Most Underrated

2. SHUG JORDAN

Shug Jordan made one terrible mistake in his career. The man coached 25 years at Auburn, won 176 games, a national championship, and election to the College Football Hall of Fame. That's a career worth celebrating—if anyone knew about it. That leads to Jordan's mistake.

He coached in the same state as Bear Bryant.

On December 3, 1957, the Associated Press poll named Auburn the national champion (the final vote came before the bowls in those days). Jordan didn't know it, but his career had peaked two weeks earlier, when word leaked that Alabama had hired Bryant away from Texas A&M. Any chance Jordan had of receiving due credit for molding Auburn into a force in the Southeastern Conference ended the moment Bryant set foot in Tuscaloosa.

Okay, maybe not the first moment—the Tigers went 9–0–1 in 1958, extending an unbeaten streak to 24 games—but to paraphrase what Rick says to Ilse at the Casablanca airport, soon and for the rest of Jordan's life. Here's looking at you, Shug: after beating Bryant in 1958, Jordan lost nine of the next 10 against him. He finished 5–13 against Bryant. His Tigers would have won three more SEC titles if they hadn't suffered regular-season-ending losses to Bryant's Tide. Instead, the 1957 league championship would be the only one Jordan won.

That makes him good enough to be underrated? Absolutely. Jordan took over an Auburn program left for dead in 1951 and finished No. 1 in 1957. Even after Bryant arrived, Jordan racked up six seasons of nine wins or more.

Jordan's personality exacerbated the problem. He may have been every bit the leader that Bryant was—Jordan served as an army lieutenant in World War II and landed at Normandy—but when he spoke at all, he spoke softly. Bryant, as intimidating as he could be, had an ego and loved the limelight.

The two coaches poked at one another, as rivals do. Bryant once famously called Jordan at 7:00 AM and when the secretary told him the coaches hadn't come in yet, he said, "What's the matter, honey, don't you people take football seriously?"

Jordan disdained coaching from a tower as Bryant did, saying he didn't want to look like an overseer on a plantation. Ouch.

But Bryant and Jordan talked often, ironing out recruiting problems that arose between their staffs, and just talking. Jordan contracted leukemia shortly after he retired. One day, some months before he died in 1980 at age 69, Jordan went to Birmingham for treatment. He walked past a restaurant where Bryant sat inside. As he watched his one-time rival go by, Bryant said, "That man has more guts in his little finger than I do in my entire body."

3. PAPPY WALDORF

Anybody can make it to the College Football Hall of Fame coaching Alabama or USC. That's the Willie Sutton path to South Bend. Sutton was the guy who, when asked why he robbed banks, replied, "That's where the money is."

The real trick is to make the Hall of Fame while coaching the mom-and-pop stores of college football. Pappy Waldorf's resume reads like the

Washington Nationals' batting order. Waldorf spent his 28-year career as a head coach at Oklahoma State, Kansas State, Northwestern, and California.

Waldorf also won big at every one of those schools. He is first all-time in winning percentage at Oklahoma State (.735). He went 7–2–1 in his only season at Kansas State (1934). Not only is he still first in career wins at Northwestern (49), but he had a higher winning percentage there (.520) than any of his successors, among them Ara Parseghian (.507) and Gary Barnett (.438). And he led the Golden Bears to 67 victories and three straight Rose Bowls.

Some coaches use fear as a motivating tool; Waldorf used love. A nicer man never lived. The son of a Baptist minister, Waldorf carried a big, round body with a voice deeper than Death Valley. He didn't speak like a sailor—or, for that matter, a football coach. He didn't have to.

"I don't ever recall him raising his voice," said Harry Agler, who played end for Waldorf and was cocaptain on his first California team. "He never swore... Some people would call him the gentle giant."

Coaches in that day brooked little dissent. Waldorf, however, listened to his players. He coached with all the militaristic bearing of a kindergarten teacher.

"Son, you went with your left foot," Agler can remember Waldorf instructing on the field. "You've got to lead with your right foot. Do it again."

That's not exactly Bryant at Junction. Waldorf understood, as few coaches of his era did, who his players were and what they had endured in the war. Waldorf couldn't threaten them with consequences. Many of them had seen the worst life had to offer. He couldn't threaten their chance at a better life. The veterans didn't need football to get their education. They could go to school on the new GI Bill.

"So many of the players were married, 29 out of maybe 85. Some had children," Agler said. "...I thought he was the perfect guy, because all the players coming back from the war were three, three and a half years older. I was an officer in the war (an army first lieutenant). I'm not going to take any horseshit from the guy. There were a lot of guys just like me. I was usually called 'Sir.'"

Waldorf appealed to his players through love. He inspired them. They wanted to win for him. And they did. Waldorf took the Golden Bears to Rose Bowls in three straight seasons (1948–50). In the 57 years since, California has spent New Year's Day in Pasadena once.

4. BO SCHEMBECHLER

Glenn E. Schembechler won 234 games in his 27 seasons as a head coach, still good enough to rank 10th all time in victories. Of the nine coaches in front of him, seven of them won national championships, and the other two, Amos Alonzo Stagg and Pop Warner, coached in the pre-poll era. That would condemn any coach in the eye of a public that wants its wins and losses delivered without nuance: *Schembechler? Good coach. Never won the big one.*

Bo would have liked to have finished No. 1. He would have liked a better record in 10 Rose Bowls than two wins and eight losses. But Schembechler never gave the impression that it bothered him all that much.

Find another coach who won 13 Big Ten Conference championships in 21 seasons. That's how Schembechler performed from 1969 to 1989 at Michigan, a Rhapsody in Go Blue.

Schembechler mastered the regular season, the grind of a 10- or 11-game schedule in which he demanded that his players work as hard and care as much as he did. You didn't have to spend more than 10 seconds with Schembechler to understand the passion that drove him.

He could be passionate about simple things. He was not complicated, and he certainly was not a sophisticate. Before Mitch Albom wrote about *Tuesdays with Morrie,* he wrote about Saturdays with Bo. Albom ghosted Schembechler's autobiography, *Bo,* and he describes with great insight the joy that Schembechler derived from a hamburger.

It may have been because eating a hamburger meant that Bo was pulling a fast one on his cardiologist, but the motivation for the passion is irrelevant. It soon became the greatest hamburger anyone had ever had.

In August 2005, I interviewed Schembechler in his office in the Schembechler Building, which houses the football program in Ann Arbor. He had begun a tradition, carried forward by his successors Gary Moeller and Lloyd Carr, of bringing in a music professor to teach the freshman players how to sing the Michigan fight song.

When I asked him why he found that important, Schembechler replied in his customary tone, somewhere between a roar and a command.

"You've heard 'The Victors,'" Schembechler said. "If you sing it badly, it really sucks!"

There would be no detail too small for Michigan football. When his players sang "The Victors" in the locker room following a victory, Schembechler saw to it that they sang well.

Schembechler cared about running the ball, and he cared about defense. His first team at Michigan, in 1969, allowed 13.5 points per game. He didn't have another team allow even that much scoring until 1981.

Schembechler finished four victories short of his mentor, Woody Hayes. That's the same number of games he lost to Hayes during the 10-Year War that Schembechler's Michigan waged with Hayes's Ohio State from 1969 to 1978.

On some level, Schembechler appreciated that. He had played for Hayes at Miami and followed him from Miami to Ohio State. Schembechler worked for Hayes as a graduate assistant in 1952, and as a full-time assistant from 1958 to 1962. Bo returned to his alma mater as head coach for six seasons, winning 40 games from 1963 to 1968.

Bo loved Woody. But he loved to beat him even more. Schembechler won the 10-Year-War, 5–4–1, and no victory in this or any other rivalry matched the Wolverines' 1969 triumph. The Buckeyes, for nine games, looked as if they would defend their national championship. But in the final game of the season, the pupil outsmarted the master. The Wolverines won 24–12, and Schembechler left the field at Michigan Stadium on the shoulders of his players.

Years later, at a testimonial dinner for Hayes, the Buckeye coach discussed his great teams. When he turned his attention to 1969, Hayes looked down the dais at Schembechler and glowered. Schembechler told the story in his book.

"Goddamn you, Bo!" Hayes thundered. "You will *never* win a bigger game than that one!"

Six weeks after the upset, the 40-year-old Schembechler suffered a heart attack on the night before the 1970 Rose Bowl, the game that Michigan reached via its 24–12 victory over No. 1 Ohio State in 1969, the biggest upset in the 103-year history of the rivalry.

Schembechler always felt as if he had gotten a second chance at life after that heart attack. In fact, he lived nearly as long after that heart attack as he had before it. He lived long enough to see that he revitalized Michigan football. He never got enough credit. Good for this list, bad for Bo.

5. TOM OSBORNE

Osborne hasn't coached a game since 1997 and has somehow grown in stature, which probably says more about his critics than it does about him.

From 1972 to 1993, in his first 21 seasons as head coach at Nebraska after nine seasons there as an assistant to Bob Devaney, Osborne had a record of 206–47–3. That winning percentage (.811) would have placed him 10th all time among major college coaches. Every single one of those 21 teams won at least nine games, part of an NCAA-record 33 straight nine-or-more-win seasons by the Huskers.

Even if Osborne's last four Husker teams hadn't gone 49–2 and won three national championships, his career would have been remarkable. But over his last four seasons, Osborne and the Huskers dominated college football. He finished at his peak, saying good-bye just as the rest of the country was learning to say hello. Osborne's reputation never got the polishing it deserved. The country had become too accustomed to Nebraska never quite having enough.

You can attribute the increase in respect to how Nebraska football has suffered in his absence. Osborne's handpicked successor, Frank Solich, won a lot but not as much as his mentor, always a ticket for dissatisfaction. Solich's successor, Bill Callahan, didn't matched Solich's record, much less Osborne's. The 2007 Huskers sent gobsmacked historians to the record book every Saturday, checking to see just how long it had been since the Huskers had lost by so much at home, or on the road, or to this team or that one. Midway through the season, Nebraska chancellor Harvey Perlman fired athletic director Steve Pederson and brought Osborne back to replace him on an interim basis. Nebraska finished 5–7, and Callahan was fired the day after the Huskers dropped their season finale 65–51 to Colorado.

Osborne returned to the athletic department out of love and duty. But he would have been just as happy to be fishing. One of the biggest reasons that Osborne is one of the most underrated coaches is that, despite all his time as a public figure, Osborne always seemed ill at ease in the public eye. Part of it is his taciturn nature, a stoicism that masked a sharp intellect and a wickedly dry sense of humor. It's a curious trait for a man who left coaching and went into politics. Osborne served as a U.S. Congressman before losing the Republican primary for governor in 2006. In both careers, Osborne dedicated himself to helping others, and the price he had to pay included tape recorders, bright lights, and boom mikes.

Osborne viewed every situation with his own clear-eyed logic. He knew he would get roasted for reinstating suspended, troubled I-back Lawrence Phillips to the 1995 Huskers late in the season. But he thought it was the right thing to do. The rest didn't matter. Osborne believed Nebraska would suffer if the Big Eight expanded into the Big 12. His voice decrying the move sounded a lonely note. History has proven him right, at least as judged by wins and losses.

On the field, Osborne proved to be a sound offensive strategist. Nebraska took permanent residence among the top rushing teams in the sport. His players won six Outland Trophies, three Lombardi Awards, and one Heisman Trophy (Mike Rozier in 1983). In Osborne's 25 seasons, 30 Huskers became All-Americans.

For years, Osborne battled with Bobby Bowden of Florida State over who would be the Best Coach Never to Win a National Championship. In 1983, the Huskers produced what may have been the greatest offense of the option era: 401.7 rushing yards and 52.0 points per game.

But Nebraska lost the Orange Bowl 31–30 and the national championship along with it. The Huskers pulled within that margin by scoring a touchdown with :48 remaining. An extra point and a tie would have made Nebraska No. 1. Osborne boldly chose to go for two and the victory. The play failed, but the decision earned Osborne respect that for the next decade tempered criticism of Nebraska's inability to finish at the top.

That changed in 1994—and 1995 and 1997. Those Husker teams featured powerful offenses and dominant defenses. Quarterback Tommie Frazier managed the neat trick of winning those first two national championships without winning a Heisman (see Chapter 4).

Just as his friend Bowden rode his charm and outgoing personality to national acclaim, Osborne's natural reticence contributed to a lack of appreciation for what he accomplished. There's also a hint of big-city-media prejudice in the skepticism that hovered over what Osborne achieved in flyover country. With the benefit of the full view of time, it is easier to see the magnificence of his career. It is worth another look.

CHAPTER 8

Players

When it comes to college football, I'm as egalitarian as the next Appalachian State fan. I enjoyed seeing Boise State become America's Darlings. Gordie Lockbaum? Been there, written about him. (Lockbaum, kiddies, played both ways for Holy Cross in the mid-1980s.)

The reason that I limited the selection of the most overrated and underrated players to the 19 winningest programs (plus Army, for historical reasons) has everything to do with the time-space continuum. Time, as in I have a deadline, and space, as in I wanted to keep this book somewhat shorter than the *Random House Webster's Unabridged Dictionary.*

Michigan

OVERRATED: DREW HENSON (1998–2000)

What happened here? Henson is one of the early examples of recruiting mania run amok. He had all the hype, in part because pro baseball kept trying to lure him away from college football. He had a father, a former assistant coach, who promoted him to the media. And Henson looked the part—handsome, tall, and wide-shouldered. In the end, after playing one season without Tom Brady, a season in which Michigan went 9–3 and shared the Big Ten championship with Purdue and Northwestern, Henson bailed

Michigan's Drew Henson had the look of a superstar NFL quarterback—he just didn't play like one.

out to chase his dream in baseball. He lasted six seasons in baseball, getting all of nine at-bats in the bigs, before returning to the NFL. As happened everywhere else in his career, potential beat reality by three touchdowns.

UNDERRATED: DENNIS FRANKLIN (1972–74)

Yeah, even my wife suggested Tom Brady, who went from sort of beating out Drew Henson at Michigan to winning three Super Bowls for the New England Patriots. And that's no knock on my wife, who grew up on Syracuse football, which will give anyone a lesson in life's disappointments. But Brady eventually got his due, and I don't mean because he has dated more starlets than George Clooney. Check out Franklin, who in three seasons of starting for Bo Schembechler went 30–2–1—*and never played in a bowl.* That's what torqued Schembechler off about Ohio State winning the vote of the athletic directors after the 10–10 tie in 1973. You either went to the Rose Bowl or you stayed home. Franklin and his teammates deserved better.

Notre Dame

OVERRATED: RON POWLUS (1994–97)

The Fighting Irish hype machine is a wonderful thing. It has helped take a small, Midwestern, Catholic institution and transform it into an American shrine. Occasionally it gets an innocent student-athlete stuck in its maw. Powlus came to South Bend from western Pennsylvania just as the NFL career of Irish legend Joe Montana came to a close. When ESPN analyst Beano Cook said Powlus would win multiple Heismans, no one flinched. Powlus played well for four seasons, overlapping between the eras of Lou Holtz and Bob Davie. He set several career passing records, including yards (7,602) and touchdown passes (52), since smashed by Brady Quinn. But the closest he came to All-American was sharing the 1994 team picture with former Irish safety Bobby Taylor.

Ron Powlus never came close to winning the multiple Heismans some predicted for him when he committed to Notre Dame as a highly touted prospect from Pennsylvania.

UNDERRATED: JOHN HUARTE (1962–64)

Huarte is regularly derided as having won the Heisman because of the color of his uniform, not what he achieved while wearing it. Baloney. As an unheralded senior in 1964, Huarte led a team that had been 2–7 the year before to within a few seconds of a national championship. He became the first Irish quarterback to throw for more than 2,000 yards (2,062, a school record that stood for 22 seasons) and completed 56 percent of his passes in an era when anything above 50 percent raised eyebrows. Huarte suffered by comparison to Joe Namath. The Jets picked Namath in the first round of the 1965 AFL Draft, signing him beneath the goalposts at the end of the 1965 Orange Bowl. The Jets picked Huarte in the second round. Namath became a superstar; Huarte became a fixture on the bench. His reputation never recovered.

Texas

OVERRATED: CHRIS SIMMS (1999–2002)

Simms surely doesn't see his father's NFL success as a burden. Yet the expectations placed upon Simms because of his bloodline put pressure on him that wouldn't have been visited upon most 18-year-old blue-chip recruits. Blame it on the media and on the fans. If his name had been Chris Smith, he would have been given more time to develop. Simms went 26–6 as a starter; only quarterbacks Vince Young and Bobby Layne won more games for the Longhorns. Simms threw for 7,097 yards and 58 touchdowns. But he never quite satisfied the fans looking for his father, who led the New York Giants to a Super Bowl victory, or the fans looking for their beloved Major Applewhite. Simms never really had a chance at Texas.

UNDERRATED: MAJOR APPLEWHITE (1998–2001)

He was scrawny, he looked 12 years old, and all he did was beat you. Major Applewhite had an accurate arm, a football brain, and the guts of a tightrope walker. Those traits endeared him to the Longhorn public, as did his first three seasons, when he threw for 7,974 yards and led the revival of

Quarterback Major Applewhite never got the credit he deserved during his college career at Texas.

Texas football. But a year after Applewhite took over the 'Horns, coach Mack Brown fell in love with a recruit from New Jersey, Chris Simms, the 6'5" son of Super Bowl-winning quarterback Phil Simms. Brown promised Chris Simms that he would play as a freshman. After two seasons, the two reversed roles in 2001. The Longhorns needed only to beat Colorado to play Miami for the national championship. However, Simms committed four turnovers in the first half, and Colorado pounced on them to take a 29–10 lead. Applewhite came off the bench and rallied Texas within 39–37 before time ran out. Texas didn't play for the BCS title, but Applewhite had secured his legend. He finished his career with eight school records, a prime example of brains over brawn.

Nebraska

OVERRATED: JOHNNY MITCHELL (1990–91)

The Husker tight end may have reaped in publicity what he sowed with his always moving tongue. In his mind, and in my notepad, and on that camera over there, there would never be another tight end like Johnny Mitchell. He had one season in which he matched his own hype. As a sophomore in 1991, Mitchell caught 31 passes for 534 yards (17.2 yards per catch), including seven catches for 137 yards against archrival Oklahoma. And then he left for the NFL at age 21, perhaps before he had prepared his body and his mind for the demands that The League places on both, especially at a hybrid blocking/receiving position such as tight end. The New York Jets took him with the 15th pick of the 1992 draft. After five largely disappointing seasons, he left the league, although as late as 2003, Jacksonville was still interested enough in him to sign him to a one-year contract. Mitchell is still regarded as a prototypical tight end at Nebraska. In terms of production, however, he never reached his potential.

UNDERRATED: OSBORNE'S CENTERS (1973–1997)

It's not exactly news that Nebraska's Tom Osborne developed some of the best offensive lines in college football during his quarter-century as head coach. But the level of excellence remains stunning more than a decade after his retirement. In 11 of Osborne's 25 years, the Huskers' starting center made at least one All-America team. While I haven't run the numbers, I feel safe in saying that no other school has reached that level of success at any position over that length of time. Not all of the All-American centers played in the NFL, and, to tell the truth, the respect for Nebraska's offensive lines was such that not all of them were the best centers in the nation, either. But when an offense churns out 300 rushing yards a game, someone up front is doing something pretty well. The honor roll, please: Rik Bonness (1974–75), Tom Davis (1977), Dave Rimington (1981–82), Mark Traynowicz (1984), Bill Lewis (1985), Jake Young (1988–89), Aaron Graham (1995), and Aaron Taylor (1996). In the 10 seasons since Osborne retired as head coach, one Nebraska center, Dominic Raiola (2000), has made All-American. That speaks for itself, too.

Ohio State

OVERRATED: MAURICE CLARETT (2002)

It couldn't be anyone else. As a freshman tailback, Clarett burst onto the national scene by rushing for 175 yards and three touchdowns in the opener, a 45–21 victory over Texas Tech, and followed with 230 yards and two touchdowns in the third game, a 25–7 victory over No. 10 Washington State. He finished the year with 1,237 yards and 18 touchdowns, and there is no doubt that Ohio State wouldn't have won the national championship without him. There is also no doubt that the odds you could have gotten on that 31–24 double-overtime Fiesta Bowl upset of Miami being Clarett's last football game would have set you up comfortably for life. *He has not played a down since.* Clarett sued the NFL for early access in 2004 and lost the case. When he showed up at the combine in 2005, he brought 20 extra pounds with him. Denver took a chance on him with a third-round pick

Ohio State's Maurice Clarett turned a sensational freshman season into a lifetime's worth of regret.

and cut him before Labor Day. He currently resides in a Toledo prison, serving seven and a half years on robbery and weapons convictions. What a waste.

UNDERRATED: PETE JOHNSON (1973–76)

Archie Griffin may have lined up behind Johnson, but the fullback played in the shadow of the two-time Heisman Trophy winner. Johnson opened four-lane highways in the line for Griffin, but the 6'1", 246-pound Johnson carried the ball, too. Four times in 1975, his junior season, he and Griffin each rushed for more than 100 yards. Johnson finished that season with 1,059 yards and 25 touchdowns, the latter still a school record. So are the 56 touchdowns that Johnson scored in his Buckeye career, which made him the most prolific scorer in scarlet and cream for 28 seasons, until kicker Mike Nugent surpassed him in 2004. My favorite stat about Johnson: in his last two seasons, he converted 54 of 74 third or fourth downs. Griffin, in the 1995 oral history *Woody's Boys,* said, "I used to see guys shy away from him, especially when we got to the pros. I used to see Pete run by guys and they would jump on his back. And I don't blame them, because, I'll tell you, you hit him head on, and you have some work to do."

Penn State

OVERRATED: ANTHONY MORELLI (2004–07)

Morelli came to State College as one of the most decorated quarterbacks ever to come from western Pennsylvania, which is like being one of the most decorated politicians in the Kennedy family. Morelli was a two-time all-state pick, considered the No. 2 quarterback recruit in the nation. Nittany Lion fans expected a lot from him, more than he probably could have produced. But after two years as an understudy to Michael Robinson, the 6'4", 232-pound Morelli never made anyone forget Joe Namath, Joe Montana, Dan Marino, or any of the other passers who sprouted in his homeland. In those two seasons, Morelli threw for 5,075 yards and 30 touchdowns. He threw 18 interceptions and took 39 sacks. In an age when quarterbacks such as his predecessor made "escapability" a word, Morelli had little of it. Overrated perhaps because of the recruiting services placing unreal expectations on him, but overrated nonetheless.

UNDERRATED: TONY HUNT (2003–06)

The tailback never made All-Big Ten or gained a lot of attention outside of Beaver Stadium. What he did gain was a lot of yards over four seasons. As a senior in 2006, the 6'2", 230-pound Hunt rushed for 1,386 yards and 11 touchdowns. He finished his career with 3,320 rushing yards. At a school that has produced Lydell Mitchell, Franco Harris, Heisman Trophy winner John Cappelletti, Matt Suhey, Blair Thomas, D.J. Dozier, Ki-Jana Carter, and Curtis Enis, Hunt stands second in career rushing only to Curt Warner. That's damn good company. To point out that he also caught 88 passes, the most ever by a Nittany Lion running back and, when he completed his eligibility, tied for 10th among all Penn State receivers, seems like piling it on.

Alabama

OVERRATED: THE 2000 CRIMSON TIDE

This is a group award, given to the Alabama team that began the season ranked No. 3 in the nation and finished 3–8. The Tide began the season at UCLA, Alabama's first game in Pasadena since the 1946 Rose Bowl, with stories of how the Tide hoped to return to California at the end of the 2001 season for the BCS Championship Game. Alabama ended the season with a lame-duck head coach, Mike DuBose, who packed up his office the week that Auburn came to Bryant-Denny Stadium and beat the Crimson Tide 9–0. After two mediocre seasons under DuBose, Alabama appeared to have turned the corner in 1999, winning the SEC and finishing 10–3, thanks to the Outland Trophy winner, offensive tackle Chris Samuels, and the blocks he threw for tailback Shaun Alexander. When they graduated, they took the team's leadership with them. After a 3–3 start in the 2000, Alabama lost its last five. Through 2007, the Tide still hadn't returned to the SEC Championship Game.

UNDERRATED: STEVE SLOAN (1963–65)

The easiest way to remain in the shadows of college football is to play in the interim between two stars. Sloan came after Joe Namath and before Ken Stabler, both Crimson Tide legends who went on to NFL celebrity for their swagger on and off the field. Sloan had no swagger, but the quiet, religious Tennessean knew how to lead. He started the Sugar Bowl after Bryant suspended Namath at the end of the 1963 season. He started several games in the second half of the 1964 season after Namath suffered a knee injury. In 1965, as a senior, Sloan led Alabama to the national championship, throwing for a school-record 1,453 yards. In the 39–28 Orange Bowl victory over Nebraska, Sloan completed 20 of 28 passes for 296 yards and two touchdowns with one interception. Two decades later, as athletic director at his alma mater, Sloan acquiesced to Auburn's wishes to play its Iron Bowl home games at Auburn. Crimson Tide fans had a hard time forgiving him.

Oklahoma

OVERRATED: MARCUS DUPREE (1982–83)

Dupree left so much unaccomplished. He showed such promise as a high school player that author Willie Morris wrote a book about the recruitment, *The Courting of Marcus Dupree*. He helped bring his hometown, Philadelphia, Mississippi, back to a nation that had written it off after the murder of three civil rights workers there in 1964. Dupree worked his way into the Sooners' lineup midway through his freshman season and rushed for 905 yards (7.0 per carry). When Dupree rushed for 239 yards on only 17 carries in a 32–21 loss to Arizona State in the Fiesta Bowl, it was hard to imagine that he had peaked. In his book *Bootlegger's Boy,* coach Barry Switzer quoted one of his assistants: "It appears Dupree is much more fond of adulation than he is of football." He didn't work hard because he had never had to. When Switzer got on him about it, Dupree quit four games into his sophomore year. He went to the USFL, tore up his knee, and became a legend for different reasons than he, Switzer, and every Sooner fan hoped.

UNDERRATED: QUENTIN GRIFFIN (1999–2002)

Bob Stoops went 43–9 in his first four seasons, winning the 2000 national championship, and the spread passing game became all the rage. The spotlight shone, first on Josh Heupel, then on Jason White, quarterbacks who picked apart defenses and the Sooner record book with ease. The national spotlight never caught Griffin at tailback, but few people ever did. The 5'7", 195-pound Griffin fit well in the Oklahoma offense. He proved as dangerous catching the ball as running it, all the while hiding behind his blockers. Get this: as a senior, Griffin rushed for 1,884 yards and 15 touchdowns, and caught 35 passes for 264 yards and three more scores. The 2,148 all-purpose yards is a Sooner record, better than Heisman Trophy winners Billy Vessels, Steve Owens, or Billy Sims; better than All-Americans Adrian Peterson, Greg Pruitt, Joe Washington, or Tommy McDonald. Griffin ranks fifth in Sooner history in career rushing yards (3,938), third in touchdowns (44), second in all-purpose yards (5,275), and second in receptions (169). He did so many

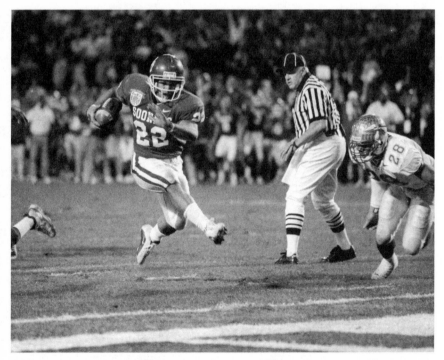

The undersized Quentin Griffin stands tall in the Oklahoma Sooners record book, ranking fifth in career rushing yards and third in touchdowns.

things well, yet his talents got lost in an offense that spewed ridiculous numbers. Texas fans may recall Griffin well. He scored six touchdowns against the Longhorns in the 63–14 rout in 2000.

Tennessee

OVERRATED: KELLEY WASHINGTON (2001–02)

Washington came to Knoxville after an abortive minor-league baseball career, and as a 22-year-old freshman in 2001, he caught 64 passes for 1,010 yards and five touchdowns. In 2002, Washington promised even greater things—all you had to do was ask him. However, Washington produced more arrogance and ego than he did yards and points. He had backed it up as a freshman, but a year later, a knee injury put him on the sideline for the first two games. He played three and then he suffered a concussion that ended his season. Wash-ington left for the NFL and clashed with Cincinnati coaches over issues of ego—his, not theirs. As he closed in on the age of 30, Washington found a niche with New England, where he became a special teams star in 2007.

UNDERRATED: RICHMOND FLOWERS (1966–68)

Flowers's father, Richmond Sr., was an Alabama attorney general who had the nerve not to fight the U.S. Supreme Court rulings on integration. In 1966, Richmond Sr. ran for governor against George Wallace's wife Lurleen, and when Flowers openly courted the African American vote, the Wallace machine crushed him. In the charged atmosphere of the day, in no way did his son, Richmond Jr., care to play for the state university. That turned two generations of the Flowers family into pariahs. The son had the last laugh: not only did he become a three-time All-American hurdler, but, in 1967, Flowers led the Southeastern Conference champions with 41 catches for 585 yards and four touchdowns. *Football News* made him an All-American. And Tennessee defeated Alabama 24–13 in Birmingham, the first of four straight victories over the Crimson Tide. "Now I can go back home, to Montgomery, and go to parties again," Flowers told *Sports Illustrated.* As a senior in 1968, Flowers, now a tailback, scored the Vols' only touchdown in their 10–9 victory over Alabama.

USC

OVERRATED: TODD MARINOVICH (1989–90)

There are few sadder stories in college football than the tale of Todd Marinovich. Raised by his father to be a star quarterback, right down to what passed his lips—no fast food—Marinovich rebelled. He didn't cope well with authority, especially the old-school discipline of Larry Smith, the USC coach who signed him. But Marinovich, the national high school player of the year, went to USC anyway because it had always been assumed that he would. As a redshirt freshman in 1989, Marinovich led the Trojans to the Rose Bowl, where they beat Michigan 17–10 and finished No. 8 in the nation. As a sophomore, however, Marinovich's relationship with the coaching staff deteriorated. The Trojans lost the last two games of the season to finish 8–4–1, and Marinovich declared for the 1991 NFL Draft. He never performed professionally nearly as well as he had at USC, where he

Destined to be a star quarterback—at least according to his father—Todd Marinovich declared for the NFL Draft following his sophomore season after disagreements with the USC coaching staff.

threw for 5,001 yards and completed 61.6 percent of his passes over two seasons. And he never performed as well at USC as he could have. As old-timers in baseball used to say: million-dollar arm, 10-cent head.

UNDERRATED: DOYLE NAVE (1937–39)

USC trailed Duke 3–0 with 2:00 to play in the 1939 Rose Bowl, and it may as well have been 30–0. The Blue Devils had not allowed a point all season. With the ball on the Blue Devil 34, Trojans assistant coach Sam Barry sent Nave, a fourth-string quarterback, onto the field. Nave had the best arm on the team, and the coaches in the press box thought the Duke secondary had been playing too soft. Nave completed four passes, the last a 19-yarder to Al Krueger for a touchdown with :40 to play, for the shocking upset. Nave hadn't played enough to earn a letter, but he got one anyway. In fact, when he graduated after the following season, Nave received a lifetime pass to Trojan games, an honor bestowed only upon those players who earned three letters.

Georgia

OVERRATED: QUINCY CARTER (1998–2000)

As a 20-year-old freshman in 1998, Carter, who had arrived in Athens after two seasons in the minor leagues, became a national sensation. He led the No. 12 Bulldogs to a 28–27 upset at No. 6 LSU, completing 27 of 34 passes for 318 yards and two touchdowns, rushing for 41 yards, and catching a 36-yard pass as well. That game would haunt Carter for the rest of his collegiate and professional career because it showed a level of play he could reach but never maintain. In three seasons in Athens, Carter threw for 6,447 yards and 35 touchdowns. But he also threw 25 interceptions, and his efficiency rating of 127.79 ranks only seventh all-time in Georgia history. Dallas selected Carter in the second round, and he underachieved in the NFL by that standard as well.

UNDERRATED: TERRY HOAGE (1980–83)

Hoage, the son of a Texas college professor and the last player signed by coach Vince Dooley in 1980, arrived in Athens as interested in his science studies as in playing football. He excelled at both. Hoage played rover, and he knew the game well enough to always appear at the right place. He intercepted passes. He blocked kicks. He became an All-American, and he became an Academic All-American while majoring in genetics. As a senior, he finished fifth in the Heisman vote. More important, in his four seasons, Georgia went 43–4–1, won one national championship and played for another. "The number one player [we signed] became a three-time All-American," Dooley said, referring to Herschel Walker. "The least recruited player we signed became a two-time All-American, and both of them became Hall of Famers."

LSU

OVERRATED: JOSH BOOTY (1999–2000)

The *USA Today* 1993 national high school offensive player of the year from Shreveport took a five-year detour into professional baseball, emerging after a cup of coffee and a World Series ring with the Florida Marlins in 1997 to play quarterback for his home-state LSU Tigers. He started 17 games in

Josh Booty never fulfilled his promise as quarterback of the LSU Tigers.

1999–2000, sharing time with the talented but raw Rohan Davey, and Booty played well enough under first-year coach Nick Saban in 2000 (2,121 yards, 17 touchdowns) for the league coaches to make him first-team All-SEC. Then, at age 25, he bailed on college football again, this time for the NFL. There are still dreamers in Louisiana who imagined what kind of quarterback Booty would have become if he had devoted himself to college football from the outset. Instead, after a career of clipboard-holding in the NFL, he's a bundle of what-if.

UNDERRATED: JEFF WICKERSHAM (1983–85)

In a decade in which the Tigers have had two quarterbacks lead them to national championships (Matt Mauck and Matt Flynn) and a third become the number one pick in the NFL Draft (JaMarcus Russell), it's worth pointing out that none of them, or anyone else in the history of LSU football save for Tommy Hodson, threw for more yards than Wickersham (6,921) in his three years (1983–85) as starter. He also took the Tigers to a Sugar Bowl and a Liberty Bowl in his junior and senior seasons, respectively. Not bad for a guy barely good enough to get drafted (10th round, Miami). Tailback Dalton Hilliard may have been the star on those offenses, but Wickersham made them run without a stumble.

Syracuse

OVERRATED: R.J. ANDERSON (2000–03)

I'll say it at the top: this is unfair to Anderson. It says something about the recent woes of the Orange, but to be overrated, a team requires some level of national expectations. Syracuse hasn't generated much in the nine years since Donovan McNabb graduated. The Orange had the best sustained success in its history in the 12 years leading from the undefeated 1987 season through McNabb: seven seasons with at least nine victories and four major bowl bids under Dick MacPherson and Paul Pasqualoni. Anderson arrived at Syracuse with some hope of being the next Marvin Graves or McNabb. His performance at quarterback varied from season to season—

and sometimes from play to play—and the inconsistency mirrored Syracuse's slide into mediocrity. A state, by the way, to which Syracuse would love to return, given the struggles of the Greg Robinson years. One example: as a sophomore in 2001, Anderson took over the starting job in midseason. The Orange won eight consecutive games and finished 10–3. As a junior, he threw eight interceptions and four touchdowns and lost the starting job to Troy Nunes. He played adequately as a senior (.600 completion percentage, 10 touchdowns, eight interceptions, 2,164 yards) but no more than that. Syracuse finished 6–6.

UNDERRATED: MARVIN GRAVES (1990–93)

There is no more beloved figure in Syracuse football than Donovan McNabb, the four-year starter (1995–98) who led the Orange to three Big East championships and a cumulative record of 35–14. Yet McNabb finished second to Graves, like him a four-year starter (1990–93), in career passing yards, attempts, completions, and nearly every passing category save efficiency and touchdowns. Granted, those are two pretty important ones. But Graves has been relegated to the musty record books because he lacked

Marvin Graves has been underrated by college football fans because of the shadow cast by the man who followed him at Syracuse: Donovan McNabb.

the one thing that cemented McNabb's legacy at his alma mater: an NFL body. While McNabb has become an icon and Campbell's Soup pitchman with the Philadelphia Eagles, Graves, all 6'1", 184 pounds of him, enjoyed a brief career in the CFL. Graves's skills proved ideal for the freeze option offense employed by Dick MacPherson and Paul Pasqualoni. In his four seasons as starter, Syracuse went 33–12–3, including a final ranking of sixth in 1992. Graves just doesn't sell Chunky Steak & Potato.

Auburn

OVERRATED: AUNDRAY BRUCE (1984–87)

Okay, rules are made to be broken. I said at the outset that I didn't believe that NFL careers should impact whether a college player is considered underrated or overrated. But when an All-American linebacker with all the physical tools that 6'6", 236-pound linebacker Aundray Bruce brought to the field becomes the first player selected in the NFL Draft, and then starts only 42 games in an 11-year professional career, don't you have to think that maybe the Atlanta Falcons could have picked him up in the second round? Or maybe the fifth? Maybe the Falcons were swayed by Bruce's performance as a senior at nearby Georgia Tech. Bruce intercepted three passes, returning one for a touchdown, and made 10 unassisted tackles in a 20–10 Tigers victory. That's one fewer interception than Bruce made in his entire NFL career.

UNDERRATED: RONNIE BROWN (2001–04)

If Brown had wanted publicity worthy of his talent, he came to the wrong backfield. Sharing the ball with a back as talented as Carnell Williams was one thing. Add to it that Williams carried the nickname "Cadillac" and someone with an Average Joe name like Ronnie Brown had no chance. But man, what a runner. Williams used speed and an ability to make tacklers miss in the open field. Brown ran with knees high and an occasional elbow thrown in for good measure. As a sophomore in 2002, he rushed for 1,008 yards, getting the bulk of the work after Williams got hurt. As a senior, he had 1,226 rushing and receiving yards combined, along with nine touchdowns. The truest measure of Brown's worth: Williams outrushed him as a junior and a senior, and was the fifth pick of the 2005 NFL Draft—three picks after Brown.

Colorado

OVERRATED: MATT RUSSELL (1993–96)

Russell was a smart, physical (6'2", 245) linebacker. As a junior in 1995, Russell led the Buffaloes with 119 tackles, 16 of them behind the line. He finished fourth in the Butkus Award voting. So far, so good. But in 1996, Russell won the Butkus Award without even being one of the best two defensive players on the Buffaloes' team. Says who? The coaches who named end Greg Jones and free safety Steve Rosga as co-winners. Russell benefited in part from a strange year for linebackers. Like Russell, Northwestern senior Pat Fitzgerald played well but basked in the reflection of his play in 1995, when the Wildcats made their magical Rose Bowl run. The other All-American linebacker, Canute Curtis of West Virginia, played well but didn't stand out. Of the three of them, Russell would be the first one picked in the 1997 NFL Draft—by Detroit in the fourth round, the 17th linebacker taken that year.

UNDERRATED: HALE IRWIN (1964–66)

It may be generally known that the three-time U.S. Open champion golfer played football for the Buffaloes. It's clear that anyone who won a U.S. Open at age 45, as Irwin did in 1990, or won the Senior PGA in 2004 the week before turning 59, is a remarkable athlete. But time—and his prowess in golf—obscured exactly how good Irwin was as a safety, as in two-time All-Big-Eight good. Irwin led Colorado in interceptions as a junior in 1965 with five. He also played some quarterback at Colorado. Irwin once was asked whether the NFL showed any interest in him. "The St. Louis Cardinals sent me a questionnaire," Irwin said, according to the book *Massacre at Winged Foot*, about his victory at the 1974 U.S. Open. "You know, how big are you? How fast are you? When I saw the one about how fast you are, I threw it away."

Reggie McNeal never had the success at Texas A&M that his counterpart Vince Young had with the Texas Longhorns.

Texas A&M

OVERRATED: REGGIE McNEAL (2002–2005)

The debate raged all through 2001—who was the best Texas high school quarterback: Reggie McNeal of Lufkin or Vince Young of Houston? McNeal went to Texas A&M and Young went to Texas. As a freshman, while Young redshirted, McNeal came off the bench to lead the Aggies to a 30–26 upset of No. 1 Oklahoma. The victory looked as if it might save coach R.C. Slocum's job. When it didn't, Dennis Franchione arrived to replace Slocum, and McNeal had to start over in a new offense. As a junior, with Young in his first full season as a starter at Texas, McNeal passed and ran for 3,509 yards and 22 touchdowns. And as a senior, McNeal fizzled. He completed more than half his passes in only five of 10 games. His yardage and efficiency went down. His leadership was questioned. When he missed the regular-season finale against Texas because of an ankle injury, the comparison of him and Young grew stark. Young led the Longhorns to the national championship. McNeal became a late-round draftee by Cincinnati, which tried without success to turn him into a slash player.

UNDERRATED: DARREN LEWIS (1987–1990)

In the history of college football, only eight tailbacks from the six major conferences—the ones that get the automatic BCS bids—have rushed for 5,000 yards in their careers. Six of them (Ron Dayne, Ricky Williams, Tony Dorsett, Charles White, Herschel Walker, Archie Griffin) won the Heisman Trophy. A seventh, Cedric Benson, was the fourth player selected in the 2005 draft. And then there is Lewis, who rushed for 5,012 yards and 44 touchdowns. Lewis peaked as a senior. He failed a drug test before the 1991 NFL Draft and fell to the sixth round. The 5'10", 230-pound player known as "Tank" washed out after two-plus seasons with the Chicago Bears and has been in and out of jail for years. That's the surest way for your athletic deeds to be forgotten. But Lewis still has the two best single-season rushing totals in Texas A&M history (1,692 yards in 1988, and 1,691 yards in 1990).

Washington

OVERRATED: SONNY SIXKILLER (1970–72)

Sixkiller had a great Native American name and an exciting game. I have tried in underrating and overrating these players not to apply current standards to previous eras. The difference between the passing game of today and what Sixkiller ran nearly four decades ago is like the difference between, well, everything of today and of 40 years ago. Completion percentages weren't revered back then and interceptions weren't viewed as the social disease they are today. But still. In three seasons under center, Sixkiller completed less than half of his passes (385-of-811) and threw 51 interceptions as opposed to 35 touchdowns. The University of Washington claims that Sixkiller won the Sammy Baugh Trophy, given by the Touchdown Club of Ohio, in 1970. There's a Touchdown Club in Columbus that gives out a Sammy Baugh Trophy to the nation's best passer. In 1970, according to the club's website, Pat Sullivan of Auburn won the award. In other words, another incompletion.

UNDERRATED: MICHAEL JACKSON (1975–78)

Trusting the tackle count can be like building on sand. Statistics and the stories based on them can crumble. But no one could have made up the numbers attributed to Jackson, an inside linebacker on Don James's first great Husky teams. His stats from his junior year alone are so outlandish that they must be true: 219 tackles for the season. Three games—not one or two—with 29 tackles apiece. Jackson is attributed with 578 tackles over four seasons. If you want to know how high is high, consider that in 30 years since Jackson left Montlake and went over the bridge to play for the Seattle Seahawks, only one Husky defender has come within 75 career tackles of Jackson. So how did he not make All-America? The deeper I dig into this book, the more I'm beginning to believe in East Coast biases.

Georgia Tech

OVERRATED: REGGIE BALL (2003–2006)

As a freshman, when Ball won the starting job in August and proceeded to complete 51.7 percent of passes for 1,996 yards and 10 touchdowns, and rushed for 384 yards and three touchdowns, he won the ACC Freshman of the Year award. You couldn't help but think, *Wait until this guy matures.* As a senior, when Ball completed 44.4 percent of his passes for 1,820 yards with 20 touchdowns and 14 interceptions, he missed the Gator Bowl because of academic ineligibility. You couldn't help but think, *Wait until this guy leaves.* His completion percentage went down every year. Ball never seemed to catch on, which deprived the rest of us of seeing All-American Calvin Johnson catch more passes.

UNDERRATED: CLINT CASTLEBERRY (1942)

There's something about the Flats, as old-time Atlantans call Georgia Tech, and pint-sized players. In the late 1990s, Joe Hamilton proved that college football still had a place for 5'10" quarterbacks. He threw for 8,882 yards and 65 touchdowns over four seasons. As a senior, Hamilton threw for 3,060 yards, rushed for 734 yards, and finished second in the Heisman voting. But Castleberry wins this by a nose, if only because time has obscured his achievements. At 5'9", 155 pounds, Castleberry lived on his ability to make tacklers miss. In the second game of his freshman season, Castleberry led Georgia Tech to a 13–6 upset at Notre Dame. Castleberry rushed for 466 yards that year, a remarkable 8.5 yards per carry. He returned an interception 95 yards for a touchdown in a 21–0 victory over Navy. The Yellow Jackets went 9–1 and finished fifth in the nation before losing the Cotton Bowl 14–7 to Texas. After the season, Castleberry enlisted in the Army Air Corps. In 1944, the plane he piloted went down near the African coast. "He'd have probably been an All-American for three years and been the greatest back in Georgia Tech history," legendary coach Bobby Dodd, an assistant on the 1942 team, said in his autobiography.

Pittsburgh

OVERRATED: TYLER PALKO (2002–06)

Here comes another western Pee-Ay quarterback whose performance failed to match his hype, which is too bad, because Palko actually put up good numbers. He threw for 8,343 yards, third behind Alex Van Pelt and Dan Marino in school history, and his ratio of 66 touchdowns to 25 interceptions would stand any coach's scrutiny. But the Panthers went 19–16 in his three seasons at quarterback. Part of the blame fell on his rocky transition from playing for Walt Harris to playing for Matt Cavanaugh, new coach Dave Wannstedt's offensive coordinator. Palko didn't have enough talent around him, either. Don't blame Palko. Blame the hype.

UNDERRATED: PETE GONZALEZ (1995–97)

He's not underrated among Panther fans as much as adored. The Miami native didn't get to play much until his fifth year when a new coach, Walt

Harris, overlooked Gonzalez's lack of physical talent and invested in his leadership and his guts. Harris's hunch paid off. Gonzalez led Pittsburgh to a 21–17 upset of No. 22 Miami, his hometown university, to make the Panthers 3–1. Not storybook enough for you? There were the 470 passing yards and seven touchdown passes, still both school records, in a 55–48 double-overtime defeat of Rutgers. Wait, it gets better. At the end of the season, with the Panthers needing two wins to reach a bowl, Gonzalez delivered. Down went No. 19 Virginia Tech 30–23, with Gonzalez throwing for 315 yards and four touchdowns. And down, in triple overtime, went archrival West Virginia 41–38. Gonzalez converted a fourth-and-17 from the Mountaineer 32 to keep the winning drive alive. After the season, in which Pitt went 6–6 following a 41–7 Liberty Bowl rout by Southern Mississippi, Gonzalez returned to obscurity. Except in Pittsburgh.

Army

OVERRATED: BILL CARPENTER (1957–59)

Carpenter won acclaim because of the uniqueness of his position on the 1958 team that went 8–0–1. The "Lonely End" may have been the first primitive version of the spread offense. Listen to coach Red Blaik's description: "(T)he far flanker so spreads the pass defense that it has much more ground to cover." Carpenter got the nickname because Blaik instructed him to stay out of the huddle. He caught 22 passes for 453 yards, a remarkable 20.6 yards per reception. But Carpenter became a threat because Heisman winner Pete Dawkins lined up in the backfield. As talented as Carpenter may have been, Dawkins drove this team.

UNDERRATED: ARNOLD TUCKER (1943–46)

Tucker made the mistake of playing in the same backfield as Mr. Inside, Doc Blanchard, and Mr. Outside, Glenn Davis. But the 1945 Army backfield, with Shorty McWilliams as the fourth, is considered one of the best in the game. Legendary coach Red Blaik praised Tucker's ability as an athlete and leader. "There was nothing to choose between him and…Notre Dame's John

Lujack," Blaik once said. And that's when Tucker was healthy. As a senior at Michigan, Tucker suffered a separated shoulder and sprained throwing elbow, yet remained in the game. Later in the season, he continued to play despite a knee injury. Tucker didn't make All-American—no one would put three players from the same backfield on an All-America team. But he did win the Sullivan Award, given to the most outstanding amateur athlete—regardless of sport—in the nation. As a measure of how underrated Tucker was, he didn't get elected to the College Football Hall of Fame until 2008, 52 years after his career ended.

CHAPTER 9

Stadiums and Campuses

Rooting for a college football team is pretty straightforward. You went there, you live there, your favorite quarterback played there. It's pretty cut and dried.

College football stadiums are different. Fans have a more visceral relationship with their stadiums. They had a good experience there or an awful one. They grew up going to the stadium. They've never been colder than that one day. They saw the greatest game they've ever seen or had their heart broken. There are memories of their visits, of holding Dad's hand walking through campus, of seeing their team run out of the tunnel for the first time.

A stadium is a more subjective experience. So it is with the stadiums that I declare overrated and underrated. My experiences at them played a small role in the stadiums discussed. But I also measured them against the image that these stadiums project after decades of play. Size and reputation play a larger role than my own experiences, since I'm usually in the press box. I've sat in the stands at one college football game in the last 20 years. I looked forward to it with great anticipation as a busman's holiday.

I hated it.

Blame it on naiveté, but it never occurred to me that people would go to a game and *not watch it*. I'm all for tailgating, but it seems to me that once the game begins, it would be a good time to wrap up the tailgate and begin to move toward the stadium. And I had the good fortune to be sitting in front of the World's Leading Authority on the Game and Its History. After a half of listening to this uninformed drivel, I began commenting to my friends on the expert commentary.

"That's wrong."

"That's wrong."

"Nope. Wrong."

That gave me a newfound appreciation for what fans endure. It also compels me to present this caveat. I can't rate all the amenities of a stadium. I can't tell you about parking, about the second mortgage necessary to afford the tickets, about the third mortgage necessary to afford good tickets. But I know the stories behind these stadiums. I know their reputations, and I know what they are really like for the opposing team when it runs onto the field. So here goes.

The Most Overrated Stadium in College Football

MICHIGAN STADIUM

This statement will be viewed with narrowed eyes by most college fans. In a sport that sustains its fans on the mother's milk of legend, generations have suckled on stories of the Big House.

The name may be part of the problem. The Big House conjures visions of a foreboding place for visiting teams, a field where opponents are sentenced to four quarters of hard labor. The reality is one of the biggest reasons that the Big House is overrated.

First of all, the Big House is more like the Big Basement. Michigan Stadium is built in a natural hole, which means that from South Main Street, the edifice that seats 107,501 doesn't look as imposing as it might. Many of the most famous stadiums in college football can be seen for miles, as if they

What Michigan Stadium has in historical significance, it lacks in good sightlines, crowd noise…and peanuts in the shell.

were a palace built to announce the royalty within. Michigan Stadium is hidden from view.

The natural bowl provides unobstructed views for the multitudes, even if the people on the top row of the south end zone are closer to I-94 than they are the 50-yard line. If you don't have a second deck, you have to go pretty far back to accommodate the population of a good-sized town in one setting.

Second, the natural bowl means one big competitive problem for the Wolverines: the noise escapes. A drunken fraternity (is there any other kind?) at Texas A&M's Kyle Field hits a higher decibel level than a sold-out Big House. Kyle Field, like Lane Stadium at Virginia Tech and Jordan-Hare Stadium at Auburn, is built straight up. The noise reverberates from one concrete side to the other, unabsorbed before it assaults your eardrums and, more important, the eardrums of the opposing offense straining to hear the snap count.

Noise at Michigan floats up, up, and away. You can choose any reason you want why Michigan has won only one national championship in the last 50 years. Blame Lloyd Carr for his antiquated offense. Blame Bo Schembechler for his antiquated offense. Shoot, blame Fielding Yost for the same reason.

But it's got a lot to do with architecture. The home-field advantage would be greater if the Big House were louder.

I can't speak to the legendary creature discomforts of the Big House, where the narrow width of the seats is surpassed on the claustrophobia scale only by the narrow distance between the benches. I spend my time there in the press box, which last got an overhaul about the time Gutenberg created the printing press.

But I'll give you another reason why Michigan Stadium is overrated. You can't buy peanuts in the shell at the Big House. Eating peanuts at an outdoor sporting event is an American liberty. It may be listed in the Bill of Rights, which I haven't read since it sent me to the canvas for a 10-count in my freshman year of college. Yes, peanut shells are messy. Hey, you're selling 110,000 seats at $49 a pop. Spring for some brooms.

The Rest of the Most Overrated

2. DARRELL K. ROYAL-TEXAS MEMORIAL STADIUM

The eyes of Darrell K. Royal stare down upon this shrine to excess. Tucked in the corner of the south end zone stands a statue of the greatest Longhorn coach of them all. Royal won three national championships at Texas and provided Longhorns fans with the outsized expectations and arrogance that only a football fan at a major school can demonstrate (see Ohio State, Alabama, etc.).

Behind the statue of Royal in the end zone is the Moncrief-Neuhaus Athletics Center, one of the first edifices to redefine the arms race in college football over the last 25 years. Let tuition skyrocket. Let students accumulate enough debt to weigh them down into their thirties. What this campus needs is to spend millions on Caligula's locker room.

(The inside of the Texas locker room goes unseen by those in the pen-and-pad set. Most college locker rooms are closed by head coaches because, well, they can. The NFL opens locker rooms. The BCS bowls open locker rooms. Shoot, USC opens locker rooms. You would think, in a sport where coaches copy one another the way pirates copy DVDs, that other coaches might think

Pete Carroll knows what he's doing. But the number of coaches who open locker rooms remains small.)

The plaza in front of the Moncrief-Neuhaus complex is where the wealthiest Orangebloods eat barbecue, drink toddys, and cheer on their 'Horns. That end zone has a wide expanse of grass. What that end zone doesn't have is a set of vertical bleachers that would seat another 10,000 ticket-buying fans as well as rain down noise upon the poor visiting team.

What saved this stadium from being the most overrated in the nation is the renovation, completed in 1999, that removed the track that separated the fans from the field. The atmosphere in Memorial Stadium used to be so dead that scientists came to study how people survived in it. Winning, which the Longhorns have made a habit of since Mack Brown arrived in 1998, has pumped some life into the stadium. But Orangebloods still greet victories not with celebration, but an air of expectations met.

One thing the stadium has going for it: an imposing footprint. To see it all lit up, miles away on I-35, is to get a sense of how important college football is on this campus. The Longhorns have won, and won a lot, at Memorial Stadium since Mack Brown arrived a decade ago, going 58–6 at home. That record could use an asterisk, though, because Oklahoma hasn't played at Texas five times in those 10 years. Brown has gone 4–6 against the Sooners at the Cotton Bowl.

And don't get the Texas fans started on the lack of parking near the stadium.

3. ORANGE BOWL

We're not leaving the Orange Bowl off this list just because, 20 years too late, the city of Miami decided to add the one thing this stadium needed—a wrecking ball. When the Miami Hurricanes decided at long last to pull up stakes in 2007, the outdated, outmoded, erector set of a football outpost was just plain tossed out.

Back in the day, when Bear Bryant roamed the sideline on January 1 and palm trees swayed in the end zone, the Orange Bowl possessed a charm unique to south Florida. The neighborhood groceries and the vendor stations along NW 3rd Street lent to the game that city-of-the-world feeling that Miami at its best always conveys.

But that time went out with the Ford administration. The Dolphins fled two decades ago, largely because they could. Even the Orange Bowl fled the Orange Bowl, which ought to tell you everything you need to know.

The Hurricanes stayed, in part because of the stadium's proximity to the campus, in part out of a sense of civic duty—even if the campus is in Coral Gables, not Miami—and in large part because the last thing this small, private university wanted or needed to do was come up with the millions it would take to build a stadium on campus.

So in the end, you put your head on a swivel when you ventured to your car in the wee hours after a night game. It seemed nearly as dangerous as a climb to the upper deck. The cinder block locker rooms had lost their charm. The plumbing had a mind of its own. It went on strike most memorably during an Orange Bowl in the late 1990s, when the ramps proved the accuracy of the ages-old wisdom, learned by every underling who ever got yelled at for something his boss did, that crap flows downhill. The press box could be depended on, throughout the advance of technology, to be one step behind the industry. It didn't have enough outlets in the age of electricity. It didn't have enough phone lines in the age of computers. It didn't have good wireless in the age of the Internet.

And it never had enough seats.

What the Orange Bowl always had in the Age of the Canes were great teams and great stars. Miami is a front-running town, and when The U won five national championships in 19 seasons, the Orange Bowl rocked to the beat and bravado of players such as Bennie Blades, Michael Irvin, Warren Sapp, et al. In the final two seasons, however, when Miami went a combined 12–13, the fans deserted the Canes. At long last, the Canes deserted Miami. The Orange Bowl won't be missed.

The Most Underrated Stadium in College Football

WILLIAMS-BRICE STADIUM

The raucous nature of Williams-Brice Stadium, where South Carolina plays, is a tribute to hope, faith, and the annual, yet-to-be-realized belief that this will be the Gamecocks' year. South Carolina has played in Williams-Brice since 1934, and actually, only one of those years has been the Gamecocks' year, if success is measured by championships.

To put it another way, Charlie Brown may eat Great Pumpkin pie before the arrival of another season like 1969.

South Carolina, under coach Paul Dietzel, went 6–0 and won the Atlantic Coast Conference. Dietzel, buoyed by such success and feeling restricted by the ACC's academic rules, pulled the Gamecocks out of the ACC in 1971 and made them an independent. Score one for pride over acumen.

That left South Carolina in the wilderness for more than two decades, until it joined the Southeastern Conference in 1992. The Gamecocks are one of four SEC schools that have never played in the league's championship game. In fact, they have never had a better record in league play than 5–3, and achieved that only three times in 16 years. Mediocrity, thy colors are garnet and black.

However, if success is defined by butts in seats, no matter the mediocrity of the product on the field, than South Carolina is a raging success. That's why Williams-Brice belongs on the list of underrated stadiums. Rain or shine, Gamecock fans show. Never have so many arrived so often to see so little happen.

The capacity is 80,250. The season ticket sales are well over 62,000. Those are just numbers. For a real sense of the devotion of Gamecock fans, take the 1998 and 1999 seasons. In 1998, coach Brad Scott began his fifth season with a record of 22–22–1. But Scott could do nothing to keep South Carolina from hitting bottom. After winning their opener against Ball State, the Gamecocks lost their last 10. Not to go all X-and-O on you, but they stunk. Yet the Gamecock fans barely wavered. Average attendance: 74,744.

The university fired Scott and hired Lou Holtz, late of Notre Dame, where he remains the only coach to win a national championship (1988) in more than 30 years. Holtz brought his more physical running offense to recruits who came to Columbia to play in Scott's passing offense. In other words, Holtz had no players recruited for his offense. The Gamecocks went winless. But in that 0–11 season, in which their losing streak extended to 22 games, the Gamecocks saw their average attendance *increase* to 78,273.

Win or lose, South Carolina fans make Williams-Brice Stadium the most underrated venue in college football.

As for the stadium itself, it's not much to look at unless you like concrete. But that's far from the point. The light stanchions that line the width of each side of the field are distinctive, and rarely are they not in use. The Gamecocks like to play at night. The fans like it, too. They tailgate on the state fairgrounds across the street and arrive at the game well lubricated. The moneyed fans don't even have to cross the street. Just outside of the stadium sits the Cockaboose Railroad, a track filled with 22 cars outfitted like luxury boxes.

And South Carolina may be the most conservative state west of the Taliban and proud of it, but I promise you there's no double entendre regarding the beloved 'Cocks that hasn't ended up on a T-shirt, a frat-house banner, or across the backside of a female student's shorts. A few years ago, the university moved to prevent any merchandise from being sold at Williams-Brice that didn't use the full nickname "Gamecocks." That went over like a lead Gamecock.

The pregame ritual is old, and anyone who would think of updating it would be escorted to the state line and thrown over it. The Gamecocks enter the field to the strains of *Also sprach Zarathustra*. You know it as the theme from *2001: A Space Odyssey.* It's outdated, it's hokey, and it's a goose-bump epidemic that breaks out from one end zone to the other every game.

There's also only one stadium in college football that celebrates touchdowns with a rooster crowing over the loudspeakers.

South Carolina may have trouble finding enough talent within its borders to compete with Florida, Georgia, and Tennessee. Holtz won, but not like he won at Notre Dame, and current coach Steve Spurrier, in his first three seasons, discovered that winning at South Carolina is more difficult than the winning he did at his alma mater, Florida. But no matter the product on the field, the Gamecocks will always have their fans. There will come a day when Williams-Brice is no longer underrated. But it will come only when South Carolina football performs as well as the people who come to watch it.

The Rest of the Most Underrated

2. AUTZEN STADIUM

Oregon football isn't a factory. It doesn't boast a tradition that resonates with anyone east of the Cascades. When the College Football Hall of Fame selected running back/wide receiver Ahmad Rashad in 2007, he increased the number of Ducks in the Hall to five, or about what Notre Dame gets elected every couple of years. Oregon has never won a national championship, and when the Ducks should have played Miami for the BCS title in 2001 and got passed over for Nebraska, the outcry could be heard only by those wearing green and Hi-Liter yellow.

What the citizens of the Emerald State do possess is pride in their Ducks and passion enough to fill Autzen Stadium on those autumn Saturdays that dawn cold and damp—which is to say, just about all of them.

That passion, when blended with the considerable donations—$40 million, anyone?—of Phil Knight and his Almighty Swoosh, have made for a ramshackle palace of a football stadium. Though barely 40 years old,

Few teams have a better home-field advantage than the Oregon Ducks do at Autzen Stadium.

Autzen Stadium is the least-known, most intimidating place to play in the nation.

The beauty of the setting just north of campus belies its danger. Autzen sits surrounded by evergreens, separated from campus by the Willamette River. The students take a footbridge over the Willamette to the stadium.

On the outside, Autzen's sloping architecture on the south side, the result of a 2002 renovation and addition, resembles a half-sun, which is about all that ever shines on this lush, green campus. It is not something an architect would have drawn up from scratch, which only adds to its charm.

On the inside, to paraphrase Groucho Marx, it's too loud to win. The students arrive early and often, and take up residency in the west end zone, where they prepare to pounce on the opposing team from the moment they step on the field for warm-ups. From there, it only gets worse.

According to *The Oregonian,* the decibel level during the Oregon-USC game in 2007 reached 127.2 decibels, or two decibels higher than the onset of pain. Tell that to the No. 12 Trojans, who lost to the No. 5 Ducks 24–17 and fell to No. 19. That's not exactly breaking news to Oklahoma, Michigan, Wisconsin, and Fresno State, all non-conference ranked teams that have lost at Autzen in this decade. In 13 seasons under coach Mike Bellotti, the Ducks are 63–16 (.797) at home.

Perhaps the most impressive aspect of Autzen is that it has proved to be so intimidating despite seating only 59,000 and change. The biggest stadiums in college football seat almost twice as many fans, which makes sense, because fans elsewhere make about half as much noise.

3. LANE STADIUM

Lane Stadium is no longer a secret. What is in the Era of Google? ESPN *College GameDay* will travel to Blacksburg at the drop of Lee Corso's pencil. The atmosphere at Virginia Tech remains underrated in my mind, largely because traditionalists who haven't been there have a hard time believing that an ACC (nee Big East) stadium can look and sound like Lane Stadium does.

This is an SEC atmosphere that somehow strayed into the ACC. Don't get me wrong—the ACC is a good league. I believe in my heart that some day, some way, the ACC champion will win another BCS bowl. The league has lost eight in a row and, believe me, Notre Dame (having lost nine consecutive bowls) is feeling the heat. To put the ACC's losing streak in perspective, the last ACC quarterback to win a BCS bowl was Chris Weinke of Florida State.

But I digress. The Hokies get loud, and they got jet-engine loud even before the addition of 11,000 seats in the south end zone. The architect, clearly a Hokie fan, built the stands straight up, a la Kyle Field at Texas A&M. The sound has no escape, especially if you're an opposing quarterback trying to call signals.

And this isn't modern-day manufactured sound, the kind that assaults you the moment you walk into an NBA arena, a Major League Baseball park, or Beaver Stadium at Penn State. You know what I'm talking about—that mix of boomer rock and hip-hop that prevents anyone inside the walls from harboring a coherent thought or carrying on a conversation.

Virginia Tech does use the occasional turkey gobble over the loudspeakers to goose the fans, but that is in honor of the school's former nickname, the Gobblers. What it isn't is the one zillionith use of the first three notes of "Start Me Up," or Jennifer Lopez imploring everyone to get loud. Some marketing genius decided that the game is not enough to entertain the fans who drove several hours and spent several hundred dollars in order to do just that.

Lane Stadium has proven to be one of the toughest home fields in college football under coach Frank Beamer (in 21 seasons, 100–29–1, .773; in the last 10 seasons against ranked opponents, 14–6, .700). That's another reason it's underrated. People have taken for granted the difficulty of playing at Virginia Tech. But, like Autzen Stadium, Lane Stadium is undersized. With a capacity of 66,233, it is less than two-thirds the size of the behemoths at Michigan and Tennessee.

The last reason that Lane Stadium remains underrated will be unknown to anyone who hasn't attended a game there. A concession stand beneath the west side sells smoked turkey legs that year after year would make anyone's top-10 list of stadium cuisine. It makes you wish more teams used to be the Gobblers.

As a turkey leg aficionado, I may be biased. As a long-time, long-term avoider of stadium food, these Flintstone-looking entrees make a mockery of waterlogged hot dogs. They are on my short list of great college stadium grub, right there with the spicy homemade sausage served at a small stand in the west end zone of the Los Angeles Memorial Coliseum and the fresh roasted peanuts that a lovely woman sells in small paper bags outside the east side of Bryant-Denny Stadium.

Before entering most other college stadiums, I make sure there's a Balance Bar in my briefcase.

* * *

The best gameday atmosphere combines fun, food, drink, and passion so well that even a fan without a dog in the hunt will want to come back. Without that, you're just committing your weekend to traffic jams and overpriced hotel rooms.

The Most Overrated Campus in College Football

OHIO STATE

I am not completely unfamiliar with the charms of burning a couch. I was once a college student, too. Couch-burning, overdrinking, making opposing fans not only feel unwelcome but fear for their safety: it's all part of Buckeye love. I have made my way through the elbow-to-elbow drunks at Hineygate—get it?—outside of the Holiday Inn on campus. If it's a Michigan game, Hineygate doesn't cross the line from party to disturbance, but you can see the line without binoculars.

There is a lot to recommend Ohio Stadium on a football Saturday, from the grandeur of the place to The Best Damn Band In The Land to the football itself. I bet of the 100,000 or so Buckeye fans who invade the campus, there are dozens who are warm, hospitable Midwestern folks. I'm sure not all of them burn couches in the street and generally make the Columbus Police Department yearn for basketball season. But some ugly stuff has happened there.

In 2002, more than 40 people were arrested in Columbus after fires were set and cars were destroyed following Ohio State's victory over Michigan. (Photo courtesy of AP Images)

The Rest of the Most Overrated

2. UCLA

First of all, if you want to be taken seriously, play on campus. Second, Bruin fans are sometimes reluctant to drive up the 110 to the Rose Bowl. You mean to tell me you could spend an entire afternoon in the Rose Bowl and you find something better to do? Third, I do have to admit, if it's not January 1, or if USC isn't on the opposite sideline, the Rose Bowl doesn't deliver everything. Fourth, as regards the Bruins in general, here's a state school with a campus that's smack dab in the middle of a gushing well of football prospects. Here's a campus that teems with beautiful scenery and even more beautiful people. Why does UCLA not finish first in the recruiting rankings every February? Why doesn't this team go 11–2 every fall?

3. NORTH CAROLINA

Gorgeous campus, stunning football facilities built under the watch of former coach Mack Brown in the mid-1990s, great academics. It just feels like, Butch Davis as head coach or no, most Tar Heel fans are sitting in Kenan Stadium with one foot in the Dean Dome, waiting for basketball practice to start.

The overwhelming focus on Tar Heels basketball makes for an uninspired college football environment in Chapel Hill, North Carolina.

4. FLORIDA

I think the Swamp is one of the best college football venues in America. There's no stadium louder, no fans more besotted with their team, than the Gators. So what's overrated? Easy—I admire Gator fans from the comfort of the Norm Carlson Press Box. I'm not sweating buckets in the late-summer Gainesville humidity. I'm guessing that Ben Hill Griffin Stadium at Florida Field is the hottest, stickiest, clammiest stadium in the SEC, which would make it the hottest, stickiest, clammiest stadium in all of college football, at least until the University of Singapore joins the NCAA. If you've read this far, it must be clear by now that I love college football, but if I'm sitting in those hothouse conditions, I better be staring at the Gulf of Mexico, beer in hand.

5. MIAMI

For the same weather as above, plus fans whose level of arrogance makes Yankee fans look as if they need self-esteem therapy. Before the 2007 season, with the Hurricanes coming off a 7–6 season and starting out under first-time head coach Randy Shannon, Miami fans expressed outrage at the suggestion that they may not be worthy of the top 25. Only when Oklahoma defeated Miami 51–13 in the second week of the season did the squawking stop. The Hurricanes finished 5–7. The only reason that Miami is ranked below Florida on this scale is that the Hurricanes begin play at Dolphins Stadium in 2008.

The Most Underrated Campus in College Football

TEXAS-OKLAHOMA AT THE COTTON BOWL

For nearly 80 years, the Longhorns and Sooners have played in Fair Park in Dallas during the Texas State Fair. Call it sheer genius. Funneling 75,000 fans through the Fair, with its carnival rides, livestock, and butter sculpture (personal favorite: Elvis singing "Hound Dog," complete with hound dog) gives this rivalry a flavor unavailable anywhere else in college football. And that flavor is fried: if it's not the Fletcher Corny Dogs, which are hot dogs with fried cornmeal coating, then it may be the fried dough, the fried chicken, the fried jalapenos or the—Lipitor alert—fried cheesecake. All of them are available on the plaza outside the Cotton Bowl. Any football fan who steps onto the fairgrounds finds his hard feelings toward Texas/Oklahoma coated in flour, deposited in a wire basket, and dunked in a vat of bubbling oil. Fried foods may "angry" the blood, as the late Satchel Paige famously warned, but they create a peaceful coexistence for one afternoon between Sooners and Longhorns. The Cotton Bowl is a stadium where time stands still, and so do the elevators. But the 50-50 split of the stadium creates an atmosphere that overcomes creaky plumbing and creature discomforts. With a stadium split down the middle—the aisles on the 50-yard lines separate orange from red—someone is cheering on every play.

The passion of Texas and Oklahoma fans makes the annual Red River Shootout one of the can't-miss games in college football. (Photo courtesy of AP Images)

The Rest of the Most Underrated

2. FLORIDA-GEORGIA

The Florida-Georgia rivalry is neck-cord-bulging intense for plenty of reasons: the shared border, the shared reverence for football, the shared history in the Southeastern Conference, which began in 1933, the same year that Florida and Georgia moved their game to Jacksonville. But the biggest reason the rivalry has become known from the First Coast to the West Coast are the acres of parking lots that surround Jacksonville Municipal Stadium. On that sacred pavement is held the event that dare not speak its name. In this age of heightened alcohol awareness, civic reputation, and trolling attorneys, the city fathers no longer embrace The World's Largest Outdoor Cocktail Party. But you still can't walk very far through the parking lot without seeing someone with a funnel and some firewater. The spirit lives because the fans on both sides of the field have that history of so many weekends in Jacksonville. Take the passion of an intense regional college football rivalry and mix it with liberal amounts of alcohol, hotel rooms, and sun. Garnish with sleep (optional). The savvy fan understands that the night to be at the Landing, the development of bars and restaurants smack on the St. Johns River in downtown Jacksonville, is Friday night. Both sides are excited and optimistic. Like the Texas-Oklahoma game, tickets are split 50-50. Unlike Texas-Oklahoma, hotel rooms in Jacksonville are at a premium. Every college football fan should see it.

3. WISCONSIN

It may be cabin fever, or rebellion against the cold. It may be the love of frigid tailgating, a tradition in Green Bay that has migrated 136 miles south. Whatever it is, the Badger athletic department ought to try to copyright it and sell it to other athletic departments. Being inside the early-20th-century relic that is Camp Randall Stadium on a chilly autumn (my redundancy beeper just went off) Saturday is just a lot of fun, as long as you have the appropriate amounts of Smartwool. Not to get all actuarial on you, but in the lifetime of most Badger fans, the only winning they have known is the current success that dates to Barry Alvarez's arrival in 1990. Badger fans are not yet spoiled, and their brat-and-beer-fueled giddiness has shown no signs of encroaching cynicism. In other words, it's good not to be Ohio State and Michigan. Success is enjoyed rather than expected. So far.

4. TEXAS A&M

Some people, especially those with orange blood, find the whole concept of the 12th Man corny. But if game-day atmosphere encompasses 24 hours, which would include Midnight Yell Practice, then the Aggies get a jump on every other game. When Kyle Field starts swaying—literally—as every Aggie fan puts his or her arm around the shoulder of the next Aggie fan and sings, you realize you've tapped into something special. The band plays martial music throughout the game (personal favorite: the theme from *Patton*), which also gives a Texas A&M game a flavor hard to find anywhere else.

Yell Leaders at Texas A&M are one of the many reasons College Station is an underrated place to watch a football game. (Photo courtesy of AP Images)

5. OLE MISS

This is tailgating raised to art form. The Grove is the oval at the center of campus. In the wee hours of Friday night/Saturday morning, fans jam in, tent pole to tent pole, tailgate to tailgate, and put out spreads that make eyes and mouths water. One look at the amount of fried chicken and you understand that there can't be a hen or a bag of flour left in the whole state of Mississippi. In the last 20 years, Oxford has become a gastronome's delight, and four-star restaurants such as City Grocery are more than happy to cater for two or 20. The Rebels don't win much, especially if a Manning isn't playing quarterback, but they know how to throw a party.

CHAPTER 10

Traditions, Fight Songs, and Mascots

The Most Overrated Tradition in College Football

THE HEISMAN CAMPAIGN

Campaigning for the Heisman Trophy is not entirely a waste of time. All of us, if you want to get all existential about it, are promoting the game of college football. (Somebody stop me before I suggest that we hold hands and sing fight songs.) But the days of Madison Avenue–style campaigns, when schools employed clever slogans and tchotchkes to attract the attention of their target audience, are as effective with the Heisman as they are with the rest of business.

Which is to say, not at all, in case you were wondering why newspapers have gone in the dumper and *Time* and *Newsweek* are about as thick as *The New Republic*.

In a way, it's too bad, if only because it's always a good idea to encourage creativity. In 1997, for instance, Washington State sent envelopes to Heisman voters that contained only a single leaf, a reference to Cougar quarterback Ryan Leaf (the question no one asked: when the leaf came down, did it fall straight into the hands of an opposing safety?). Those of us who received the envelope waited anxiously for Kentucky to adopt the same tactic in support of quarterback Tim Couch.

In 1990, Brigham Young sent out blue paper "ties," complete with a rubber band to go around the neck, in support of quarterback Ty Detmer.

Clever tactics, yes, but in the day of the Internet, when more and more of the public gathers news over cell phones, the key to winning a Heisman is no longer the clever stunt. In 2001, Oregon bought billboard space in Times Square to promote quarterback Joey Harrington. Even as late as 2007, Rutgers promoted tailback Ray Rice by giving out small binoculars with the slogan "Run Ray Run" printed on the carrying case. Cute idea, but redundant. At that point, the voters knew that Rice finished third in the nation in rushing in 2006, and they also knew that if he didn't produce similar numbers in 2007, they would train their new mini-binoculars elsewhere.

Rice played three consecutive early-season games in which he gained fewer than 100 yards and that was that.

The rules to win a Heisman today are play well, play for a successful team, and play a tough schedule. Little else is relevant. Name recognition is important, but not as critical as it used to be. The last two winners, Florida quarterback Tim Tebow (2007) and Ohio State quarterback Troy Smith (2006), enjoyed little Heisman support before the season. But they not only played well enough, they did something else to win. Smith kept the Buckeyes at No. 1 through the regular season. Tebow performed as the best hybrid without a Toyota insignia. He ran like a fullback, threw like a quarterback, and played like a throwback. The Gators didn't win the SEC East, much less defend their national championship, but they won enough to keep Tebow's name afloat.

There is a lot of suspicion across the country that ESPN in general, and the guys on air on Saturday in particular, decide who wins the Heisman. As a voter for more than 20 years, I can tell you why I think that suspicion is a load of manure. Those theories are fine in a vacuum. What they don't take into account is professional jealousy.

Campaigning for the Heisman Trophy run amok: a gigantic banner promoting Washington State's Jason Gesser hung from a building in Seattle in 2002. (Gesser finished seventh in the voting.) (Photo courtesy of AP Images)

First of all, most voters are covering games. They are not sitting at home watching *GameDay.* Second, writers and TV people don't like being lumped together in any way, shape, or form. TV people think writers are slobs who are as interested in free food as they are disinterested in steam irons. Writers think TV people are leeches whose idea of reporting is to pull up the writer's story on the Internet.

The last thing any writer would do is vote for a Heisman candidate because Mark May—or Lee Corso or Kirk Herbstreit or Craig James or Doug Flutie—said that candidate is a front-runner. If anything, that would cause the writers I know to cast a sidelong glance at that candidate and make sure he knew how to put on his pads without help.

The smart Heisman candidates nowadays dispense with the toys and gifts and instead prefer to give out information. They design websites to promote the candidate and then design e-bombs to dispense the address of the website to the voting populace. They set up weekly conference calls for their candidates so that writers around the country can interview them and continue to spread the word about their candidacy. They write emails every week trumpeting how well they played—and if they didn't play well, they write an email describing the extenuating circumstance that kept them from extending themselves into the end zone.

The Heisman campaign of 2008 is all about buzz. It dispenses with the gimmicky. It doles out more meat and potatoes than it does junk food. In short, it is simply a sports information director doling out sports information.

The day when an SID could pull a publicity stunt to make his player's name is over. One of the great examples of that kind of stunt occurred in the late 1960s, when Notre Dame quarterback Joe Theismann (rhymes with cheeseman) became Joe Theismann (rhymes with Heisman). The idea, the brainchild of former Notre Dame SID Roger Valdiserri, almost worked. Theismann finished a distant second in 1970 to Stanford quarterback Jim Plunkett, who took his team to the Rose Bowl.

The Rest of the Most Overrated

2. THE BOWL REWARD

If you backed me into a corner and threatened to take away my Philips Pronto TSU3500 remote—you know, the one that integrates the TV, DVD player, iPod, and the toaster—I would admit how much I love the abundance of bowls. There's something about turning on the TV during the week between Christmas and New Year's Day and watching college football, no matter the time of the day.

But my addictions aside, let us not confuse 32 bowl games with the tradition of rewarding a team for a good season. Of the 64 teams that received bids after the 2007 regular season, 23 of them had records of 7–5 or 6–6. The increase in bowls has rewarded mediocrity, a privilege that the nation more famously reserves for *American Idol.* In fact, the absence of a bowl bid is worse than a bowl game is good, which is the exact opposite of the way it was a generation ago.

It used to be that plenty of very good teams were not good enough to gain a bowl bid. In 1978, with 15 bowls, teams in the six major conferences had to win eight games to get an invitation. Washington went 7–4, tied for second in the Pac-10 with a 6–2 record, and stayed home. And if you didn't play in one of the major conferences, you had to win your league championship or forget about a bowl.

Nowadays, of course, a bowl bid is a badge of not much. It doesn't keep the mob away from the embattled coach's door. In 2007, several teams—Georgia Tech, Southern Mississippi, Texas A&M, and UCLA—played bowl games without head coaches because they had been fired. The school didn't think they got the job done, but the bowls did?

No, it's simply that winning enough to get to a bowl game doesn't take nearly the effort that it once did. Bowls have been cheapened in the process, and perhaps the sport has as well.

Me? As Alvy Singer said in *Annie Hall,* "My brother thinks he's a chicken."

Someone said, "Why don't you turn him in?"

"I would," Singer replied. "But we need the eggs."

The plethora of bowls have changed college football and not always for the better. But for that one week when you hit the remote and there's always a game awaiting you, you have to admit—we need the eggs.

3. THE PREGAME TEAM WALK

Former Auburn athletic director David Housel once described his school's Tiger Walk as "the most copied tradition in all of college football." That's exactly why it has become one of the most overrated traditions in all of college football. When everyone adopts something cool, it becomes uncool (with the exception of Facebook).

When every team adopts the pregame walk, it loses its juice. Tennessee, Virginia Tech, Georgia, and Ole Miss, among others, have a pregame walk. Even Alabama—Auburn's archrival and self-appointed superior to everything

Auburn's "Tiger Walk" down Donahue Drive is one example of the overrated "team walk" tradition.

blue and orange—has adopted a pregame walk. At least until the Crimson Tide fans realize that Auburn made it famous.

Other teams had a pregame walk before Auburn. Stanford used to walk from the physical education building, where its locker rooms were, down a tree-shaded street to Stanford Stadium. But that's all Stanford had. Only when the NFL came in and gussied up Stanford Stadium for Super Bowl XIX did the Cardinal get to shower without walking. Williams College, a Division III powerhouse, doesn't have a pregame walk. It has a postgame walk—if it beats archrival Amherst, the Ephs, in their uniforms, walk downtown to a local barber shop and celebrate their victory. Cold beverages are consumed.

I understand the power of the walk. I have watched from the Neyland Stadium press box as Vol Walk makes Peyton Manning Pass look like a Tennessee fan's arteries after a few hundred trips to Calhoun's Barbecue. The team squeezes down the street toward the stadium. Vol Walk began in 1990, the year after the most famous pregame walk in college football.

In 1989, the year that Alabama broke precedent and broke its holier-than-thou stance, the Crimson Tide played at Jordan-Hare Stadium for the first time. That Tiger Walk is the only time I have feared for my safety in nearly 30 years as a journalist. I have covered events in Russia, Spain, Germany, England, and 39 states. I have walked through the Los Angeles Memorial Coliseum parking lot at 2:00 AM. I have been sneered at by Lloyd Carr and yelled at by Gene Stallings.

I've been around.

But nearly 20 years later I remember standing amidst those crazed Auburn fans and having the adrenaline kick in, the adrenaline that said, "Forget taking notes. You need to move." The Tiger fans got so hopped up on excitement—and maybe a drop or two of the grape—that I don't know how that football team made it through that crowd without a riot. Auburn converted that energy into a 30–20 defeat of unbeaten, No. 2 Alabama.

That, to me, was a walk. The next year came Tennessee and others followed to the point that it's no more distinctive than dressing female students in skimpy outfits and having them lead cheers. I think most other schools do that, too. What all those other schools have done is make Tiger Walk into A Good Walk Spoiled.

4. SOD CEMETERY

Once upon a time, before Florida State won two national championships, before the Seminoles dominated the 1990s, before Bobby Bowden combined cornpone humor with a sense of comic timing in ways that Jeff Foxworthy could only dream about, Florida State wasn't a good football school. From 1972 to 1974, for instance, the Seminoles lost 20 consecutive games, and this wasn't the ACC schedule that Florida State fans know. In those days, Florida State lived a MAC-like existence, playing more games on the road than at home, playing three weeks in a row on the road, all in the chase of paycheck games.

Bowden changed all that. How he did it on the field is a story for another time. It was the fields on which he did it that made all the difference. In 1981, Bowden took Florida State to play No. 17 Nebraska, No. 7 Ohio State, Notre Dame, No. 3 Pittsburgh, and LSU—in a row. The Seminoles won three of them—beating the Buckeyes, Irish, and Tigers—and created a persona. They would go anywhere and play anyone and they would win.

Bowden took that reputation and burnished it. Never mind that the Seminoles came off the road and lost their last three games by an average of four touchdowns. And when they won those road games, they would take a piece of the opposing field back to Tallahassee with them. The Seminoles planted their conquered turf in a Sod Cemetery on the edge of their practice fields. The practice actually dates to 1962 and an 18–0 upset of Georgia. Such was the opinion of the Seminoles at the time that a victory over the Bulldogs, in the middle of their second consecutive three-win season, was considered an upset.

The Sod Cemetery served its purpose as Florida State clawed its way to the top of college football. By the 1990s, however, it began to look like those end-zone celebrations that we all know and abhor. As the late Paul Brown said to his Cleveland Browns, "Act like you've been there before." Why brag about a road victory? You're Florida State. You expect to win.

It could be that, after consecutive 7–6 seasons, the Seminoles will take their dirt when and where they can get it. But the Sod Cemetery, like playing five consecutive games against national powers on the road, is one gimmick whose time has passed. The Seminoles no longer need to prove that they belong in the big time. They just need to prove they can return to it. There's a big difference. The Sod Cemetery should be allowed to die a peaceful death.

5. MISSISSIPPI STATE'S COWBELLS

Make all the cow college jokes you want. Mississippi State loves it. The Bulldogs embrace their inner farmer, right down to their choice of noisemaker. Legend has it that prior to World War II, when Mississippi State got invited to the Orange Bowl twice in a five-year span, a cow wandered onto the field during a game against Ole Miss. Mississippi State won the game and for years afterward students continued to bring a cow to the game as a talisman.

As the years went by, the students found it easier to bring cowbells to Scott Field instead of the cow. A couple of professors began welding handles to cowbells, and, if Al Gore gets around to doing a book on noise pollution—

An Inconvenient Sound?—he can point to that invention as the source of noise pollution in northeast Mississippi.

Opposing teams complained, which just made Bulldog fans all the more determined to get cowbells. Finally, in 1974, the Southeastern Conference outlawed the use of "artificial noisemakers" at its football games. Hmmm, who *could* the league have had in mind?

With that rule passed, the SEC pretended it had solved the problem, save for one small issue. The league enforces the cowbell ban with all the zeal of Captain Louis Renault closing down the casino in *Casablanca*. You remember that:

> Renault: "I'm shocked, shocked to find that gambling is going on in here!"
> Croupier (handing Renault a wad of cash): "Your winnings, sir."

In other words, the league sprains neck ligaments looking the other way, even after supposedly putting teeth into the rule in 2002, when the league voted to back the rule with penalties. Mississippi State points out that the SEC's rules don't apply to nonconference games, but even when the Bulldogs' big rivals come to Starkville, the cowbells manage to find their way past the ever-alert gendarmes. The cowbells ring, and cows can hear them clear back to Jackson. Attend a game in Starkville, and you will hear the cowbells for days afterward.

They are unique to Mississippi State, and their presence lends a charm to the sport. What the cowbells don't do—and the reason that they are over-rated—is affect the game. Mississippi State doesn't win at home any more than it wins on the road. In head coach Sylvester Croom's four seasons, the Bulldogs are 7–15 at home against I-A competition. On the road, they are 7–14.

While it is true that under Croom's predecessor, Jackie Sherrill, Mississippi State won 15 in a row at Scott Field from 1998 to 2000, the cowbells rang just as loudly in Sherrill's last three seasons (2001–03), when the Bulldogs went 6–13 at home.

Ring all you want, but the records don't lie. The cowbells don't make one bit of difference on the field.

The Most Underrated Tradition in College Football

SCRIPT OHIO

Players are bigger, players are faster, playbooks are thicker, tuition is higher, tickets are more expensive, and somehow, the marching bands are the same. Marching bands have the half-life of nuclear waste, although most of them do sound better. They wear uniforms straight out of an MGM musical. Their songs may as well be straight out of an MGM musical, too. My favorite recent memory is The Ohio State University Marching Band playing the theme from *Titanic* at halftime of the 2007 BCS Championship Game, on the Buckeyes' way to a 41–14 loss to Florida.

In other words, mood music.

As you can tell, I'm not a fan. Marching bands leave me as unmoved as a Rice fan at bowl time, so believe me when I tell you that the best tradition in college football involves a marching band. Not just any band, mind you, but The Best Damn Band In The Land, as they say at Ohio State. When they're not playing prophetic Celine Dion tunes, TBDBITL has made me a sucker for "Script Ohio," which it performs before games or during halftime.

Script Ohio rolls out to an obscure—in 49 states, anyway—19th-century French poem set to music, "Le Regiment de Sambre et Meuse." They could perform it to "We Don't Give a Damn About the Whole State of Michigan," and it would still be riveting. The precision of the marching makes the script flow as if it were written by your fourth-grade teacher. In fact, the Ohio State band has gotten an A-plus in penmanship since it began performing "Script Ohio" in 1936.

The band has gotten larger since then, and the original i-dotter, a cornet player, quickly gave way to a sousaphone player because he would be easier to spot. But not much else has changed. It is riveting theater; perhaps because of history, perhaps tradition, perhaps the anticipation of seeing the drum major lead the human dot from the side of the last "o" to his place above the "i." All 102,000 people in the Horseshoe have seen it before, and so what? We watch the ball drop in Times Square every year, and every year brings the same thrilling comfort.

And it is a thrill. Boys and girls in Ohio grow up dreaming of dotting the "i."

"The first time I saw Script Ohio," said assistant band director Jonathan Waters, "I was 10 years old, watching an Ohio State football game. They showed the band on TV, and the "i"-dotter. Every one of these kids in the sousaphone section will tell you that it happens that way for them. I was a saxophone player in my middle school band and switched to sousaphone, or tuba, because I wanted to come to Ohio State and dot the "i." And that story is like that for so many kids in our band."

Dr. Jon R. Woods, the longtime director of the Ohio State band, said the state's high schools are awash in sousaphone players. Not to question your attachment to band recruiting websites—can ESPN's Hot 150 Snare Drummers be that far away?—but when other band directors are looking for sousaphone players, they know they can come to Ohio.

"To have a great band, or a great stereo system, you have to have a good bass sound," Dr. Woods said. "The Script Ohio routine has become so famous, it's the best recruiting tool there ever was to get a bass sound. Every year we get more sousaphone players to try out for our band. We get 40 to 50. Most of my colleagues will say, 'Would you just give us the people you don't take?' We always have 28 sousaphones and we probably turn away another 25 to 30 good ones, so we have a great bass line in our band, which really helps the whole sound of the band."

The sousaphonists are accorded the honor by a point system. Band members accumulate points by marching and by winning challenges for positions in the band. Clint Phillips, who last marched in TBDBITL in 2006, dotted the "i" three times in his band career.

"Dotting the 'i' was one of the most incredible experiences I have ever had," he told me for a story on ESPN.com. "The excitement and intensity running through your body is just unbelievable.

"While marching through the Script that day, I took some time to look around the stadium a little bit and the emotions started to overcome me. When I got to the bottom of the little 'o' of Script Ohio, I stopped playing and clearly heard someone on the sideline yell, 'You're about to dot the "i"! Go get 'em!' I leaned forward a little to slap the drum major's hand,

Unless you're a Michigan fan, you're bound to feel some goose bumps during Ohio State's Script Ohio halftime performance. (Photo courtesy of AP Images)

and my friend marching behind me, Wes Clark, was yelling and screaming for me."

It's one thing for the drum major to lean back and strut. All he carries is a baton. It's quite another for a guy wearing a sousaphone.

"When you first start your strut, you want to make sure to get a good push with whichever leg you choose in order to start your momentum," Phillips explained. "Once you're in motion, your next goal is to get your legs up as high as you possibly can. In order to help make your legs look higher, you want to lean back. The farther you can comfortably lean back without losing your balance, the better. How far you lean back is all up to the person dotting. It isn't that difficult to strut while wearing the sousaphone. In my experience, I find it easier to strut while wearing it. It helps you get accustomed to the strut with the horn, and also helps keep your momentum."

Phillips said that the strut leaves "i"-dotters susceptible to shin splints and pulled hip flexors, not to mention waves of emotion.

"When I got to the top of the 'i,' I bowed to the east side of Ohio Stadium with tears in my eyes," Phillips said. "I did my kick turn to face the west side and did the low bow and couldn't hold the tears back."

Once in a rare while, the sousaphonists will vote to grant someone within or without the university the honor of dotting the "i." In 2006, golfer and former Buckeye Jack Nicklaus joined a short list that includes fellow Ohioans Woody Hayes and boxer Buster Douglas as well as Bob Hope.

Every legend has a secret that it would rather not tell. The secret of "Script Ohio" is that the first band to write "Ohio" in script was…Michigan's, in 1932. Ohio State band fans point out that Michigan may have formed an "Ohio" in script but that they didn't perform "Script Ohio."

(The secret that Wolverine fans don't like to tell is that the guy who wrote "The Victors" came from…South Bend, Indiana.)

The Rest of the Most Underrated

2. ARMY-NAVY ALMA MATER

You can make a very good case that service academy football is about as relevant as Cold War politics. The evidence is clear: national championship football has become a demilitarized zone. To put it in horticultural terms, Army, Navy, and Air Force exist somewhere between the Poinsettia Bowl (where Navy plays when it qualifies) and the Ivy League (where many of these players might have landed if they chose to wear civvies all week).

As tough as it is for the Ivy League to find players, it's a day at the beach compared to finding recruits who are academically eligible for a service academy *and* willing to commit to serve their country for five years after they graduate.

The football is not what it once was, when Army won national championships and Midshipmen won two Heisman Trophies in four seasons (1960, 1963). And in terms of tradition, it doesn't matter at all. The Army-Navy game is still a tough ticket. How can that be?

Because two teams that represent the best of the nation's young people give everything they have for 60 minutes.

Because the pageantry of seeing both student bodies march into the stadium would be worth the price of the ticket.

Because when the game ends, the two teams illustrate an allegiance to something bigger than their football uniforms. When the game ends, players and coaches from both sidelines go together to stand before the band of the losing team, where they stand at attention, hands on hearts, as it plays its alma mater. In 2007, as in the previous five seasons, that means that the Army band played "Alma Mater" first.

And then, as Navy sports information director Scott Strasemeier put it, "The winning team sprints across the field, and the losing team gets over there." The teams and their coaches were then paid the same respect as the Navy band played "Blue and Gold."

No one is sure when the tradition began, except that it is a young one.

"It's within the last quarter-century," said author Jack Clary, the unofficial historian of the rivalry. "It goes at least into the '80s. It wasn't there in the '60s and '70s. Specifically when, I don't know."

The respect on display at the end of every Army-Navy game is one of the great traditions in all of sports. (Photo courtesy of AP Images)

Clary recalled a time when the winning student body rushed the field. But at some time during the Reagan administration, when the service academies, like the armed services themselves, again became a source of pride to a nation that had left behind the anguish and torpor of Vietnam, the teams began to honor each other. Television, always a sucker for emotion, brought that feeling into millions of homes across the nation.

To see the players from both teams standing together, many with tears in their eyes—tears of pride, tears of victory and loss, tears of realization for the seniors that their carreers are over—is to see one of the grand spectacles of college athletics.

"Now some people, including myself," Clary said, "have stayed through some bad games just to see them. It's become the highlight of the game."

3. HOWARD'S ROCK

Okay, here's the deal: we take a rock from across the country, see, and we mount it on a pedestal and stick it behind one end zone, and when the players come into the stadium, they'll come through the end zone and rub the rock! The crowd will love it! Who's with me?

Without context, without emotion and tradition, college football's rituals are silly. But without ritual, emotion, and tradition, most of organized religion would be reduced to a couple of feel-good anecdotes and the Golden Rule. The story of Howard's Rock is how one man's trash soon became college football's treasure.

Back in 1948, Presbyterian College head coach Lonnie McMillian referred to Memorial Stadium as "Death Valley." That might be because from 1930 to 1947, Clemson opened every season at home against Presbyterian and went 15–1–2. Soon after, Tigers coach Frank Howard began referring to his home stadium as Death Valley.

In the mid-1960s—no one is quite sure when—a Clemson alumnus named S.C. Jones went to Death Valley, California, picked up a white flint rock, and brought it back to campus. When Jones presented it to Howard, the coach was so touched that the rock sat on the floor of his office for the next couple of years.

Finally, Howard directed Gene Willimon in the athletic department to get that rock out of his office. Willimon served as executive secretary of IPTAY, or "I Pay Ten a Year," the Clemson booster club that had its roots in the Depression, when $10 a year was quite a sum. Willimon didn't want to get rid of the rock. He knew a good booster prop when he saw one. Willimon placed the rock on a stand in the east end zone, where the Tigers came down a hill into the stadium, in 1966. A season would pass before Howard suggested to his players that they rub it.

"If you're going to give me 110 percent, you can rub that rock," Howard told the Tigers before their 1967 game against Wake Forest. "If you're not, keep your filthy hands off it."

Clemson won 23–6 and gave birth to a two-and-a-half-pound tradition. With the exception of a couple of seasons in the 1970s, the Tigers have rubbed Howard's Rock before every home game. In 2000, they replaced the old pedestal with elegant carved granite.

For a rock.

Yet it works. You get 81,000 fans on their feet, the Clemson band playing "Tiger Rag," thousands of orange and white balloons floating skyward, and the football team running down the hill toward the end zone, pausing to touch the rock, and what you have is gen-yew-wine college football at its earsplitting best. Other schools have begun to imitate Howard's Rock, which is the sincerest form of copyright violation. Maryland, for instance, has a turtle statue. Every school with a giant videoboard has made its team's entrance on the field a production, usually something right out of a Vegas show. Clemson did it first and does it best.

With a rock.

4. AGGIE YELL PRACTICE

Yell Practice at Texas A&M takes place at midnight, and it has a secret code. What purpose does football serve if not to keep alive the little boy in us all?

You have to see Yell Practice at Kyle Field at midnight before a Texas A&M home game to believe. The Yell Leaders—five Aggie undergrads elected by the student body—do just what their title suggests. God protect the man who suggests that they are cheerleaders. Let us not forget that A&M used to be an all-male military school, and it is deep in the heart of Texas. It may be the friendliest campus in America—it's an Aggie tradition to say "Howdy!" to friends and strangers—but machismo rushes through the university's veins. That's why, since 1931, Aggies have had Yell Leaders, not cheerleaders.

They lead the Aggie student body in "old Army yells." They use hand signals that every true Aggie learns before he learns how to find Evans Library. They lead the Aggie War Hymn, which begins "Hullabaloo! Caneck! Caneck!," words penned by an Aggie while serving guard duty in Europe during World War I.

And, as their website says of Yell Practice, the Yell Leaders "tell fables of how the Aggies are going to beat the everlivin' hell out of our opponent for the next day." This is on the official website of a state university in a red state. If that's not what makes America great, I don't know what is.

Midnight Yell Practice is not limited to the night before home games. It is held on Thursday nights at the Grove on campus. For big away games, the Aggies hold Yell Practice on site, such as the steps of the State Capitol in Austin before Texas A&M plays Texas, or, as Aggies refer to it, t.u. (lower case is not a typo).

When the lights go out at Yell Practice, as when the football team scores a touchdown, an Aggie kisses his date.

The hippest, happeningest thing about Yell Practice is that in this cynical, postmodern age, Texas A&M still needs a place as big as Kyle Field to hold it. One of the biggest worries among athletic departments across the nation is a way to keep the student body engaged in athletics. Student ticket sales are flat or declining at most schools. Schools aren't dumb. Today's student ticket buyer is tomorrow's luxury-suite renter. They want their students engaged by sports.

Most schools are concerned about this issue. At Texas A&M, winning the Big 12 South may be an issue (last division title: 1998) but school spirit never is.

5. THE LACK OF SIGNAGE AT NOTRE DAME STADIUM

For the most part, colleges have resisted the temptation to sell the naming rights to their stadiums to corporations (colleges sell naming rights to academic buildings to wealthy donors; why that is acceptable but Chevrolet Michigan Stadium is not is a mystery best left unsolved).

Inside the stadiums, however, an onslaught of advertising awaits the fans, from placards across the façade to video advertisements on the big screens that hover over the end zone. Like most professional sporting events, a college football game can feel like watching a game on a shopping channel.

Except at Notre Dame.

There are no signs at Notre Dame Stadium. There are no logos painted on the field, no rolling electronic billboards on the sidelines, no corporate signage in sight, save for one NBC logo on one scoreboard. Consider it the mole on Marilyn Monroe's flawless cheek. There is one sign in Notre Dame Stadium that is a trademark. It is posted over the stairs that the Fighting Irish take to enter the field. As the players come down the stairs, they tap the sign that says "Play Like A Champion Today."

It is not as if Notre Dame doesn't know what its walls would be worth. On the Notre Dame website, fans may buy the Play Like A Champion Today message on T-shirts, hoodies, fleece jackets, caps, lapel pins, towels, tumblers, coffee mugs, playing cards, magnets, key rings, pennants, footballs, and, yes, even in the original sign format.

These people know how to make a bank deposit. But they also know where the value lies in Notre Dame football.

"It's just been a long-standing tradition to keep the environment within the Stadium bowl as clean as possible," said John Heisler, the senior associate athletic director. "[It's the] same reason there are no logos on the field or names of teams in the end zones. There really isn't even any discussion about this. If we deal with potential corporate relationships, we make them understand right away that there is no signage in the stadium and it's not up for debate."

The decision to leave the stadium unadorned has given it a timeless feel. In 1997, Notre Dame Stadium underwent a $50 million renovation that added 21,000 seats and modernized The House That Rockne Built. But without the signage, the stadium looks the way it always has. The only difference is that with the additional seats, fans in the stadium see less of Touchdown Jesus.

It's a sacrifice worth making. Not every school could do this. In fact, it may not be a coincidence that the only school that has its own national network also has enough resources to withstand the urge to mine the gold in them thar bleachers.

Notre Dame Stadium would be an icon just from the history that has taken place on its grass. Notre Dame football has risen to the top without the benefit of playing in a conference. The fact that the stadium remains so "clean" elevates it, like the Irish team, into a league of its own.

* * *

What I know about music in general could be written on a Post-It note with room left over for a grocery list. Fight songs, I know. I've heard them every autumn Saturday for a long time.

A good fight song has to open with an uptempo hook that announces to the crowd, "Hey! Get fired up! We've got a team to beat!" The lyrics have to be easy enough for a kindergartener to memorize. After all, the next generation of fans must be brainwashed early.

I am a sucker for lyrics that specifically refer to championships. Michigan wants to be "Champions of the West." When the song was written more than a century ago, Michigan was considered in the west. It would be a couple of decades before the west moved to California. It certainly had nothing to do with the Rose Bowl, which, given the Wolverines' recent record in Pasadena, is probably a good thing. Bo Schembechler went 2–8 in the Rose Bowl. Gary Moeller and Lloyd Carr went 2–5.

Alabama, on the other hand, is 4–1–1 in Rose Bowls. The Crimson Tide's song exhorts the team to "Remember the Rose Bowl, we'll win then." Maybe the Wolverines can borrow that line.

The Most Overrated Fight Song in College Football

"GIMME A G, GO GATORS" (FLORIDA)

The Gators' fight song is so unmemorable that it's not even the most popular school song on campus. That song is "We Are the Boys from Old Florida," which Gator fans sing at the end of the third quarter.

Try as they might, not even the Florida cheerleaders can make people love the Gators' fight song.

The Rest of the Most Overrated

2. "THE FIGHT SONG" (ARKANSAS)

"The Fight Song"—that's its name, sort of like The Beatles' *White Album*, the only difference being that one is a musical masterpiece and the other sounds like a dance hall song from a bad Western. I could have sworn Lili von Shtupp sang this one during her act in *Blazing Saddles*.

3. (TIE) "SONS OF WESTWOOD" (UCLA) AND "BIG C" (USC)

The same song with different lyrics. I mean, I know that the schools are brothers in the same educational system, but c'mon.

4. (TIE) "ROCKY TOP" (TENNESSEE), "COME JOIN THE BAND" (STANFORD), "FIGHT FOR LSU" (LSU), "SOCK IT TO 'EM" (CLEMSON), "GLORY" (GEORGIA), AND "THE EYES OF TEXAS" (TEXAS)

Schools that adopt popular tunes as their fight songs should be automatically disqualified, although I'm willing to give LSU a pass, because I saw the Golden Band from Tigerland in the French Quarter the night before the 2008 BCS Championship Game. It was early, and the band jaywalked (jaymarched?) across a four-lane street in the Quarter, amassed in front of a bar, and played the first four notes of "Hold That Tiger!" at a slightly slower tempo. Very Preservation-Hall-like.

Tennessee, with "Rocky Top," has no excuse. I like country music as much as the next Alabama native, but a song from *Hee Haw*? As a Stanford alum, I considered giving the Farm a pass for using "All Right Now," because the official fight song sounds like the theme song from a show on Nick Jr. Texas writing new lyrics to "I've Been Working on the Railroad," and Georgia borrowing "Battle Hymn of the Republic"? Wasn't the latter a Union song out of the Civil War?

If you can't beat 'em, sing their song.

The Most Underrated Fight Song in College Football

"THE VICTORS" (MICHIGAN)

Only because you can't rate it highly enough. The Wolverines sing it in the locker room after every victory, a task that Schembechler took so seriously that he brought in a music professor to teach his players how to sing it. That practice continues to this day.

Fight songs don't get any better than Michigan's "The Victors."

The Rest of the Most Underrated

2. "RAMBLIN' WRECK FROM GEORGIA TECH" (GEORGIA TECH)

How have the Thought Police missed this one? In three verses, there are nine uses of the word "hell," one verse devoted entirely to drinking rum, and one reference to "gamblin'." The school would never be able to sing this if NCAA president Myles Brand were alive today. In other words, "I'm a Ramblin' Wreck from Georgia Tech and a hell of an engineer," is as close to perfection as an opening lyric can get.

3. "NOTRE DAME VICTORY MARCH" (NOTRE DAME)

I love how the song builds in energy and excitement, and lyrics that implore the team to "wake up the echoes" and "shake down the thunder" bring in tradition and a sense of power that define any program that wants to be great. It's not underrated, but if you talk about fight songs and don't include the Irish, you have no credibility.

4. (TIE) "WAR EAGLE" (AUBURN) AND "YEA, ALABAMA" (ALABAMA)

Both have great opening hooks—Alabama in five notes, Auburn in seven—that stay in your head long after the game is over.

* * *

The best mascot should be feral, regionally symbolic, and unique, and if it's only two of those, then they better really stand out. I like Tigers as much as the next zoo-going dad. But you can't go three clicks on the remote on a college football Saturday without finding a team of Tigers playing somewhere.

The Most Underrated Mascot in College Football

CHIEF OSCEOLA AND RENEGADE (FLORIDA STATE)

If the Seminole tribe takes pride in being the symbol of Florida State athletics, that's good enough for me, especially because the pregame ritual, where the Seminole slams that flaming spear into the stadium grass, never gets old.

Chief Osceola and Renegade are a highlight of the pregame festivities at Florida State.

The Rest of the Most Underrated

2. UGA (GEORGIA)

Uga may not be underrated in the traditional sense. He remains one of the most recognizable mascots in college athletics. But he's underrated as a defender. The 1996 photograph showing him lunging at Auburn receiver Robert Baker during the Dogs' 56–49 overtime victory is an SEC classic. I'm pretty sure Mississippi State tried to recruit him as a nickel back.

3. THE STANFORD TREE (STANFORD)

Former Cardinal athletic director Ted Leland used to be a judge for the student competition to be the Tree. He told me one candidate planned to set himself on fire during the tryout. "Only at Stanford," Leland said, "would a student write a five-page paper explaining why he would be in no danger."

4. BEVO (TEXAS)

How to make lemonade when Texas A&M gives you lemons. In the early days of the rivalry, Aggies rustled the Texas Longhorn and branded him with the score, 13–0, of their victory. Texas students took their own branding iron and turned "13–0" into "Bevo," and the Longhorn has had that name ever since.

5. RALPHIE (COLORADO)

You've got a 1,300-pound bison named Ralphie sprinting down the sideline. I know there are 11 student handlers running with her—five who try to steer with ropes, six who run the perimeter—but if Ralphie wanted to veer off and take out the visiting team's bench, do you really think five students with ropes could stop her?

The Most Overrated Mascot in College Football

CHIEF ILLINIWEK (ILLINOIS)

On one side, you have a tribe of Native Americans that has asked that Chief Illiniwek not be used as a symbol for Illinois athletics (for the record, the tribe asked before USC humiliated Illinois 49–17 in the 2008 Rose Bowl). On the other, you have a bunch of 60-year-old white guys who want to relive their days of watching a guy do an Indian imitation straight out of a B-movie western. Gee, that's a tough call.

The Rest of the Most Overrated

2. THE ORANGE (SYRACUSE)

Then again, you have to implore Illinois not to do what Syracuse did when it retired its Indian, which is to have a student don a costume that looks like something you wear when you're handing out coupons outside an Orange Julius.

Nothing says college football better than…citrus fruit?

3. THE WAR EAGLE (AUBURN)

The bird flies around the stadium and lands on its master's arm. I'm sorry. I need more. It would be impressive if he delivered a present to his master, like, say, Uga. Don't think the War Eagle hasn't considered it, either.

4. BRUTUS BUCKEYE (OHIO STATE)

One man's tough nut is another's nut. Virginia isn't the Peanuts. California isn't the Almonds. In fact, The Ohio State University may be the only school with produce for a mascot. Is the Syracuse Orange the color or the fruit?

5. MR. COMMODORE (VANDERBILT)

I don't know about you, but I just don't think it's right to adopt a '70s Motown group as a mascot.

Selected Bibliography

"Selected Bibliography" is a fancy name for the list of books I used to research this book. It may not be every book; if not, this is nearly all of them, with an asterisk explained in the paragraph below. I have listed only books; articles and game stories from the web, both those written by me or by others, are not listed here, nor are the myriad university websites and media guides that I used to check name spellings, statistics, birth dates, game dates, etc.

Rather than list the individual years of the volumes I used, I will say up front that *Best Sports Stories,* the series of top American sportswriting edited by Irving T. Marsh and Edward Ehre and published annually by E.P. Dutton from 1944 to 1980, continues to be the foundation of my research and my library. I thought I had every volume, but 1958 has walked off my shelves. I better go look for it.

Ashe Jr., Arthur A. *A Hard Road to Glory: Football,* New York, Amistad Press, 1993

August, Bob, and Anderson, Dave, et al. *The Heisman, Sixty Years of Tradition and Excellence,* Bronxville, NY, Adventure Quest, 1995

Barnhart, Tony. *What It Means to Be a Bulldog,* Chicago, Triumph Books, 2004

Barra, Allen. *The Last Coach,* New York, W.W. Norton, 2005

Bisheff, Steve, and Schrader, Loel. *Fight On!*, Nashville, Cumberland House, 2006

Blaik, Earl H. with Cohane, Tim. *You Have to Pay the Price,* New York, Holt, Rinehart and Winston, 1960

Bowden, Bobby and Ellis, Steve. *Bobby Bowden's Tales from the Seminoles Sideline,* Champaign, IL, Sports Publishing, 2004

Briley, John David. *Career in Crisis: Paul "Bear" Bryant and the 1971 Season at Alabama,* Macon, GA, Mercer University Press, 2006

Broeg, Bob. *Ol' Mizzou,* Huntsville, AL, The Strode Publishers, 1974

Brown, Ben. *Saint Bobby and the Barbarians,* New York, Doubleday, 1992

Brown, Gerry and Morrison, Michael, eds. *2007 ESPN Sports Almanac,* New York, ESPN Books, 2006

Browning, Al. *Third Saturday in October,* Nashville, Cumberland House, 2001

Bryant, Paul W., and Underwood, John. *Bear: The Hard Life and Good Times of Alabama's Coach Bryant,* New York, Little, Brown, 1974

Bynum, Mike, ed. *Pop Warner: Football's Greatest Teacher,* Gridiron Football Properties, 1993

Cameron, Steve, and Greenburg, John. *Pappy: The Gentle Bear,* Lenexa, KS, Addax Publishing Group, 2000

Cohane, Tim. *Great College Coaches of the Twenties and Thirties,* New Rochelle, NY, Arlington House, 1973

Cohn, Lowell. *Rough Magic,* New York, HarperCollins, 1994

Cromartie, Bill and Brown, Jody. *The Glamor Game,* Nashville, Rutledge Hill Press, 1989

Danzig, Allison and Brandwein, Peter, eds. *The Greatest Sport Stories from The New York Times,* New York, A.S. Barnes, 1951

Dodd, Robert L. *Bobby Dodd on Football,* Englewood Cliffs, NJ, Prentice-Hall, 1954

Dodd, Robert Lee "Bobby" and Wilkinson, Jack. *Dodd's Luck,* Savannah, GA, Golden Coast Publishing, 1987

Ellis, Steve and Vilona, Bill. *Pure Gold,* Champaign, IL, Sports Publishing, 2006

Feinstein, John. *A Civil War: Army vs. Navy,* New York, Little, Brown, 1996

Gilbert, Bob. *Neyland: The Gridiron General,* Savannah, GA, Golden Coast Publishing, 1990

Goldstein, Richard. *Ivy League Autumns,* New York, St. Martin's Press, 1996

Groom,Winston. *The Crimson Tide,* Tuscaloosa, AL, The University of Alabama Press, 2000

Hesburgh, Theodore, with Reedy, Jerry. *God, Country, Notre Dame,* New York, Doubleday, 1990

Hester, Wayne. *Where Tradition Began,* Birmingham, AL, Seacoast Publishing, 1991

Holtz, Lou, with Heisler, John. *The Fighting Spirit,* New York, Pocket Books, 1989

Jenkins, Dan. *Saturday's America,* New York, Little, Brown, 1970

Kerasotis, Peter. *Stadium Stories: Florida Gators,* Guilford, CT, The Globe Pequot Press, 2005

Libby, Bill. *Heroes of the Heisman Trophy,* New York, Hawthorn Books, 1973

Liebendorfer, Don. *The Color of Life is Red,* Stanford, CA, Stanford University Press, 1972

Majors, Johnny, with Byrd, Ben. *You Can Go Home Again,* Nashville, Rutledge Hill Press, 1986

Mandell, Ted. *Heart Stoppers and Hail Marys,* South Bend, IN, Hardwood Press, 2006

Manning, Archie and Peyton, with Underwood, John. *Manning,* Harper Entertainment, 2000

Martin, Buddy. *The Boys From Old Florida,* Champaign, IL, Sports Publishing, 2006

McCambridge, Michael, ed. *ESPN College Football Encyclopedia,* New York, ESPN Books, 2005

Miller, Jeff. *Going Long,* New York, McGraw-Hill, 2003

Mule, Marty. *Sugar Bowl: The First Fifty Years,* Birmingham, AL, Oxmoor House, 1983

Naftali, Alan. *Woody's Boys,* Wilmington, OH, Orange Frazer Press, 1995

Namath, Joe Willie with Schaap, *Dick. I Can't Wait Until Tomorrow... 'Cause I Get Better Looking Every Day,* New York, Random House, 1969

NCAA Football's Finest, Indianapolis, National Collegiate Athletic Association, 2002

NCAA Official 2007 Division I Football Records Book, Indianapolis, National Collegiate Athletic Association, 2007

Nelson, David M. *Anatomy of a Game,* Cranbury, NJ, Associated University Presses, 1994

Nelson, Lindsey. *Hello Everybody, I'm Lindsey Nelson,* Beech Tree Books, New York, 1985

Newcombe, Jack, ed. *The Fireside Book of Football,* New York, Simon & Schuster, 1964

Rappoport, Ken. *Wake Up the Echoes,* Tomball, TX, Strode Publishers, 1988

Schembechler, Bo and Albom, Mitch. *Bo,* New York, Warner Books, 1989

Sperber, Murray. *Shake Down the Thunder,* New York, Henry Holt, 1993

Staff of the Lincoln Journal Star. *A Salute to Nebraska's Tom Osborne,* Champaign, IL, Sports Publishing, 1998

Switzer, Barry and Shrake, Bud. *Bootlegger's Boy,* New York, William Morrow, 1990

Vaught, John. *Rebel Coach,* Memphis, Memphis State University Press, 1971

Ward, Arch. *Frank Leahy and the Fighting Irish,* New York, Van Rees Press, 1944

White, Steve. *One Game Season,* Collegeville, MN, Steve White, 1995